We are the Pilgrims, master; we shall go
Always a little further: it may be
Beyond the last blue mountain barred with snow,
Across that angry or that glimmering sea,
White on a throne or guarded in a cave
There lives a prophet who can understand
Why men were born: but surely we are brave,
Who take the golden road to Samarkand.

The Golden Road to Samarkand
James Elroy Flecker

Contents

Picture Credits

Picture credits (in order of appearance):

1. Courtesy the Mayne family
2. Courtesy the Davis family
3. Courtesy the Nash family
4. Courtesy Special Forces Roll of Honour –
   https://www.specialforcesroh.com
5. IWM BU 1162
6. Courtesy the Appleyard family
7. IWM A 14970
8. IWM NA 674
9. Courtesy Fondation de la France Libre
10. Public domain
11. Courtesy Service historique de la Défense
12. Courtesy Service historique de la Défense
13. Courtesy Verney family
14. Courtesy Gibbs family
15. Courtesy Gary Hull
16. Courtesy Gibson family
17. Courtesy Gibson family
18. Courtesy Gibson family
19. Courtesy Gibson family
20. Courtesy Graham & John Alcock
21. Courtesy US military
22. Courtesy US military

Author's Note

There are sadly few survivors from the Second World War operations depicted in these pages. Throughout the writing of this book I have endeavoured to be in contact with as many as possible, plus surviving family members. If there are further witnesses to the stories told here who are inclined to come forward, please do get in touch, as I will endeavour to include further recollections in future editions.

The time spent by Allied servicemen and women as Special Forces was often traumatic and wreathed in layers of secrecy, and many chose to take their stories to their graves. Memories tend to differ and apparently none more so than those concerning operations behind enemy lines. The written accounts that do exist tend to differ in their detail and timescale, and locations and chronologies are sometimes contradictory. That being said, I have endeavoured to convey an accurate sense of place, timescale and narrative to the stories depicted here. Where various accounts appear particularly confused, the methodology I have used is the 'most likely' scenario: if two or more testimonies or sources point to a particular time or place or sequence of events, I have treated that account as most likely.

The above notwithstanding, any mistakes herein are entirely of my own making and I would be happy to correct them in future editions. The best means by which to make contact with me is via my website – www.damienlewis.com

Or you can message me on X or Instagram @authordlewis.

These are true stories. Any sections of speech are taken from contemporary accounts of reported dialogue, diary entries, letters, or memoirs written by those involved. Any number of the documents I have consulted – war diaries, scribbled notes, signals logs, letters home – were written under the most difficult circumstances and often in haste. Doubtless, they were never intended for publication. Accordingly, I have standardised spelling, corrected grammar and simplified acronym use, to make the book easier to read (i.e. 'Amm' is rendered as ammunition; 'Ack' becomes acknowledge). References to the source documents can be found in the notes at the end of this book.

Chapter One

THE DIEHARD ESCAPEE

June 1943, Lampedusa

Grasping his Thompson sub-machine gun, SAS Captain Roy Bridgeman-Evans lowered himself into the folbot – a collapsible canvas-hulled canoe. It was a warm Mediterranean night in June 1943, the calm waters lapping softly against the dark hull of the Motor Torpedo Boat (MTB) that had brought them to within striking distance of their target. Ahead, a further clutch of folbots, crewed by commandos of the Special Boat Squadron (SBS), set out to reconnoitre the beach. They were followed by another craft crammed with raiders, and led by SAS Captain Raymond Couraud, a French-American who had served in the French Foreign Legion with distinction earlier in the war.

Gently pushing off from the MTB's hull, Bridgeman-Evans and his men, including Lieutenant Anthony Greville-Bell, plus Sergeant Robert Lodge, set out for the shoreline. They slipped the blades of their paddles into the night-dark water, careful not to create any noise that might alert enemy sentries. This was the third such mission that Bridgeman-Evans had commanded, including a recent recce of the Galite Islands, which lie off the North African coast. But those previous attempts had ended in failure, the British raiders being spotted by the enemy before they had any chance to achieve their objectives. They were hoping for better fortunes tonight, here at the Italian island of Lampedusa, set deep in the Mediterranean.

It was the early summer of 1943 and the Allied invasion of Sicily – codenamed Operation Husky – was drawing ever closer, after which Allied forces would advance onto the Italian mainland, or the 'soft underbelly of Europe' as Winston Churchill had called it. With Lampedusa lying between the coast of North Africa and Sicily, the danger was that it would serve as an early-warning post for the enemy. The island garrison was known to be on high alert for any Allied invasion fleet that might set sail. Hence Bridgeman-Evans and his men being ordered 'to destroy the powerful radar installed on the island as well as an ammunition and gasoline depot'.

In a mission codenamed Operation Buttercup, a flotilla of three MTBs had set sail from the British-held island of Malta, arriving off the Lampedusa coast shortly before nightfall. The fact that it was still light had worried Sergeant Lodge, who noted in his war diary 'the uncanny feeling' of their approach 'in full visibility'. While those manning the MTB had argued they could not be seen at such a distance, 'we had our doubts.' His misgivings were to prove well-founded, for shortly all hell was to let loose.

As darkness descended, Lodge recalled the 'absolute calm' of the scene. 'Heaven and sea seemed glassy, the air still and warm.' Navigating their fragile craft through the water, they proceeded with utmost care, small 'whirlpools of phosphorous sparks' seeming to cast an eerie glow upon their boat. Ahead of them, Couraud and his men had made it to shore, where they discovered a narrow beach lying at the foot of steep cliffs. As Bridgeman-Evans and Lodge approached the coastline, they were hoping for a signal from those at the vanguard to guide them in. But there was nothing.

They nudged the rocks with their paddles, noted Lodge, as they skirted the shore, searching for where the others had made landfall. But even as they were doing so, a series of blinding green flares erupted into the night sky, rendering everything into a lurid-tinged near-daylight. Then there was a yelled challenge from the cliff-tops, and the first burst of gunfire cut through the night.

A cry echoed across the water, as one of the raiders gave voice to the shock and frustration all were feeling: 'Fuck.'

Moments later more machine guns opened up, bullets ripping into ground and sea all around the raiders. Ashore, Couraud and his men were forced to execute a desperate dash for cover, seeking safety behind some scattered boulders. But even as the raiders tried to return fire, searchlights cut through the darkness, sweeping the terrain to all sides. Probing out to sea, the Italian operators sought to illuminate the MTBs, plus any of the small boats that might still be in the water.

As Lodge recalled, they were dead in the water if they got nailed in the searchlight's fierce glare. With more light quartering the seas, their first thought was that this was an enemy patrol boat, perhaps one of the feared German E-boats, powerful and well-armed motorboats. That would have 'spelled the end', Lodge observed. They had 'about a mile' to reach their MTB, the crew of which dared not risk moving closer for fear of being trapped in the searchlight's glare.

Drifting on the flat calm, Bridgeman-Evans ducked down to avoid a burst from Lodge's machine gun, as the SAS sergeant sought to shoot out the bulbs of the powerful searchlights. The SAS traded fire with the shore-based defenders, but still the blinding stabs of illumination drew ever closer to the thin-skinned craft. With its canvas sides and collapsible frame, the folbot would prove easy meat for any of the cliff-top machine guns.

Back on the bullet-riddled beach, Couraud sensed that the game was up. The element of surprise was lost, if it had ever been theirs' in the first place. With a storm of rounds pinging off the boulders, he gave the order to pull out. The mission was being aborted. Under intense fire, he and his men made a dash for their folbot, managing to manhandle it back into the water, and grabbing their paddles as they went.

With Couraud and his team making a desperate bid to escape, Bridgeman-Evans gave the only order that he felt he could: the mission was being abandoned. He and his men were to head back to the MTB at all possible speed. With fiery arcs of tracer cutting into the water, and the beams from the searchlights quartering the seas, they began to paddle for their lives. A few moments later, one of those beams of light sputtered out, shattered by a round fired from one of the raiders' weapons. That might buy them a little extra time. Frantically, they continued to paddle, fearing that at any second the enemy would find their range and rake their craft with murderous fire.

It was an hour before the first of the raiders made it back to the nearest of the MTBs, during which the motorboats were constantly under fire. By now a searchlight had picked out the nearest ship, and 'we had to move fast' Lodge noted, or it risked being shot to pieces. Eager arms hauled the exhausted men, plus their boats, aboard. Once the first vessel was full, the MTB 'deployed a large plume of smoke to blind the enemy and conceal themselves from view as they zig-zagged through the salvos'.

After their desperate getaway, Lodge slumped down exhaustedly against one of the MTB's torpedo tubes. While he fretted about 'the several thousand pounds of high explosives near my head', he was too tired to move. Two of the raiders were never to make it back to the waiting ships. One of the folbots that had gone ahead would never return. The missing men were Sergeants Alexander 'Ginger' Milne and Archibald Sinclair. While an MTB searched for them for most of that night, no trace was ever found.

Upon their return to Malta, Bridgeman-Evans and his men were debriefed by Major Oswald Cary-Elwes, a standout figure of the 2nd SAS Regiment, which had been formed just a few months earlier. This was a third failed mission in succession, and what Bridgeman-Evans chose to report of the night's events would rankle. He stated that 'against his will and his own orders, it was Lee who had given the order to withdraw'. Raymond Couraud had served with the Special Operations Executive (SOE) before joining the SAS, and he had been forced to change his name to 'Ray Lee', for the Gestapo had discovered his true identity. For Bridgeman-Evans to have accused Couraud (Lee) of having scuppered the night's raid would enrage the former French Foreign Legionnaire no end.

Another of Bridgeman-Evans's men, Lieutenant Anthony Greville-Bell, was equally aghast at the tone of their mission commander's report. 'You can criticise Raymond on some points, but not call him a coward. In battle, I'd rather have him on my side . . . and if he finds out what Roy said, he will kill him,'

Greville-Bell observed. With Couraud and Bridgeman-Evans at loggerheads, Major Cary-Elwes sought to defuse the situation and fast. Sensibly, he opted to separate the two men. Right then, a submarine was preparing to leave Malta, carrying a force charged to raid another Italian island. Seizing the opportunity, Cary-Elwes dispatched Couraud to join them, while Bridgeman-Evans would be given a completely separate mission.

Whether or not Bridgeman-Evans stood by his assessment of the Lampedusa raid, and Couraud's supposed culpability, was irrelevant. He'd managed to upset several of the men under his command, a number of whom had already labelled him as something of a 'snob'. In an egalitarian unit like the SAS, where merit mattered above rank or social class, this was not a good reputation to garner. Until recently, the men had found Bridgeman-Evans's high-born gentleman's persona somewhat amusing, but his critical comments about the battle-hardened Couraud had changed their perceptions.

It would take a lot for the SAS captain to regain their trust.

Fortunately, the chance to do so would come soon enough. Barely a month later, Bridgeman-Evans and Lodge would be back in action, hungrier than ever to strike a blow against the enemy.

As the ten men of what was codenamed the 'Brig' patrol climbed aboard the Armstrong Whitworth Albermarle aircraft, Colonel Bill Stirling, commander of 2 SAS, and the older brother to the regiment's founder, David Stirling, shook hands with each in turn, wishing them good luck. At his side was his deputy, Major Geoffrey Appleyard, but the roaring of the engines scuppered any chance for chat. Stirling was there in person to send them off, this being a vital mission behind enemy lines in support of the Operation Husky landings, which were just a few days old. Across the runway, another group of SAS parachutists were boarding a second Albermarle on a sister mission. They made up the 'Pink' stick – a stick being a patrol of paratroopers – and Major Appleyard would be accompanying them to the drop zone.

It was 7.30 p.m. on the evening of Monday 12 July 1943. The place, Kairouan airbase in Tunisia, North Africa. Developed as a transport aircraft, the Albemarle had been fitted with a hatch at the rear of the narrow fuselage, from which men could jump, transforming it into a makeshift paratrooper aircraft. It was far from ideal, but beggars couldn't be choosers, and airframes were in high demand at this stage of the war. Once inside, the men took up their positions for what would be a three-hour flight. Bridgeman-Evans was in command of the Brig mission, with Captain Patrick Dudgeon serving as his deputy.

As Bridgeman-Evans was jumper number ten, he'd be the last man out. This would be his first parachute jump into combat, and for many on that flight it would be their *first ever jump*, whether into combat or not, and their nerves were on edge. The rushed nature of their mission had meant that corners were cut, and consequently men who had had woefully little parachute training were being dispatched into the skies over Sicily, come what may. Little wonder they kept anxiously checking and rechecking their various jump straps and buckles, the knots in their stomachs growing tighter by the second.

Preparations for the mission had been fraught. Even Appleyard, who was to oversee the whole operation, had got only the briefest notice, the warning to deploy 'coming through on a Saturday evening at nine o'clock', leaving barely half a day to make their preparations. In a desperate rush, equipment had been drawn from the stores and the drop-canisters stuffed full of supplies. While each man wore American-style coveralls and carried a Colt .45 automatic pistol on his person, their main armaments, plus all of their explosives and ammunition, were jammed into those containers, which were to be dispatched from the aircraft along with the men. Driven by the urgency to deploy, stuffing those drop-canisters to the brim was seen as being the quickest means to get airborne.

Until recently, many of these men had been serving with 62 Commando, otherwise known as the Small Scale Raiding Force (SSRF), a unit that had executed a string of seaborne raids behind enemy lines. The SSRF sat under the umbrella of the Special Operations Executive, more often referred to as 'The Ministry for Ungentlemanly Warfare'. SOE was a clandestine unit founded by Churchill, and formed to do all the things that are forbidden in war: assassinations, bribery, corruption, money laundering, raising guerrilla armies and more. But once 2 SAS began recruiting, it was men like these that Bill Stirling had turned to, to establish the core of his new regiment. Experienced, tough, super-fit and able to think and act on their own initiative, they'd proved their worth many times over. They were the natural choice to emulate what David Stirling and Colonel Blair 'Paddy' Mayne, now the commander of 1 SAS, had achieved across the North African deserts.

Tonight's mission was critical. Following victory in North Africa, the Allies were launching a series of thrusts into Italy by sea and by air. In order to get to the Italian mainland, Sicily first had to be conquered. With that aim, on 9 July 1943, just three days earlier, British and American troops had landed on the southern shores of the Italian island, in a combined airborne and amphibious assault.

As Allied forces fought their way ashore, so the men of 2 SAS were to be deployed behind the lines, in a series of missions codenamed Operation Chestnut. Their orders were to land 'by parachute in north-east Sicily to harass the enemy by attacking communications, roads, signals and convoys, by destroying cables, harassing headquarters and reporting on movements of enemy troops'. Designed to cause as much chaos and confusion as possible, the aim was to blunt the enemy's will and their means to fight.

Acting as an advance party, the Brig and Pink sticks were to establish an operational base, before calling in the rest of the squadron by radio, plus their Eureka homing beacons, which would guide in the aircraft. Bringing in the full squadron was seen as being key to the success of the mission. 'If no signal message is received,' read their orders, 'aircraft will, on night D+6/7 carry reinforcements to area of DZs, but if contact is not established with the Eureka, troops will not be landed and aircraft will return to base and repeat this part of the operation on the next night.' 'D+6/7' denoted the sixth/seventh night after the advance party's insertion, while 'DZ' was short for drop zone. In other words, SAS headquarters would keep dispatching the remainder of the squadron by air, until proper contact was established and they could be parachuted in.

Thirty minutes after the Albermarles had taken to the dark skies, the men of Bridgeman-Evans's stick hooked up their static lines to the hawser stretching the length of the aircraft's ceiling, buddy checking each other, making sure their straps and buckles were tight, before settling back for the remainder of the flight.

Most sat in silence in the cramped confines of the fuselage, amid the deafening roar from the aircraft's twin Bristol Hercules engines. Despite the racket, Sergeant Lodge, by now a seasoned elite operator, somehow managed to close his eyes and grab some rest, despite the high stakes of tonight's mission for him in particular.

Lodge was in truth a German Jew. Born Rudolf 'Rudi' Friedlander to a wealthy Jewish family in Munich, he'd grown up in relative comfort, studying Law and Economics at Munich university, and graduating with a PhD. But due to the prejudice suffered by Jews once the Nazis came to power, in 1934 he'd moved to Holland, retraining as a carpenter, before relocating to England the following year. Gaining steady employment, he'd travelled the country with work. Fortunately, other members of his family were able to join him before war's outbreak, his father settling in Newcastle-upon-Tyne, where Friedlander was a frequent visitor.

But from the very outbreak of the war Friedlander had been determined to enlist in the British Army. Nursing a deep hatred of Germany under Hitler, he was desperate to help rid the world of the evils of Nazism. Accepted into the Auxiliary Military Pioneer Corps, a non-combat unit, he spent months in London during the Blitz, clearing debris and putting his carpentry skills to good use. But eventually, Lodge 'sparked the interest of SOE', and the Ministry of Ungentlemanly Warfare 'earmarked him for future employment'. That was how he'd been recruited into the Small Scale Raiding Force, a unit closely affiliated with SOE.

When brought into the ranks of the SAS in February 1943, Friedlander had had to choose a more English-sounding name, in the event that he might be captured. Being Jewish was a death sentence. He'd opted for 'Robert Lodge', the surname being that of his then fiancée, Win Lodge. The new name was designed to protect him, but 'with his thick, jam-jar glasses and big, heavy, kindly looks', Lodge was under no illusion as to how thin was his cover, and the risks of 'what might happen if he were taken captive'.

With Lodge being all of thirty-four years old, he was the same age as his commander, Bridgeman-Evans. Both were decidedly ancient, in a unit that mostly boasted men in their early twenties. They also shared a wealth of military experience, both having soldiered in the SSRF before joining the SAS. Yet there the similarities ended. Bridgeman-Evans hailed from a very different kind of background to Lodge. While the latter had escaped the horrors of Nazism, and been forced to adopt a nom de guerre in order to fight in freedom's cause, the former had suffered no such trials and tribulations. In fact, Bridgeman-Evans had been born with something of a silver spoon in his mouth. Even so, he was possessed of an uncommon courage and a hunger to fight, as events were about to prove.

Standing at six feet tall, with brown hair and grey eyes, the SAS captain hailed from Richmond in Surrey. Born in 1908 to a successful and prosperous cigar merchant, he'd attended boarding school in Sutton Valence, Kent, after which he'd joined his father's tobacco firm, Fribourg and Treyer. At the outbreak of war he'd volunteered for officer training. Having been a member of the OTC (Officer Training Cadets) while at boarding school stood him in good stead. Once he'd graduated from officer training school at Shrivenham, Oxfordshire, he was commissioned as a second lieutenant into the 36th Anti-Aircraft Regiment, Royal Artillery.

After spending two years on anti-aircraft duties, Bridgeman-Evans was desperate to get into some real action. Volunteering for the SSRF, he'd been interviewed by Major Geoffrey Appleyard, under whose intense scrutiny he had to somehow argue that he had the right attributes to join this elite fraternity. 'I had the feeling that he had summed me right up,' Bridgeman-Evans would remark of his interview with Appleyard, 'and that if I had told a lie, he would have known it right away.' Accepted into their ranks, on 26 October 1942 he was posted to Anderson Manor, Dorset, to undergo specialist training.

Bridgeman-Evans had very big shoes to fill. He was following in the footsteps of some quite extraordinary men, including some of the SSRF's legendary founders – Major Gus March-Phillips and Lieutenant Anders Lassen. Along with Appleyard, March-Phillips and Lassen had been involved in a string of daring missions, gaining them a reputation as fearless and audacious warriors. Sadly, March-Phillips had been killed in action during a raid on the French coast, just a month before Bridgeman-Evans joined the unit. With March-Phillips's loss, Lassen had moved on to the SAS and SBS. In time he would become one of the war's finest soldiers, being the only member of the British special forces ever to win a Victoria Cross, Britain's highest award for valour.

Bridgeman-Evans had joined the ranks of the best of the best. He had a lot to live up to.

The Albermarle droned onwards, pushing north across the Mediterranean and drawing ever closer to the DZ, lying not far from the small Sicilian village of Sperlinga. As the aircraft approached the coastline flak reared up before it, while 'a heavy barrage' was visible on the ground, as Allied forces traded blows with their adversaries. Then, as if from nowhere, streaks of burning tracer lit up the night sky, arcing towards the aircraft, the pilot banking hard to avoid being hit. The men shifted about nervously, being eager to get down on the ground.

It was approaching 11 p.m. when Bridgeman-Evans, who was wearing headphones that linked him by intercom to the pilot, was given a verbal warning: they were ten minutes away from the DZ. He alerted his men to make their final preparations. They pulled on their jump helmets and checked and rechecked their straps, even though they knew all should be good from the last time they had done so. Nerves were playing their part, especially for those who had never jumped before.

As they arranged themselves in line, the cover was removed from the drop-hole. Immediately the fuselage was swept by a blast of cold air, the noise swelling into a deafening crescendo. The ten men shuffled closer, their eyes fixed on the red light above the exit hole, waiting for the 'green for go'. The first, Corporal Wilkins, steeled himself.

'Action stations in two minutes,' Bridgeman-Evans yelled, after receiving word from the pilot.

Expecting to hear another call to bring them to 'action stations', the green light suddenly flashed on, catching many by total surprise. From somewhere, a voice cried 'Green light! Jump!' A moment later Wilkins was gone, plummeting through the hole and being sucked into the moonlit night. No sooner had he disappeared than the next man, Private Alan Sharman, leapt into the void. And then, at number three, Captain Dudgeon, too, was gone.

As Bridgeman-Evans readied himself to go, there seemed to be a delay further along the line. The man at number six, Sergeant

Hawkins, hesitated. Whatever might have caused this Bridgeman-Evans couldn't tell, but after a second or so Hawkins too slipped from view. Once Sergeant Lodge had dived out, Bridgeman-Evans took a gasp of breath and plummeted through the hole, the silk canopy of his parachute snapping open with a resounding crack as he was buffeted by the aircraft's slipstream.

With his parachute oscillating through the night sky, Bridgeman-Evans could tell that they had been dropped at a far greater altitude than intended. Beneath him lay a distant, barren landscape of jagged hills and knife-edged crests – not at all what he had been expecting. He glanced upwards, searching for the parachutes beneath which would be suspended their all-important drop-canisters, crammed full of their weaponry and kit. They were packed with everything they needed to survive and to operate. But worryingly, not a single 'chute was anywhere to be seen.

Twisting and turning in his harness, he sought out the rest of his stick. What he noticed filled him with dread. Those few men that he could see appeared to be drifting further and further away, the group of parachutes appearing as a jagged and dis-jointed scattering, not as a neat line strung across the sky. Caught on high-altitude thermals, they were floating off in all directions, and there was not a thing that he could do about it.

Bridgeman-Evans felt certain that they had been released at far too great a height and very likely in the wrong place. The lack of a call to 'action stations' suggested that something had gone wrong with the drop, but there was little time to worry about that now. He needed to concentrate on getting down in one piece. He focused on the ground, bracing himself as it came racing up to meet him. Moments later, he hit the dirt with a thud, rolling to one side. Quickly he struck the release button that unfastened his chest harness, gathering in his 'chute, while searching about for any sign of the others.

Jumping at such altitude, there was every likelihood that they would have been seen by the enemy. Lodge, who'd gone immediately before Bridgeman-Evans, had spied 'many lights' and thought he'd detected 'far-off voices'. He was certain he'd heard the barking of dogs.

What neither Bridgeman-Evans nor Lodge could know was that there had been an electrical fault on the Albermarle, resulting in the green light coming on far too early. When one of those in the Albermarle's cockpit had gone to warn the ten parachutists to prepare for 'action stations', he'd found the hold deserted, for all had jumped. Worse still, none of the canisters containing their kit had been dropped alongside the men. As a report from the time noted, 'Brig party were landed . . . at approx. 2200 hours. The containers were not dropped in same run as personnel, so there is considerable doubt if they found them. If they did not do so they will have no explosives and no arms except .45 Colts.'

In short, Bridgeman-Evans and his team had jumped at the wrong time and at the wrong altitude over the wrong location, and apart from what little they carried on their persons, were bereft of all supplies and weaponry. What should have been a heavily armed SAS stick had descended into enemy territory armed with nothing more than a pistol each, plus a few magazines of ammo.

Making the best of a bad job, Bridgeman-Evans was able to locate Sergeant Hawkins, and a while later they were joined by Lodge. By now it was around midnight, which meant that first light was some five hours away. Giving the order to move out,

Bridgeman-Evans directed them to scout in three directions, to try and find the others. An hour and a half later, their group of three had become five, having located Corporal Haywood and Private Mason. Those five men had made up the second half of the stick. Where the front five might be, including Captain Dudgeon, was anyone's guess.

Bridgeman-Evans got his group moving, for they needed to seek out the canisters. Without them, and the equipment they contained, their mission was pretty much doomed. With the moon having slipped below the highest peaks, he spurred his men on. If they could reach the high ground and find somewhere to lie up, come sunrise they might be able to see where the canisters had fallen. It seemed inconceivable that none could have been dropped. The men marched uphill 'in single file, carrying our 'chutes', until they came to a high ridge, with below it an orchard and a clutch of farm buildings. It was there that Bridgeman-Evans decided to wait out the remaining hours of darkness, hoping for something more positive come daybreak.

Sunrise brought with it a scene that none of them had expected. Rather than providing some decent cover, the orchard lay on an exposed hillside. To make matters worse, there was absolutely no sign of the canisters. Shortly, they heard cries from below and the sound of people on the move. A patrol of Italian soldiers was approaching along a narrow lane. Fortunately, the five fugitives had not yet been seen. Creeping forward, they searched for more suitable cover. Finding some bushes, they crawled deep inside. Down in the valley more enemy troops could be seen, clearly hunting for the men who had dropped through the night sky. Then, to their rear, a lone Italian soldier appeared on the crest of a ridge. He stood there, scanning the terrain for any signs of his prey.

They seemed to have enemy on all sides. Bridgeman-Evans held a council of war. Some argued that the cover they had crawled into was of no use. It would only be a matter of time before the enemy chose to search the bushes, and then they would be discovered. One of the men had a carrier pigeon with him, their only means of establishing communication, for of course their radios had been packed in the drop-containers. Hastily, Bridgeman-Evans scribbled a message, attached it to the leg of the bird and let it fly.

Spying a stone wall not too far away, the men made a break for it. At least it might give them cover from fire, if they had to shoot it out with the enemy. Reaching it, the fugitives hid their 'chutes as best they could, before taking shelter behind the largest stones, where they hoped they might 'outlast the day undiscovered'.

The Italian troops searched the area, drawing ever nearer. Some thirty minutes after they had moved, a voice was heard yelling out from behind. Turning his head, Bridgeman-Evans saw immediately that they were in dire straits. A group of Italian carabinieri – part of the Italian armed forces – had the SAS party pinned in the sights of their rifles. They were demanding their surrender. Fleetingly, the thought crossed his mind to put up a fight, but they were sure to be gunned down. The accurate range of their Colt .45 pistols was a maximum of 50 metres. Boasting rifles and machine guns, the enemy could simply hang back and pick them off at their leisure.

With a heavy heart, Bridgeman-Evans gave the order to give themselves up.

Having been taken captive, the five soldiers were driven a short distance to the town of Capizzi. At the local police station, they were given water and told to wait. It was now that Bridgeman-Evans realised the full extent of the errors made in executing the drop. If they were at Capizzi, that meant they had been released some 15 kilometres north-east of their intended destination. But in a sense all of that was immaterial now. The mission, as far as Bridgeman-Evans was concerned, was very much over.

Shortly, the Town Marshal – the police chief of Capizzi – arrived. Resplendent in his Fascist uniform, he had the appearance of a 'fat bully with a red choleric face', Lodge noted. Bridgeman-Evans was dragged into the marshal's office, whereupon he was relieved of all 'belongings and money', including the 150,000 lire he had been given at the start of the mission, 'for which no receipt was given'. Ignoring the marshal's aggressive demands for information, the SAS commander offered only his name, rank and service number, despite his inquisitor's increasing anger and frustration. Finally, he was marched from the room, to be replaced in turn by each of his men. None divulged anything more than the big three – name, rank and number.

Interrogations over, the captives were thrown into cells, Bridgeman-Evans being separated from the others to spend most of the day alone. When darkness fell they were again brought before the marshal. They were to be moved to Nicosia, he announced, a village lying to the south-west, not far from where they had been dropped the previous night. No reason was given. But ominously, standing behind the marshal were a number of carabinieri, holding a long chain. The marshal warned Bridgeman-Evans that they were to be shackled together for the journey, to prevent escape.

The SAS captain protested in the strongest possible terms. By way of response the marshal said they could travel unchained, but only if Bridgeman-Evans pledged not to escape. On both sides of the war, if an officer gave his word – his bond – not to try to execute a getaway this was often viewed as sacrosanct. But Bridgeman-Evans refused to do so. As a member of the SAS it was his duty to escape, and this was a promise he was not prepared to give. Refusing to offer his bond, he was manacled along with the others.

Bound in chains, the five prisoners were driven to Nicosia and taken to the police station. There, a new marshal greeted them. He seemed to be the complete opposite of his colleague in Capizzi, becoming furious when he saw how the captives had been treated. Ordering them to be unchained, he had food and wine brought. When they had eaten their fill, they were taken to cells with comfortable mattresses, and there they were allowed to rest.

But sadly, their stay in Nicosia was to be short lived. The next day the prisoners were on the move again, this time by a truck bound for Randazzo, a town lying 50 kilometres to the east, so further away from the Allied advance. As they got on the move they could see the destruction that had been wrought by Allied warplanes – the burned out carcasses of trucks lined the road, while bridges were cratered from direct hits. Often they were pulled from the truck as Allied aircraft flew low overhead, which added considerably to their time on the road. It was the evening of 14 July by the time they reached Randazzo, where they were once more taken to the local police station. Waiting for them was a group of officials. Just as in Capizzi, they were to face more inquisitions.

Bridgeman-Evans entered the interrogation room first. The only light came from some candles, the flames flickering on a desk covered in a dark blanket. Standing behind it, almost in shadow, were two Italian Army officers. Immediately they began to bark out a series of questions, mixing seemingly innocuous enquiries about his regiment and his length of service with more pressing ones regarding the nature of his mission. Just as he had done before, Bridgeman-Evans stubbornly gave them only what was required of him under the Geneva Convention: his name, rank and service number. Nothing more.

The Italian officers became infuriated at their lack of progress. They warned Bridgeman-Evans that as he was wearing American coveralls, he was technically not in British Army uniform, and could be treated as a spy and shot. If he talked, they suggested clemency might be extended to him and his men. The threat did little to persuade the SAS commander to relent, for they'd been trained to expect such treatment and in the means to resist. He was a serving British officer, Bridgeman-Evans argued, and his inquisitors would get nothing but name, rank and number.

Once all the captives had been interrogated – each like Bridgeman-Evans, remaining stoic in their responses – they were paraded through the streets of Randazzo, before being taken to the local jail. There they were thrown into 'a cell full of vermin', as Bridgeman-Evans would describe it. The place was disgusting. There were no beds, merely clumps of flea-infested straw on a bare stone floor. A heavily barred window offered little chance of escape, but through it they could observe the roadway, and the German units streaming by. Whether they were headed for the front line or retreating, no one could tell. But at least all five of the SAS men were together.

There they remained for several days, surviving on starvation rations of macaroni, bread and water. Mason, whom Lodge had nicknamed 'The Old Sailor', or 'Pops', had been a merchant seaman before the war, and was by far the oldest among them. He made their captivity somewhat more bearable, for he kept them entertained with his humorous tales and quick wit. When Mason had been interrogated by the Italian officers and asked what he had intended to do with the money he had been carrying, he'd replied, 'Buying beer, sir,' much to the fury of his inquisitors, who threatened to have him shot.

The monotony of their incarceration was broken by the sound of aircraft – Allied planes flying attack missions. Bombs landed close to the jail, the concussive blasts causing their cell to shake. The danger of being killed by their own side seemed very real.

Permission was given to get some exercise in the jail's courtyard. Immediately thoughts turned to escape. Bridgeman-Evans and his men scrutinised the high brick wall, seeking out any means to scale it. But some of the other prisoners – 'an old man with two leg stumps, and a young rascal', both of whom were imprisoned 'for theft or begging' – warned against it. Recently, they warned, a prisoner who had 'tried to scale the walls' had been gunned down. Another idea was to attack the guard force and so engineer a breakout. But eventually all resolved that 'better opportunities' were sure to come, and in any case they baulked at falling upon their guards 'in cold blood'.

A week after their capture, on 19 July, the prisoners were moved yet again, only now they were lumped together with a number of other Allied prisoners. They were mostly RAF aircrew mixed with airborne troopers, but among them was one familiar face – Private Sharman, one of their fellow patrol members. Incarcerated in a stout-walled stone barn, which was 'heavily guarded' by Italian infantry, plus with 'sentries on the roof', the chances of making a breakout seemed negligible. So Bridgeman-Evans and his men let Sharman regale them with tales of his fortunes.

Sharman had been the second to go from the Albermarle, and he'd carried one of the Eureka homing beacons. Having jumped from what he believed to be close to 3,000 feet – six times the normal altitude for making such a parachute-borne insertion – he'd landed in a ravine. 'The rest of the stick appeared to drift round the mountains and out of sight . . . Although I searched for two hours, I was unable to contact any of them,' he would report. Hiding the cumbersome Eureka, Sharman had climbed the nearest mountain, remaining there for forty-eight hours, 'in the vain hope of seeing something of the others'. Deciding to head south towards Allied lines, he was spotted by an Italian patrol and chased, having to hide in a ditch for several hours.

Once the danger had passed he pressed on, walking through the night and sticking to the hills and mountains. Below him, he could see 'enemy transport on the road, both German and Italian, and there were many Italian soldiers on foot obviously retreating, some with arms and some without'. As the terrain seemed to be free of enemy troops, Sharman decided to risk moving during daylight hours. 'This was a mistake because I walked into an Italian patrol of eight men, almost convinced them I was German, but finally had to show my pay book . . . This of course gave me away.' The Italian troops took Sharman captive, and subsequently he was questioned by the same marshal who had earlier interrogated Bridgeman-Evans and his men. During the process Sharman learned, as suspected, that the Italians 'had observed the parachute descent'.

So from the very outset, the Brig mission had been pretty much doomed to failure.

Sharman's news of enemy units retreating was music to his fellow captives' ears. It meant that the invasion had to be going well. Surely, they reasoned, it was only a matter of time before Sicily capitulated and they would be liberated. But on the afternoon of 21 July, nine days after their capture, the SAS prisoners were once more on the move. They were herded aboard a truck, which proved to be 'full of Italian sailors', and were crammed in so tight there was little chance to leap off. They learned they were bound for the port city of Messina, which lies in the far northeast of Sicily, situated a mere six kilometres across the Strait of Messina from the Italian mainland. Upon reaching the harbour, they were placed aboard an Italian landing craft for the short voyage to the mainland, along with scores of other Allied POWs.

It was a scorching day as the vessel set sail. Despite the sunshine, the mood was bitter. Bridgeman-Evans and his fellow captives had allowed themselves to believe that the Italians lacked the logistical and organisational skills to transport large bodies of POWs across the sea to Italy. They had been proved wrong.

Despite being imprisoned on an Italian warship, Bridgeman-Evans remained alert to any means of escape. As they steamed north, with the sun beating down upon them and the Italian coastline stretching out far into the distance, he gazed across the glimmering blue of the sea. The SAS captain was on the search, studying closely the Italian coastline. As they neared the port of Gioia Tauro, which lay about thirty kilometres from Messina, a plan of escape began to coalesce in his mind.

Once landed at Gioia Tauro, the mass of Allied prisoners were formed up to march towards the town's railway station. As they got on the move, their Italian captors became severely harassed and harried, much to the amusement of their captives. Via a kind of unspoken understanding, some of the prisoners walked too quickly, while others hung back, mostly out of sheer devilment, for they could see the guards getting increasingly frustrated. Soon, as Lodge observed, the mass of prisoners had become a straggly line, stretching way back along the street, as the guards rushed back and forth 'like sheepdogs round their flock'.

Eventually, they reached the railway station where they were hustled into a yard, to await a train. As Bridgeman-Evans well appreciated, that train was going to spirit them to a Prisoner of War camp, which meant that he had little time if he was to put his escape plan into action. He shared his thoughts with Lodge, and shortly they were joined by Mason – 'Pops' – plus Sharman, who was likewise eager to make a getaway. Of the six SAS captives, those four just needed the right opportunity to present itself. (Neither Bridgeman-Evans nor any of his men make any mention of their two SAS comrades at this juncture, Sergeant Hawkins included, so either they had been separated during captivity, or they were disinclined to attempt a breakout.)

That evening a regiment of 'crack' German troops arrived at the station, en route to the fighting in Sicily. Bridgeman-Evans called out to one of the officers, who wandered over to the British prisoners, and shortly they were engaged in surprisingly amicable discussion. The focus of the conversation became their 'common contempt' for the Italian soldiery, as they made a 'mockery' of their martial prowess. Finally, Bridgeman-Evans asked the German officer when he imagined the war might end.

'When we have won,' he replied, laughing.

The station was being guarded, but the sentries – already

stressed from the chaotic march – were thinly spread. With the POWs complaining about lack of food and water, the guards were forced to seek some out, which served to lessen their vigilance still further. Sensing this was the moment to chance it, the four fugitives gathered out of sight, sandwiched between the station itself and the perimeter wall. For the moment unobserved, one by one they climbed over the wall and dropped into the street on the far side. The time was 10.30 p.m. on 22 July.

With no shouts of alarm coming from behind, Bridgeman-Evans figured that phase one of his escape plan had worked. They were out. For the first time in ten days, he and what remained of his Brig stick were free. First priority was to put as much distance as possible between themselves and the railway yard, before it was discovered they were missing.

As they set out into the darkened streets, Lodge suggested they proceed in pairs, himself and Bridgeman-Evans at the front, the other two bringing up the rear. Lodge was fluent in German, of course, so it made sense for him to take the lead. As they headed south, he began to converse in that language, making sure anyone they passed would overhear. The few locals that were about at this late hour glanced at them with indifference. Their American coveralls, combined with the lack of light and Lodge's Teutonic mutterings, made them appear like a group of German soldiers. In this way they managed to slip away from Gioia Tauro. Pressing further south, and keeping the sea to their right, they headed for the spot at which Bridgeman-Evans had noted there was the means to attempt their escape.

They were making for a small fishing village, one earmarked by the SAS commander as holding out the maximum promise of executing a daring getaway. But ahead of them, looming out of the darkness, was a long viaduct. If they were to reach their destination before first light, there was no way to avoid it. Standing on guard, and clearly observing the four fugitives' approach, was a group of Italian soldiers. Should the escapees move off the road now, or otherwise display their discomfiture, then the game would be up. There was no option but to attempt to bluff their way through.

Lodge continued nattering away in German to Bridgeman-Evans, even though the latter could barely understand a word. While the other escapees remained mute, the SAS captain uttered the odd, unintelligible reply, to keep up the illusion that he and Lodge were deep in conversation. They drew closer, the tension mounting with every step. Finally, the Italian soldiers stepped forward to bar their way. There was nothing the four escapees could do other than brazen it out and trust to Lodge's boldness.

He greeted the enemy with a smile. '*Freund*,' he announced, amiably. '*Amico. Soldati tedeschi.*' They were friends. German troops.

Lodge explained that they were German soldiers on their way back to their barracks. Fortune favours the brave. It was a dark night, and the Italians had no torches with which to examine the four shadowy figures. Eventually, they were forced to accept Lodge's explanation and they stepped aside. He turned to the others and beckoned them forward. As they filed past, the Italian soldiers continued to eye them closely. Conscious not to look in any way discomfited, Lodge chatted away, while Bridgeman-Evans nodded vigorously. Shortly, the fugitives had passed along the length of the viaduct and were enveloped in the darkness of the open countryside. The bluff had held good.

But it had been touch and go. Accordingly, Bridgeman-Evans led the men off the road, so as to continue their journey cross-country. As they pressed on they stuffed their pockets with grapes and pears from the vineyards and orchards that lay to either side of the road, for they had little food or water. Pops Mason, ever the joker, kept wandering off to cram his pockets with more purloined fruit. When Bridgeman-Evans grew impatient, and Lodge threatened Mason using 'pretty bad language', Mason merely quipped coolly: 'Oh, you are all far too keyed up.'

It was first light in the early hours of 23 July when they reached their destination. They'd arrived at a cliff. Beneath lay a small fishing village. On the beach were what appeared to be a number of rowing boats. Those were what Bridgeman-Evans had spotted from the Italian landing craft, and the reason why he had brought them all here. But disconcertingly, the beach was under guard by Italian soldiers, and a couple of sandbagged machine-gun bunkers could be seen, with huts for the gun crews lying close by.

Even so, Bridgeman-Evans's plan was the best shot they had at getting out of there. If they could steal one of the boats and row it the few miles back to Sicily, they should be able to link up with the advancing British and American forces. With dawn fast approaching, they needed to find somewhere to hide. Come nightfall, they would put their plan into action.

Halfway down the cliffside there was an old, ruined building set on a ledge cut into the rock face. With infinite care the four escapees descended, careful not to slip, or to disturb any stones or boulders that might tumble down and betray their presence. Eventually they arrived, to discover the ruins made the perfect hideout. While a stone wall shielded them from view, there were gaps in it from which they could observe goings-on in the village and on the beach.

Taking turns to rest or keep lookout, they endured the long hours of daylight, maintaining an eagle-eyed watch on 'the movements of sentries and boats' and discussing their chances of getting away. They ate the fruit they'd pilfered, mustering their strength for the trials that lay ahead. With dusk descending upon the beach, Bridgeman-Evans seemed cautiously optimistic that they could steal a boat without being spotted. As the night grew thicker, they decided to make their move, for the terrain below was by now cloaked in darkness.

Cautiously they made their way down the cliff face. It was slow going, and took far longer than they'd anticipated. They had misjudged just how high up they were, for they needed to descend some 700 to 800 feet. With the cliff dropping sheer in places, they were forced to backtrack repeatedly, seeking out a route via which they might descend in relative safety.

Finally, they made it safely to the sand. Bridgeman-Evans had already earmarked what looked like a suitable craft, which lay close to the water's edge. In the darkness it was impossible to tell whether the fisherman had left his oars in the boat. They would just have to take their chances. The target vessel lay some 350 yards away. Between them and it there were several points of possible discovery, including the Italian sentries patrolling the beach, as well as the machine-gun positions they had spied from their lookout. There was only one way that they might bypass both. They would have to get onto their bellies and crawl.

With a soft sea breeze wafting over them, the fugitives edged their way across the sand, stopping momentarily whenever they heard a sentry close by. They inched their way towards the water's edge, hoping that the rolling surf would mask any noise they inadvertently made. Their senses on high alert, their nerves on edge and with beads of sweat running down the backs of their necks, they pressed on, moving with infinite care.

With Bridgeman-Evans in the lead, eventually they made it to where sand met sea. Turning a sharp right, they moved off again, their target drawing closer by the second. And then they were there. Quickly, Bridgeman-Evans took a peek inside. Their luck was in: the oars had been left by the fisherman. If they could only get the boat into the water without being discovered, then they would be on their way.

But the vessel seemed to be a lot bigger and heavier than it had looked from the cliff, and it appeared to be locked in place by some sort of pulley and wire system. If they could free it, it would still need to be dragged a distance along the sand before it could be launched. How they might get it into the sea without attracting the attention of the enemy was anyone's guess. Malnourished, and out of breath from their epic crawl across the sand, the task seemed daunting. But they would just have to give it a go.

Fortunately, Private Mason, the old sailor, knew just what needed to be done. Expertly, he released the craft from its wire bindings, and, as quietly as he could, issued instructions to his comrades. They would have to drag the boat towards the sea from kneeling positions, to avoid being silhouetted against the skyline. It proved nigh-on impossible, but, bit by bit they made progress. Stifling their grunts, the four escapees edged the heavy wooden craft towards the sea until, finally, the hull hit the water, dropping from a steep fall of sand with a gut-wrenching crash.

Each of the escapees held their breath, convinced that the

enemy must have heard. But the only noise to break the still of the night was the lapping of the sea against the hull. As Bridgeman-Evans appreciated, this was the make-or-break moment. They would need to push the boat some distance out to sea before climbing aboard. It was not long before they were up to their chests in seawater.

Their nerves on edge, one by one they scrambled aboard and prepared to get moving. In the process they inadvertently banged the oars against the hull of the boat as they tried to fix them into their metal housings. Their impatience was to prove their undoing.

Suddenly, shouts of alarm echoed across the beach. The sentries must have heard all the din. A volley of rifle shots rang out, bullets cutting through the darkness. Seconds later one of the machine guns opened fire, as a storm of rounds raked the water to either side of the craft. Shortly, the enemy gunners found their aim, bullets slamming into the boat, tearing splinters away and peppering it with holes, which started to gush in gouts of seawater. In desperation, Bridgeman-Evans ordered his men to jump out, and to try to swim the boat further away from shore, using its wooden bulk as cover from the murderous fire.

They jumped in and began to swim for their lives. The flashes of rifle muzzles could be seen all along the shoreline. As many as a dozen sentries were letting rip, their bullets whistling over the heads of the fugitives as they struggled through the choppy sea. Bullets continued to smack into the boat, ripping chunks out of its sides.

And then a cry of agony rang out. Sharman had been hit.

With bullets continuing to fly and the harsh rattle of the machine guns filling their ears, Mason climbed back into the now semi-submerged craft and, with the help of the others, hauled Sharman inside, lest he slip beneath the waves and drown. As the boat was now filling with water, and with all in danger of being killed, Bridgeman-Evans was forced to face the harsh reality – their escape attempt was doomed. The only thing to do was to try to get back to the beach, before they were all shot dead, or drowned.

Immediately he began to shout. *'Amico! Amico!'*

With Lodge's help, and with both of them yelling out words of surrender, Bridgeman-Evans tried to swim the boat back towards the beach. But their efforts did little to stop the Italians from shooting. With bullets continuing to fly, the SAS captain broke away and with all the strength he could muster he began to strike out for the beach alone. Though he was exposing himself to the worst of the fire, he had to try to stop the enemy soldiers, before all were killed. Frantically he pumped his arms and kicked his legs, as bullets cut apart the sea, raising mini geysers. He had to stop the enemy from shooting his men, no matter what. On he went, with only one thought in his mind: *a second's delay could mean death for them all.*

Somehow, Bridgeman-Evans reached the shallows without being hit. Moments later his feet made contact with the seabed. Dragging his soaking body out of the water, he raised his hands to show he was unarmed and called for the Italians to stop shooting. In an instant he was surrounded by enemy soldiers. He turned his head and gazed out to sea, as bit by bit the firing petered out. Gradually, the stricken boat approached the shore-line, being hauled by Mason at the front, who had taken to the water once again. Lodge was the first to emerge from the surf, raising his hands in surrender. One by one the men were encircled by Italians and dragged onto dry land.

Finally, and wincing with pain, Sharman stood up in the boat. As he was about to climb down, an Italian called for him to raise his hands, but Sharman was unable to do so, due to his wound. The Italian soldier fired his rifle, the bullet hitting Sharman in the thigh, causing him to fall from the boat into the shallows. A few moments later he was unceremoniously dragged ashore, crying out with the pain.

All four fugitives were surrounded by nervous Italian soldiers now. Locals, curious to see what all the fuss was about, came crowding onto the beach. One, a fisherman, seemed incensed. He was boiling up with 'fury and hatred', Lodge recalled, and the Italian troops had to physically restrain him, or he 'would have attacked us'. The SAS sergeant could only assume that the boat, lying there peppered with bullet holes, was his.

Bridgeman-Evans and his men were taken to a nearby hut, where an Italian medic patched up Sharman's wounds before placing him on a stretcher. After being given a little food and water, the captives were led up a path to where a truck would take them back to Gioia Tauro. As the three thoroughly dejected prisoners climbed aboard the vehicle, they watched Sharman being placed in a separate truck and driven off to hospital. With that, the four escapees had become three. And they were very much back in enemy captivity.

Upon their return to Gioia Tauro, Bridgeman-Evans, Lodge and Mason were taken before the Town Marshal. It was around three o'clock in the morning. After ordering some food and drink, he began to question them regarding their escape attempt. Who had assisted them? Who had arranged for them to get the boat? Surely, they hadn't simply helped themselves and stolen it? Getting nowhere with his questioning, the marshal ordered the prisoners to be taken to a small windowless cell, and kept there for the next several days on meagre rations.

It was now that Mason really served to bolster the men's spirits, resorting to the comic tales of when he'd been at sea. Pops proved an amazing morale booster, Lodge reflected, as he regaled them all with his 'dry cynical humour'. But from time to time the conversation grew more fractious. Whenever Bridgeman-Evans steered the discussion towards politics, Mason expressed his fiercely-held views; 'he was for socialism, good and proper,' Lodge noted. Bridgeman-Evans countered by accusing Mason of having a 'warped mind'. Mason's retort was suitably cutting: 'Warped mind, my foot – I haven't got a large private income to fall back on . . . like you, sir.'

The fact that these men could speak so plainly with each other, regardless of rank, reflected how the SAS was a meritocracy. For a private soldier to feel free to argue, to the point of criticism, with his officer, was perfectly normal in such a unit. They were all in this together, and merit mattered far above rank. Those chosen for the SAS needed to be a certain type; their strength of character and self-possession were more important than their social background or the position they held in the chain of command. They were self-starters and free-thinkers, able to act independently, having the tenacity and drive to continue with a mission when the odds were very much against them. Those attributes were exactly what the SAS founders, David Stirling and Blair 'Paddy' Mayne, had looked for when forming the unit in the North African desert, in the summer of 1941.

Six days after their recapture, the prisoners were on the move again. Taken once more to Gioia Tauro railway station, they were placed aboard a train bound for a prisoner of war camp at Capua, a city lying 470 kilometres north of Gioia Tauro, and beyond Naples. Under escort by a group of Italian soldiers, the journey became a chronicle of disorganisation and chaos, as their guards repeatedly missed connections, leading to long delays. To add to their discomfort, Mason, who had always served to keep their spirits up, had fallen ill.

At one point they were made to trek a considerable distance along a railway track to meet a connecting train. Mason had to be half carried, held up between Bridgeman-Evans and Lodge. They proceeded, 'but very slowly,' Lodge would reflect, noting that 'old Pop was now really ill'. All presumed he'd gone down with malaria, a sickness that had dogged members of 2 SAS, for their training base at Philippeville, Algeria, lay adjacent to a stagnant, mosquito-infested swamp. Despite doses of quinine to combat the disease, many had fallen victim to the debilitating sickness.

Malaria causes fevers, delusional confusion, headaches, muscle aches, shivering, vomiting and more. The final part of the railway journey was spent in a horribly cramped carriage, that was until a kindly German officer took pity on Mason, who was by this time seriously unwell. The SAS captives were moved to a cattle truck, in which were riding a group of German troops, and where there was room for the ailing Mason to stretch out.

As the train steamed northwards, Lodge was able to chat to some of the German soldiers. Their conversation proved fascinating. Some were quite open in their opinion that the war was not going well for Nazi Germany. Lodge had to force himself to speak English, as opposed to his native German, for fear they would realise that he was a fellow countryman, with all the dire problems that would bring. Worried sick that he might doze off and 'speak German in my sleep,' he fought to keep himself awake. One man confessed to Lodge that he longed for the war to end, so he could return to his sweetheart in Hamburg. A decent-enough man, still he had been so brainwashed by Nazism that he accused 'international Jewish finance' of causing 'all the evils' of the war.

Finally, they arrived at Capua, their end destination. Thankfully, Lodge's cover had held good. He and Bridgeman-Evans helped Mason get down from the railway truck. Here, they were to be incarcerated in Campo 66, a POW camp situated on a vast plain, with the ancient volcanic peak of Mount Vesuvius glowering in the background. More a transit camp than a proper POW facility, its harsh conditions would give rise to an Allied investigation, entitled 'Ill-treatment of British prisoners of war at Camp PG 66 Capua, Italy, April 1941 to June 1943.'

Here Bridgeman-Evans and his SAS comrades were to be sep-arated. As an officer, Bridgeman-Evans was taken away to join fellow captives of a similar rank. Lodge and Mason were to be incarcerated with the 'other ranks', as non-officers were termed. And so, after enduring so much, the three musketeers were sep-arated.

Undaunted, Bridgeman-Evans's thoughts turned once again to escape. Although Sicily was yet to fall, there was no doubt in his mind that an Allied victory was inevitable. Even now, Allied commanders would be turning their attentions to the invasion of the Italian mainland. Getting out of the camp and heading south to meet them was an obvious plan of action. The only problem was just how to engineer a breakout.

As with most POW camps, the senior officers at Capua ran an 'escape committee'. Should any man have an idea as to how

35

to get away, then he had to put it before the committee in order to gain approval. 'All suggestions had to be authorised, approved and controlled by them,' as the Senior British Officer (SBO) at Capua, Lieutenant Colonel Richard Guy Webb, would declare. The reason to seek the escape committee's approval was to ensure that whatever scheme someone might be hatching didn't compromise other plans that might be in motion. The escape committee could also provide tools, maps and other aids to those given the green light.

Breakouts had to be carefully timed, for 'any attempt at escape meant redoubled vigilance and closing of loopholes previously overlooked,' including 'prowling in the buildings at night, dogs in the grounds', as Lieutenant Colonel Webb warned. Right away, Bridgeman-Evans volunteered to assist with the escape committee's work, for he had unique skills to offer. While training with the SSRF/SOE at Anderson Manor, he'd been schooled in the use of specialist codes, by which intelligence could be secreted within innocent seeming letters. With the Italian censors blind to the hidden content, those letters could be sent out via the Red Cross. Bridgeman-Evans was able to pass on such expertise to Webb. 'Captain Roy Bridgeman-Evans . . . taught me the system,' as Webb would later acknowledge.

Though his skills were proving useful, the SAS captain remained hungry to escape. By a stroke of good fortune, there was another SAS officer on the Capua escape committee, Lieutenant St John Carslake Brooke-Johnson. Brooke-Johnson had carried out a string of sabotage operations behind enemy lines in North Africa, until, in February 1943, he'd been captured, along with SAS founder David Stirling. He recognised in Bridgeman-Evans the type of candidate to join an escape initiative that was already well underway. The SAS captain would join a team digging a tunnel '25 yards long, starting from the canteen', via which a mass of prisoners were planning to break out.

Crucial to the tunnelling work was thirty-four-year-old Lieutenant Frederic Long, of the Royal Artillery, who had been serving with 3 Commando at the time of his capture. On 14 July 1943, his unit had been charged to assault the Punta dei Malati bridge near Lentini, a town in south-eastern Sicily. After intense fighting, in which many of the 3 Commando men had been killed, they were forced back into the surrounding hills. There, Long had been captured. Like Bridgeman-Evans he had a burning desire to escape and to get back to the war. From now on, Long and Bridgeman-Evans would form an unbreakable partnership in their repeated escape attempts.

Sadly, Capua's tunnel escape plan was doomed to failure. Just forty-eight hours before its scheduled completion the men learned that they were to be moved on. Bridgeman-Evans, Long and others were to be transported 445 kilometres north – so further away from the Allied advance – to another camp. On 28 August the tunnel that they had carved out with infinite care had to be abandoned. It was incredibly frustrating.

Their destination, known as Campo 19, lay about four kilometres south-east of the Italian city of Bologna, and just two hundred kilometres short of the German border. In terms of places of incarceration, it was about as far away from Allied lines as one could get. Some of lesser fortitude might have given up on their hopes of escape, but not Bridgeman-Evans. His two foiled escape attempts – one by rowing boat, the other by tunnel – only seemed to stiffen his resolve. The very day after his arrival at Campo 19, he was looking for a route out of there. Together with

Long, he set about devising another daring plan and putting it into operation.

Relying upon their Capua experiences, 'on 29 August we started another tunnel,' Bridgeman-Evans noted. Excavations were well under way when world events conspired to scupper their second tunnel escape plan. On the evening of 8 September 1943 – ten days after Bridgeman-Evans, Long et al. had started their new tunnel – the POW camp commandant, an Italian colonel, gathered the prisoners together. He had important news to impart, he announced. That very day Italy had surrendered unconditionally to the Allies, even as the British and American landings were in progress on the southern Italian mainland.

There were some in Campo 19 who had seen this coming. Brigadier Ronald Gervase Mountain, the camp's SBO, had long anticipated such a change in their fortunes. A seasoned career soldier, having served in the First World War, Mountain had been captured at the port city of Mersa Matruh, in North Africa, in June 1942. Along with many other SBOs in Italy, he'd been able to receive regular news via a clandestine radio set secreted in the camp. He was well aware that Sicily had fallen and that Allied troops were advancing onto the mainland. To him, the surrender of Italy had come as no great surprise.

Brigadier Mountain was also aware of what would become known as the 'Stay Put Order', an instruction emanating from MI9, the British secret service unit responsible for escape and evasion activities. The directive, issued months earlier, compelled all British prisoners held in Italian camps to remain where they were and await liberation, no matter what might occur in the wider theatre of the war. According to its authors, Italy was to be conquered quickly, meaning the camps would be rapidly overrun. But as Brigadier Mountain appreciated, German forces were showing little sign of evacuating the country, now that the Italians had effectively switched sides. Instead, there was every indication that they would fight for every inch of Italian soil, especially since Hitler had not the slightest inclination of abandoning the country.

Indeed, the Führer had vowed that Italy would not fall. He'd dispatched one of his most trusted deputies, Field Marshal Albert Kesselring, as the supreme commander in Italy, complete with some of the most battle-hardened of German forces. Kesselring, a decorated First World War veteran, had distinguished himself in the Spanish Civil War, before spearheading operations against Poland, Holland and France, after which he'd gone on to oversee the invasion of the Soviet Union, earning Hitler's highest regard.

Brigadier Mountain had an acute appreciation of all this, believing there was no way that Berlin would allow some 80,000 Allied POWs simply to return to their own lines. Whereas many SBOs issued the Stay Put Order blindly, expecting it to be complied with rigorously, and under threat of court martial, Mountain had very different ideas. To him it was unconscionable. He little doubted that Campo 19 would be taken over by the Germans, whereupon the POWs would be shipped off to camps in Nazi Germany. In short, he was not prepared to endorse such a nonsensical order.

Having learned of Italy's surrender, Mountain approached the Italian camp commandant for a private word, arguing that 'the British POWs in the camp should be protected against possible molestation by the Germans'. In particular he asked that 'gaps in the outside wire fence should be cut at certain places, and that armed support and anti-tank guns should be provided', to safeguard the prisoners.

Gathering the POWs together, he briefed them that at dawn the following morning they would break out en masse. Accordingly, the former POWs packed their few belongings and grabbed whatever Red Cross parcels were available, for they would need as much food as they could carry for what lay ahead. Rumours began circulating that German troops were already on the move to take over the camp. Italian guards warned that German forces were massing at the camp perimeter. With not a moment to lose, at 4.30 a.m. all prisoners were roused and told to make their way to the gates.

Grabbing his gear, Bridgeman-Evans joined the mass of POWs as they 'made a dash . . . for the gate at the north-east corner of the camp'. The Italian soldier guarding the exit told them there were no German troops outside, but refused to open the gates. A moment later, Brigadier Mountain made his way to the front and demanded that he do so. After all, the Italian Army had surrendered and technically, the British were now in charge. Faced with such an argument, the guard relented. Mountain then proceeded to unlock the gates and push them wide open, urging his men to make a break for it.

No sooner had the first man stepped into the darkness outside, than all hell let loose. Lying in wait for the escapees was a body of German troops. Just as the former POWs made a break for freedom, the enemy opened up. With the deafening sound of rifle and machine-gun fire filling their ears, those at the front ran for their lives, determined to make a break for it. In the darkness and confusion, some were hit and fell while others dived for cover. As yet more sprinted into the darkness, making for the nearest ditches and the safety of a tree line, bullets tore past their heads and ripped up the ground on all sides.

Finally, the enemy troops seemed to realise that the escapees were unarmed. They stopped shooting at them directly, instead firing over their heads. Still, it was enough to put an end to Brigadier Mountain's escape plan. With immense reluctance, those at the rear were forced to fall back, their chances thwarted. Many who had made it into the woods were rounded up, while those who had reached the road were stopped in their tracks, raising their hands in surrender. Miraculously, only one man had been killed, a Captain Johnson, who would die of his injuries. While there were many wounded, just four had managed to escape the onslaught and slip away.

As one survivor of the breakout would report: 'The Germans herded the remainder of us back inside the camp, and assumed control ... I was informed that the German authorities had excused themselves for opening fire without challenge on the ground that we were understood to be provided with arms.' No one had the slightest clue as to how such a misapprehension could have arisen, and it was of little consolation to those who had been shot.

For Bridgeman-Evans, it meant that a third escape attempt had been foiled. With German troops now taking over the camp, he feared they would be taken to Germany, making escape ever less likely. Sure enough, just forty-eight hours after the mass breakout, a convoy of trucks rolled up at the camp. The POWs were to be driven to the nearest railway station, for onward transport to Germany. Yet there was still one last opportunity for escape here at Campo 19, if only Bridgeman-Evans could seize it.

With immense foresight, Brigadier Mountain had made sure

41

to get rid of the camp roll, just as soon as the Italian surrender was known about. That meant that the Germans had no idea just how many prisoners were held there. With no list of names, enemy soldiers did their best to round up the prisoners and force them onto the waiting trucks, but some sixty managed to secrete themselves in various hiding places – in lofts, unfinished tunnels, even crammed into cupboards – intending to wait out the enemy's departure.

Sadly, for Bridgeman-Evans and Long, there was not a space remaining, much that they might try to find somewhere – any-where – to hide. Along with hundreds of other prisoners, they were hustled onto the waiting trucks for the journey to the nearest station. Upon arrival, they were herded into the carriages of a long train, which they learned was bound for the Moosburg POW camp (Stalag VII-A), 45 kilometres north of Munich.

En route to Moosburg, the train would be forced to wend its way through the Alps, via the Brenner Pass, a knife-cut gap in the mountains that links Italy to Austria. That offered a last chance of escape, before the train would descend into the nation of Hitler's birth, Austria, and from there into Germany itself. Long before they were crammed aboard that train, Bridgeman-Evans and Long were planning their means to breakout.

Before departing Campo 19, they'd hidden on their person 'part of a band saw and other tools left by a carpenter' who had been working in the camp. Once the train got underway, they and their fellow prisoners wasted little time putting those tools to work, using the saw to attack the carriage's wooden floor. As the train trundled its way ever northwards, snaking through the hills and valleys of Italy's Apennine mountains, they laboured feverishly. Finally, they had cut a hole large enough for a man to squeeze through.

Glancing through that jagged gap, they could see the ground below rushing past at what seemed like breakneck speed. To drop through while the train was moving would mean certain death. The only way to do this would be when they had come to a standstill. Obviously, that limited just how many might try to break out. As Bridgeman-Evans would later recall, 'We drew lots as to who should go through the hole first, as we could only drop one man each time the train stopped. I was ninth on the list . . .'

Each time the train halted, one man would slip onto the tracks, seizing his chance to dash off into the countryside. First one, then two, and eventually five prisoners managed to escape in that way. All down that long train, other POWs were likewise busy. As Bridgeman-Evans would later report, '150 British officers got off that train in one way or another.' Among them was Lieutenant Brooke-Johnson, the SAS officer who had been on the escape committee back at Capua. But being so far down the pecking order, Bridgeman-Evans was never to get his chance, and neither did his good friend Long.

On 13 September, two days after its departure, the train reached Moosburg, and the prisoners were disgorged into Stalag VII-A, the largest POW camp in Nazi Germany at that time. Crammed full of 'French, Serbs and Romanians', as Bridgeman-Evans would describe it, the French prisoners 'have the place well organised for escape'. Indeed, 'eight officers were got out by the French the day after we arrived. Unfortunately they were recaptured.'

It had been two months since Bridgeman-Evans and his SAS party had been taken captive. In the interim, there had been five escape attempts, one by boat, two by tunnel, one by the mass breakout and a final one by cutting a hole in the train carriage floor. All had been for naught, and despite all his best efforts Bridgeman-Evans had now crossed the border into Hitler's Reich. It was the measure of the man that he remained unbowed, despite the fact that the nearest Allied lines were now over a thousand kilometres away, in southern Italy, or a similar distance north-west, across the Channel, to Britain. All he needed was to find the right opportunity, Bridgeman-Evans reminded himself.

A few days after reaching Stalag VII-A, Bridgeman-Evans and Long were on the move once more. At least now the direction of travel boded well for their fortunes. This time they were headed 400 kilometres almost due west, over the border into France, to Strasbourg. Their end destination was the POW camp situated at Fort Bismarck, a satellite camp to Stalag V-C. Built in the 1890s, Bismarck formed part of a ring of huge fortifications that encircled the city of Strasbourg. Fort Bismarck had been garrisoned by the French Army until the June 1940 fall of France, after which the Germans had transformed it into a POW facility. Situated to the west of the city, it was an unforgiving, glowering place, most of which was set underground.

It had certainly never been designed as a POW camp. Within its massive walls, subterranean passageways and cell-like rooms, Fort Bismarck was initially designed for housing bodies of French troops. Constructed so as to be impregnable, the parts of the fortress that emerged from the depths were ringed by thick walls, the tops of which were entangled by barbed wire. Strategically placed watchtowers had been constructed by the Germans, and the entire 'camp' was encircled by a dry moat, one or two heavily guarded bridges connecting the dark heart of the fortress-prison to the outside world.

Conditions at Fort Bismarck were appalling. 'The overcrowding here was terrible,' Bridgeman-Evans would report. 'There were

35 officers to a room. We slept on three-tier wooden bunks.' That only served to fuel his hunger to break out, and that of his equally-determined escape partner, Long. Together, they began to search for a way to be free of the place, first making contact with the camp's escape committee.

The camp's SBO was Lieutenant-Colonel Johannes de Beer, a South African who had been serving with the Duke of Edinburgh's Own Rifles when captured. He boasted an exceptionally well-run escape set-up. There was a rigorous system in place should anyone have any ideas about how to break out of such a daunting set of fortifications. 'The committee interviewed all applicants with original schemes, registered the schemes and controlled priorities with reference to each type of scheme,' de Beer noted.

The Fort Bismarck escape committee had managed to procure a good deal of equipment that could prove useful to a potential escapee – mostly items picked up by officers while in transit. 'Escapes from Fort Bismarck ... were effected entirely with materials ... smuggled into camp,' de Beer would report. These included an incredible range of kit, namely 'maps, compasses, wire cutters and pincers, steel saws, torches, money, blankets for civilian suits, passes and rubber stamps ...'

With such support to hand, all Bridgeman-Evans and Long needed was a plan. After studying the routines of the camp they settled upon an idea. It was blindingly obvious – so much so, that it was a wonder that no one had yet tried it. But then again, the most obvious ideas were often the most effective, while being equally often overlooked.

By late September 1943 the two conspirators were ready to put their idea before de Beer and his committee. By careful observation, Bridgeman-Evans and Long had noticed that 'about 12 foot of wire next to the guardroom formed a complete "blind spot" from . . . machine-gun posts at either end of the camp and from both sentries, provided they were at the end of their beats'. If they could time it right, using wire cutters to snip the barbed wire in that exact spot, then they could slip through the fence and make their bid for freedom. It really was that simple.

Without hesitation, de Beer gave his approval. What was more, the escape committee suggested how they might cover for the two escapees at roll-call. A window opened out onto a dry moat, along which the prisoners walked to be counted, before crossing a bridge back into the fort. By cutting the wire at the window, 'two officers who had already been counted would be able to emerge from the window and be counted again. In this way it was hoped that two officers would get out each night.' In other words, if Bridgeman-Evans and Long were successful, pairs of escapees would follow in their footsteps for as many nights as was possible, before the breakout was discovered.

By Friday 1 October 1943, Bridgeman-Evans and Long were poised to put their plan into action. Gathering their escape pack, which consisted of a compass, wire-cutters and rations containing 'three tins of processed cheese, one tin of sardines, one block of chocolate, one bag of porridge . . . cocoa, margarine, condensed milk, raisins and sugar', they were ready to go. They also carried five pounds of 'escape cakes', made up of crushed biscuits, and 'Klim', a type of powdered milk. After their rations ran out, they intended to 'live off the land'. One massive thing in their favour was that Bridgeman-Evans was fluent in French, his wife, Suzanne, being a native of France. There should be few problems conversing with the locals.

46

Patiently they waited for the right moment. Posting lookouts to keep an eye on the sentries, they made for the blind spot, where they awaited the signal that it was good to go. Eventually, they received a discreet thumbs-up from the lookouts and, moments later, both men were hoisted up to a point where they could access the wire. With adrenalin pumping, Bridgeman-Evans snipped the nearest rolls that crowned the wall, and an instant later he'd scrambled over. Seconds later, Long followed, pulling the wire back into position, before dropping down beside his comrade. Quickly, the two fugitives crawled towards some bushes at the side of the guardroom, where they concealed themselves from view.

'The whole thing took about a minute,' Bridgeman-Evans would later report. And it had all been done in broad daylight. They were out, but now came one of the most trying periods of all – the wait for nightfall, before which they couldn't risk making any further moves. For well over an hour they lay perfectly still, hardly daring to breathe lest they give themselves away. Finally, with darkness upon them, the two fugitives emerged from the thicket and began to crawl away.

They had gone just a few yards when suddenly they heard voices near by. Looking up, they could see a pair of German soldiers emerging from the guardroom, setting out on what had to be a patrol. Alarmingly, each had a very large German Shepherd dog on a leash. Bridgeman-Evans and Long held their breaths and lay perfectly still. If the guards turned around they would surely be seen.

Fortunately the sentries and their dogs walked on, seemingly oblivious to the two escapees who lay on the ground just a few yards away. Catching their breath, Bridgeman-Evans and Long crawled off in the opposite direction. Once they reckoned they'd gone sufficiently far, they stood up and slipped away into the night.

Having studied one of de Beer's maps before breaking out, and committing it to memory, they had a good idea of which way to go. Walking across country to avoid any roads, they headed in a westerly direction – deeper into Nazi-occupied France. Just outside the town of Molsheim, some 18 kilometres distant from Fort Bismarck, they found a patch of dense scrubland in which to rest up. The two men knew that sleep was essential if they were to remain alert, and that constant vigilance would be key to making this escape attempt successful. They also needed all the strength they could muster for what promised to be a very long trek indeed.

Their escape plan was rudimentary in the extreme. By pushing west, further into France, they hoped to come across some friendly locals who might in turn put them in touch with the French Resistance, and so find a way of getting spirited back to Britain. It was not much of a plan, but as they were over 2,000 kilometres distant from the nearest British territory on mainland Europe, Gibraltar, and the Channel separated them from Britain, it was the best they could think of. No matter what happened, Bridgeman-Evans was now in control of his own destiny, and with Long at his side he had a trusted escape partner. Not since his abortive escape from Giaio Tauro, and the rowing boat shoot-up at sea, had the SAS captain felt so free.

After getting some sleep, the two men were on the move again, making another 12 kilometres on foot. Finding some woods near the town of Urmatt, they concluded, sensibly, to travel only during the dark hours, as there was far less likelihood of being seen. They'd pushed far enough from Fort Bismarck to be able to relax the pace a little. That decided, they rested in the woods. Come nightfall they pressed on, heading across hilly, densely wooded country, towards the town of Schirmeck. There, they took a short break. It was 3 October 1943, as they set out once more, stumbling through the darkness, unable to see more than a few feet ahead of them, due to the thick woods.

Unbeknown to the two fugitives, Schirmeck was the site of Natzweiler-Struthof, one of Nazi Germany's so-called *Nacht und Nebel* – 'night and fog' – concentration camps. It was there that a number of fellow SAS soldiers would be brutally tortured – and very possibly murdered – by the Nazis, after being captured during operations in the Vosges Mountains, the very area that Bridgeman-Evans and Long were presently passing through.

The going proved exhausting, the conditions tough. The terrain over which they were travelling was hilly and awkward. Shrouded in dense rain, fog and freezing mist, the Vosges in autumn were horribly inhospitable. Even so, they persevered, creeping through thick groves of trees, flitting across lower-lying fields, and all the while detouring around the lakes and highest peaks. The near total darkness proved disorientating, causing them to stop repeatedly to check their compass, another gift from de Beer's escape committee. As a result, they were not covering nearly as much ground as they had expected.

At 5.30 a.m., around first light, they found themselves struggling through the seemingly impenetrable forest that lies at the foothills of Mount Donon, the highest peak in the northern Vosges. Having lain up, they 'marched to Celles-sur-Plaine . . . 20 kilometres south-west of Schirmeck', Bridgeman-Evans would report. Celles-sur-Plaine was a small rural town situated on the banks of a large lake. It was there, having covered some 75 kilometres since their escape, that they decided to change tack, for they were desperate to make contact with the French Resistance.

Spying an isolated house on the outskirts of the town, the two fugitives made an approach. Gently, they tried the handle of the door. Finding it unlocked, they stole inside. They were greeted by the shocked face of a man – the house's sole occupant. In his fluent French Bridgeman-Evans was able to explain their predicament. It was quickly established that the homeowner was a true French patriot and was prepared to help. Although he had no contacts with the Resistance, he offered food, maps and crucially, civilian clothes, for their onward journey.

Accepting the man's generosity, and sensing he was genuine, Bridgeman-Evans and Long stayed with him for three days, mustering their strength. On 7 October they bade him farewell and set off once more, heading south-west towards Pont d'Arches, a small village located a short distance from Epinal, on the banks of the Moselle river. The intervening terrain proved to be an expanse of wild country and forest. For forty-eight hours they pushed through this wilderness, before striking it lucky once more. At Pont d'Arches they managed to contact another friendly local, who likewise was prepared to help.

Accepting his hospitality, plus a bundle of French francs to pay their way, they hurried onwards, reaching the western flank of the Vosges mountains, whereupon they descended into easier, more hospitable terrain. Reaching the small-town of Aillevillers-et-Lyaumont, for the third time they tried their luck with whoever might live in of one of the outlying houses. The man of the house introduced himself as 'Nicholas Vogelsang'. Once it was established that the two fugitives were escaped prisoners of war, they were welcomed with open arms. But frustratingly, he too claimed not to know anyone connected with the French Resistance.

Increasingly worried that nobody seemed able to provide a means of escape, Bridgeman-Evans had a flash of inspiration. From his time with SOE, he knew that the SNCF – *Societé nationale des chemins de fer français*; the French national railway company – was a hotbed of Resistance activities. Many of its employees were said to be active members of the *Résistance Fer* – the Iron Resistance, or Railway Resistance. The *Résistance Fer* specialised in reporting German rail movements to the Allies, and sabotaging key rail infrastructure and rolling stock. Surely, their host had to know someone associated with the French railway, he argued.

Nicholas Vogelsang declared that he knew of just such a man. Soon enough, that individual arrived. While he declined to give his name, he was a seasoned railway worker, and he confirmed that he knew of the kind of network that the British escapees were looking for. This was immensely heartening. For the first time in what seemed like an age, they felt their fortunes were on the up; finally they seemed to be in the hands of people who knew what they were doing. Before leaving, the railwayman took photographs of the two escapees, so false ID documents could be drawn up.

Two days later, on 12 October, they received a second visitor, a man who gave his name as Emil Horn. He'd travelled from the town of Belfort, he explained, some 50 kilometres to the south-east and close to the Swiss border. Sure enough, he carried with him fake identity cards complete with Bridgeman-Evans and Long's photographs. Plans were being formulated to spirit them back to Britain, Horn announced. Shortly, they would be on their way. Bridgeman-Evans and Long could hardly believe their luck. By simply knocking on a random door in a small rural town in Nazi-occupied France, they'd managed to find a route back to Allied lines, or so it seemed.

Of course, they had few options other than to put their faith in their new-found friends. These brave Frenchmen were risking not only their own lives, but those of their families, in an effort to spirit Allied soldiers and airmen away from the forces of Nazi Germany. On balance, Bridgeman-Evans and Long had to presume they were in the best of hands.

On 16 October Emil Horn took them to the nearest railway station, where they boarded a train heading to Belfort, his home town. Bridgeman-Evans was under no illusions that if they were caught, then he and Long would be treated as spies, for they were carrying fake identification documents and were dressed in civilian clothes. In a sense, this was now the most dangerous part of their journey, for they could expect little clemency from their enemies. Warned of the dangers that lay ahead, they were told to follow Horn's instructions to the letter, so as to minimise the possibility of being arrested along the way.

The town of Belfort lies 20 kilometres short of the Swiss border. But it wasn't to neutral Switzerland that the escapees were headed. While they needed to get back into the fight, they were being sucked into the cloak and dagger world of the escape lines, those secretive networks that criss-crossed western Europe, spiriting Allied escapees towards the promise of safety, but menaced by the Gestapo and the SS at every turn. Few explanations were offered, or expected, as to where exactly they were heading or why.

Upon arrival at Belfort, Horn led them to 16 Faubourg de

Lyons, a three-storey house set in an affluent part of the town, and owned by another Resistance operative, one Albert Zangelen. Having spent so much time in POW camps and then living rough during their escapes, it was a relief for the two fugitives to be in a place that somehow felt 'normal'. Here, they met Paul Rassiniers, a teacher and the 'head of the de Gaulle section', which was a branch of the wider French Resistance. Once Rassiniers had allocated them a guide, they were off again, this time heading to Paris, some 450 kilometres north-west of Belfort. Just why they had been sent to Belfort remained unclear, but they sensed it was to ensure that they were bona fide Allied POWs, and not Nazi plants.

After an overnight train journey to the French capital, their guide led them a merry dance through the city streets. All around them the Paris streets were hustle and bustle, as people went about their daily business. Seemingly at every turn Nazi banners hung from official buildings. The two escapees were in the thick of it now, deep inside the Nazi powerbase in Europe, yet slipping by as unremarked as any French citizen might. With their civilian attire and fake identification papers, they looked – and, more importantly, had started to feel – very much the part. That was absolutely critical, to enable them to blend in.

Now and again they passed groups of German soldiers, but none seemed to take the slightest notice, as Bridgeman-Evans and Long strolled by. Eventually, they reached the busy square that was the Place de l'Opéra. The world-famous Palais Garnier opera house drew the eye, though its grand auditorium would be crammed with Nazi party officials these days. The square was thronged with Parisians, ignorant of the fact that there were two elite British officers in close proximity. Here, their guide bade them farewell, whereupon they were passed to another, in a pre-arranged handover.

From the Place de l'Opéra they were taken to 69 Rue Victor Hugo, a five-storey apartment building in Colombes, a suburb lying to the north-west of central Paris. Upon arrival, they were handed over to Georges Guillemin. Guillemin informed them that he was a senior member of the Bourgogne network, an escape line 'whose mission was to transport Allied pilots shot down in France to England, via Spain, to allow them to resume the fight'. As Guillemin explained, he had made preparations to do exactly that for Bridgeman-Evans and Long.

The Bourgogne network had been set up by Lieutenant Georges Broussine, a FFL (*Forces françaises libres*, or Free French) officer, working in close liaison with MI9, the British escape and evasion outfit. A medical student before the war, Broussine's route to join the Free French had taken well over two years, following the defeat of France. Held in prisons in both France and Spain, he'd finally made it to Britain, where he 'officially joined the FFL on 10 September 1942'. After intense training, Broussine had been dropped back into France, in February 1943, to set up the Bourgogne escape line. It would eventually lead to the repatriation of almost three hundred Allied servicemen.

By the time Bridgeman-Evans and Long had been passed over to his network, the escape line was busy, having already conveyed close to sixty Allied servicemen to freedom. Their new contact, Guillemin, informed them that they were to be split up. That very night Bridgeman-Evans was to leave for Perpignan, a city lying on the French south coast, and just ten kilometres short of the Spanish border. Long would travel via a different route. That way, there would be better chances of at least one of them making it through.

As Guillemin explained, the plan was to hand Bridgeman-Evans over to local guides, who would lead him across the Pyrenees, to Spain. Once over the border, he could then make his way to the nearest large city, Barcelona, and from there to Madrid and the British consulate. The consulate staff would be able to make arrangements for him to get to Gibraltar and, ultimately, via ship or plane, back to Britain.

The initial route that the Bourgogne escape line had used to take escapees across to Spain had been via the Pyrenees, but with winter setting in, bad weather had hit the mountains and it was deemed too dangerous. It would be plagued by snows and blizzard-like conditions. Instead, a passage over the hills near Perpignan was seen as being the safest route, for they were far less rugged or exposed.

After bidding his goodbye to Long – they had spent two months on the run, or imprisoned together, in Italy, Germany and France – Bridgeman-Evans set off on what he hoped would be the final leg of his journey. He was to join an escape group that included Flying Officer George Lents, a twenty-three-year-old French Spitfire pilot serving with the RAF, plus five other Frenchmen. That evening, the seven fugitives 'left Paris by train for Perpignan with a young man and a girl as their guides'. They arrived in the French port city the following morning.

From there they were 'taken by tram to a small hotel near a park on the outskirts of town'. That evening they linked up with local guides and walked through the night, heading south, edging ever closer to the border with Spain. With freedom so close, it was imperative that Bridgeman-Evans and his companions remained vigilant. The area over which they were trekking was heavy with German patrols, on the lookout for groups such as theirs. Thankfully, their guides seemed highly experienced and knew which routes to take to avoid the worst of the danger. Placing all their trust in those escorts and using the cover of near total darkness in which to move, the seven escapees were led through areas of thick scrubland, across ravines and tumbling streams, as they pushed ever onwards towards the Spanish border. Retiring to secluded places in which to hide during daylight hours, as soon the sun set they were up and on the move again, the promise of freedom drawing them ever on.

And then, without even realising it, they had slipped across the border.

On the evening of 21 October they reached the town of Figueras in the far north-east of Spain. From there, their guide took Lents and Bridgeman-Evans 'on a series of trains to Barcelona', which was only a three-hour train ride from Madrid, the Spanish capital. Spain being neutral, Bridgeman-Evans was as good as home and dry.

Due to the intense secrecy of such escape lines, Bridgeman-Evans's story then becomes somewhat opaque, until, on 1 November 1943, a telegram arrived at SOE headquarters in the UK. Hailing from the British consulate in Madrid, it read: *'Captain Bridgeman-Evans formerly of STS 62 and later made prisoner of war after parachuting into Sicily is now in Madrid and will proceed to Gibraltar Tuesday night, November 3rd, en route for United Kingdom. MI9 have been informed by Military Attache here. Please inform Colonel Stirling. Am informing Gibraltar.'*

Unpacking that a little, 'STS 62' was SOE Special Training Station 62, more commonly known as Anderson Manor, the Dorset training base of the SSRF, the unit Bridgeman-Evans had served with, before joining the Special Air Service. 'Colonel Stirling' would be Bill Stirling, Bridgeman-Evans's commander at 2 SAS. Four days later, on 5 November, Bridgeman-Evans left Gibraltar by plane, arriving in the United Kingdom the following day.

Displaying all the qualities required of an SAS officer, Bridgeman-Evans had finally made it home. The freedom he had craved from the moment of his capture was now his. Through steely determination, the unyielding conviction never to give up, and braving many abortive escape attempts plus numerous setbacks, he had finally made it through. He could now rejoin his unit and get back into the fight. It had taken three and a half months since the fateful parachute drop into Sicily, but through audacity and guile he had made it, assisted along the way by those brave locals who were equally determined to rid the world of the scourge of Nazism.

Operation Chestnut, the mission Bridgeman-Evans and his men had spearheaded, proved something of a damp squib. The capture of most of the Brig team and poor communications with the Pink group meant that only a small number of SAS were dropped in. Some sabotage work was carried out, before the advancing British and American forces caught up with them at the end of July 1943, but the cost in terms of men captured or declared missing was high.

Sadly, the highly experienced and much respected SAS commander Major Geoffrey Appleyard, erstwhile of the SSRF, who had accompanied the men to their drop zone, had been killed later that night, when the Albermarle he was riding in failed to arrive back at its base. The circumstances are unclear as to exactly what transpired, but it's highly likely that the aircraft was shot down by friendly fire.

Bill Stirling, 2 SAS's commander, remained typically upbeat and philosophical about Operation Chestnut's failures. In a detailed and instructive appraisal, headlined simply 'Lessons', he wrote that this was the first major mission 'carried out by the 2nd Special Air Service Regiment from the air, and it suffered from those disadvantages which are unavoidable when plans must be made hurriedly, training fundamentally altered, or omitted entirely, and the operation carried out by men who, with few exceptions, were unaccustomed to conditions pertaining in this particular type of warfare'. The fact that his men had been given so little – or no – time to perfect the art of parachute jumps was galling, but he was determined the right lessons would be learned.

Stirling identified two key elements that lay behind Chestnut's failure. First, the SAS had not been permitted to select their own DZs. Instead, 15th Army Group had chosen them from studying aerial photos. In future, the SAS mission commander would get to select his DZ personally, and ideally after carrying out a reconnaissance flight over the terrain, Stirling declared. Secondly, the SAS had been prevented from choosing their targets. Instead, they'd been given 'a roving commission for destruction', being ordered to wander about and find whatever targets might exist on the ground. With the immense loads each man had to carry, this was far from ideal. In future, SAS teams should pre-select their targets.

For his escape from Fort Bismarck and earlier escape attempts, Roy Bridgeman-Evans would be awarded the Military Cross. His citation reads:

Captain Bridgeman-Evans was captured near Capizzi when attempting to carry out a special air operation on 13 July 43. He was chained to his men and condemned to death. He was moved to Gioia where he climbed over a wall with three of his men. They crawled past sentries and rowed out in a boat which was sunk by M.G. fire in 5 minutes. One of the men was hit and Capt. Bridgeman-Evans swam back to get the Italians to stop firing. He was then moved to Capua where . . . he dug a tunnel 25 yards long. He then moved to Bologna where he started another tunnel. When the Germans took over the camp he was moved to Germany . . . He finally escaped from Fort Bismarck, Strasbourg, on 1 Oct 43 with Capt. Long, by cutting a hole in the wire in broad daylight, after which they made their way without help across the frontier . . . from where they were helped by an organisation.

After the war Bridgeman-Evans returned to work as a tobacco and snuff blender at the family cigar merchants, Fribourg and Treyer, in Haymarket, London. In 1954 he became a founder member of the Worshipful Company of Tobacco Pipe Makers & Tobacco Blenders, one of the City of London's renowned Livery Companies, who 'promote fellowship and philanthropy, and play an integral role in the governance of the City of London'. As a founder, he was a member of the Court (the governing body of the Livery Company). He was on the Court from 1954 to 1966, when he progressed to become Master of the Company. He died on 6 April 1985, in Four Elms, Kent.

After an arduous crossing over the Pyrenees, Frederic Long also made good his escape, making it safely to Gibraltar. He arrived back in the UK shortly after Bridgeman-Evans, on 11

November 1943. Long was also to receive the Military Cross for his exploits: 'Capt. Long was captured at Lentini (Sicily) on 14 July 43 by German paratroops. He was taken via Messina to Capua and then to Bologna. He was associated with Capt. Bridgeman-Evans in the tunnel attempts at Capua and Bologna and also in the attempt to escape from the Modena-Brenner train. They finally made their escape together from Fort Bismarck.'

Private Sharman, shot while trying to escape in the rowing boat, 'spent two weeks in a field hospital . . . and five more weeks in hospital at Vibo Valentia', a city in southern Italy. On 9 September he was liberated by an advanced party of British troops and 'was able to give Brigade HQ . . . information about the German retreat'. After liberation, Sharman rejoined the military, serving with the 21st Independent Parachute Company – an elite airborne pathfinder unit – with whom he operated with distinction. He was taken prisoner again, at Arnhem, where he had parachuted in ahead of the main force, to mark the drop zones and landing zones for those troops who would follow.

Brigadier Ronald Mountain DSO MC, the unflappable Senior British Officer of Campo 19, Bologna, saw out the war at Oflag XII-B, near the town of Hadamar, in Germany. He was Mentioned in Despatches in recognition of his 'gallant and distinguished services as a prisoner of war'. He retired from the army in 1947 and died in 1983 at the age of eighty-six.

Barely a fortnight after Bridgeman-Evans and Long's meeting with Paul Rassiniers, the head of the de Gaulle section of the Lorraine resistance network, the Frenchman was captured by the Gestapo. Interrogated and tortured for a total of twenty-one days, Rassiniers was beaten incessantly, suffering a broken jaw, a crushed hand and the loss of a kidney. He was eventually sent to

Buchenwald concentration camp before being moved to another, Nordhausen-Dora. He survived the war and died in July 1967.

Georges Guillemin, the escape line leader who organised Bridgeman-Evans and Long's final getaway, was 'denounced by a traitor and arrested . . . on October 29 1943', just twelve days after the British escapees had left Paris. Tortured continuously for weeks, he remained stoic, never betraying any of his compatriots, thus allowing the escape line to continue its work right until the end of the war. Guillemin was sent to various concentration camps including Auschwitz, Buchenwald and Flossenburg, before enduring a six-day 'death march' to Dachau, where he was eventually liberated.

Sergeant Robert Lodge – the German Jew, Rudi Friedlander – was to escape captivity in Italy 'walking the length of the Apennines to reach Allied lines on 23 December 1943'. After spending a period of time in hospital, he rejoined the SAS on 9 May 1944. For his escape he received a Mention in Despatches. He was dropped into the Vosges area of France – the same area that Bridgeman-Evans had escaped through – in August 1944, on SAS Operation Loyton. There, Lodge was to meet an untimely end.

The Maquis camp in which he was staying was betrayed – the Maquis being rural resistance groups. After twice covering their retreat with a Bren gun, Lodge's body was later found near the town of Moussey, with his hands bound behind his back. Despite protestations from the Germans that Lodge had killed himself, it was clear that he had been murdered. As the commander of 2 SAS would conclude: 'Sgt. Lodge's case is a clear one in which he was bayonetted after capture and later shot.'

Lodge was buried in Moussey cemetery. The inscription on his gravestone is a quote from a letter he wrote to his father, shortly before he was killed. 'Our sacrifice will not be futile if the survivors have learned the lessons of this disastrous war.'

The determination of men such as Bridgeman-Evans and Lodge to escape captivity and get back into the war typified the SAS. Bridgeman-Evans had persisted in a series of daring escape attempts, using all possible means – on foot, by bluff, by sea, by underground means, by train and finally, by going over the wire and joining an MI9 escape line. In doing so, he risked death repeatedly, his dogged persistence embodying the triumph of the human spirit. If any of Bridgeman-Evans's men had ever had cause to doubt him, his actions in leading their escape attempts in the summer and autumn of 1943 put such worries to rest.

The deaths of SAS stalwarts such as Sergeant Lodge and Major Appleyard were tragic losses, but they only served to spur their comrades to finish what had been started, and to rid the world of Nazi tyranny once and for all.

Chapter Two

FLIGHT FROM THE REICH

August 1943, Paris, France

Having been introduced to the mysterious Madame Fontaine, thirty-two-year-old Sergeant Jacques Mouhot knew instantly that she was a woman of her word, for her 'honesty shone in her face', he would observe.

They'd met in a busy Metro station, part of the Paris underground network, where they could melt into the crowd should the need arise. Once Mouhot had outlined his bona fides and his intentions, Madame Fontaine confirmed that she would be able to help. They agreed to meet some days later at the Gare d'Orsay, the railway station lying on the south bank of the River Seine, in the heart of Paris.

At that Quai d'Orsay rendezvous, Madame Fontaine handed Mouhot a train ticket for Toulouse, plus the address of a contact who could help him with his onward flight. Toulouse lay some 600 kilometres to the south and just a hundred short of the Spanish border, and Spain spelled relative freedom for men like

Mouhot, an SAS veteran and a serial escapee. He sensed that this was it. His epic journey to freedom, which had taken him across Crete, Italy, Germany and France, was coming to an end.

This time he would be carrying official papers, and better still he was traversing his native country, for Mouhot was a French recruit to the SAS. Surely, he told himself, there could be few upsets along the way.

It was July 1943, and the forces of Nazi Germany occupied the whole of France. Up until November 1942 they had kept their troops to the north and west, allowing the puppet government in Vichy to administer the south and east – what was known as the 'Free Zone'. But on 8 November 1942, Allied forces had mounted the first ever Anglo-US amphibious operation, in what was known as Operation Torch. As Allied troops hit the beaches in Morocco and Algeria, the Axis forces found themselves caught between the British Eighth Army in the east, and the Operation Torch amphibious assault in the west. Ultimately, this would lead to the defeat of Rommel's Afrika Korps and their Italian allies in North Africa.

Fearing that the Allies would use that newly seized territory as a springboard from which to invade France's Mediterranean coast, Hitler ordered his troops into the Free Zone, thereby bringing the whole of France under Nazi control. Ironically, that had made travelling across the length and breadth of the French nation a little easier, for there was no need for checkpoints between the Occupied and Free Zones, as Mouhot well appreciated.

As Mouhot settled into his seat in the train carriage, Madame Fontaine appeared again. Surreptitiously, she handed him an envelope, telling him not to open it until the train had left the station. With that, she bade him farewell. Expecting to find further instructions inside, Mouhot was astonished to discover instead a thousand French francs, which was more than enough money to see him on his way. The generosity of the gesture was overwhelming.

As Mouhot had fervently hoped, the train journey passed without incident. On arrival in Toulouse he made for the address Madame Fontaine had given him, arriving at the house of a local doctor. After staying there for the night, the following morning his host drove him 70 kilometres further south, to the town of Foix, which lies in the foothills of the Pyrenees. He was now just 35 kilometres from the border with Spain.

Reaching Foix in the late afternoon, Mouhot was passed to another member of the escape network, someone he would describe simply as 'The Architect'. With no room in that man's house, he was taken to a small hotel in which to spend the night. But the hotelier, suspecting why Mouhot was there, refused to accommodate him, for his hostelry was full to bursting with German troops. Should they decide to ask Mouhot any difficult questions, then one wrong word, one slip of the tongue, and he might well be unmasked. The hotelier simply couldn't take the risk.

Instead, he took Mouhot to his own home, where the SAS fugitive was allowed to bed down for the night in the bathroom. Early the following morning, The Architect was back. He came bearing instructions, informing Mouhot that he would be 'leaving that night to cross the Pyrenees'. The last stage of his epic escape was about to begin. Late that afternoon they set out, The Architect driving Mouhot into the open countryside, as the flanks of the Pyrenees reared up before them. Eventually, they halted.

The Architect pointed to a patch of trees. 'Go into that little wood,' he announced. 'A van will come and take you.'

Bidding farewell, Mouhot did as he'd been instructed, taking cover behind a bush that offered him a view of the nearby road. As he waited he could hear odd, 'suspicious noises', which caused him to hunker down nervously. Increasingly, those mystery sounds troubled him. It seemed as if hidden figures were lurking in the undergrowth near by. Were they enemy patrols, on the lookout for escapers and evaders such as him? He couldn't imagine who else it might be.

Fearful that he would be thwarted at this eleventh hour, Mouhot burrowed deeper into the densest patch of undergrowth. He simply could not be caught, especially after all the abortive escape attempts, and particularly now, when freedom was so close. Fifteen months earlier his daring and audacious mission with the SAS had come to a bitter and fateful end, just at the moment when he and his fellow raiders had been so close to evading an enemy that had hunted them so relentlessly. That had been in June 1942 . . .

As unexpected as it was unwelcome, the warning yell had echoed across the sunbaked hillside. 'The krauts!'

Mouhot lifted his head, instantly alert. Scrambling for his Beretta sub-machine gun, he chambered a round and looked where his commander, SAS Captain Georges Bergé, was indicating. Sure enough, on the ridge that dominated the terrain was what appeared to be a large body of German troops, advancing cautiously, scanning the bush on all sides for signs of their quarry. After twenty-three German warplanes had been destroyed at the Cretan airbase of Heraklion, five day earlier, a manhunt for those responsible had been launched, the enemy determined to capture the saboteurs.

Mouhot glanced to one side. Concealed in the bushes were two more SAS troopers, corporals Jack Sibard and Pierre Leostic, otherwise known as 'The Kid'. Just seventeen years old, and the youngest of the six-man patrol that had embarked on 'Operation Number 10 (D)', Leostic had lied about his age when enlisting. Sibard, at twenty-one, was a grizzled veteran by comparison. They too had heard Bergé's warning and had grabbed their weapons. There seemed to be no easy way they could make a break for it, as more bands of enemy troops appeared.

Keeping low to the ground, Bergé belly-crawled through the thorny brush, moving away from the nearest threat. He'd gone no more than a few yards before he saw that it was hopeless. More German troops were coming from that direction. Their only option was to make a stand where they were, and hope that their ammunition might last until nightfall, when the cover of darkness might give them a chance to slip away. That understood, Bergé quickly organised his companions into the best defensive positions possible.

As the enemy drew closer they began to unleash bursts of fire into the bushes, the clatter of their rifles echoing across the dusty basin. There then followed the crump of explosions, as the nearest troops lobbed grenades. Most detonated harmlessly, for the range was too far to make grenade blasts count. The four SAS men hadn't yet been seen, but somehow the enemy seemed to know the rough whereabouts of where they were hiding.

Regardless, Mouhot seemed to feel little sense of fear or alarm. He'd been through enough already in this war for panic to have become an alien emotion. During the moment of waiting for action, unaware of what might happen, he'd find himself fully focused on the coming fight, with 'all my senses alert'. As soon as battle was joined, instinct would take over, as his reflexes played out 'almost mechanically, without effort'.

Armed with such a mindset and cool, steely nerves, Mouhot joined his commander behind the cover of a low wall, while Sibard and Leostic lay in a nearby ditch, so they could cover all sides. Suddenly 'a lone German trooper pressed forward', his eyes scanning for any sign of their quarry. Bergé raised his weapon and let off a short blast, knocking the enemy soldier to the ground. Seeing this, his comrades kept back, reluctant to advance for fear of meeting the same fate.

For the next twenty minutes the standoff continued, the Germans firing into the bushes all around the SAS men, who responded with short, well-aimed bursts. But inevitably, their ammo started running low. There was only one way this was likely to end. Spying what he thought was a chance to break out, young Leostic's impatience got the better of him.

Jumping up, he shouted, 'Follow me! To the south! There's no one there!'

As Leostic went to make his move, Mouhot could see the danger he was about to blunder into. 'Hide, you'll get shot,' he yelled.

Bergé added his warning: 'Don't move, Leostic!'

Despite the warnings, the young man was not for turning. It was to prove a fatal error. As he dashed forward, emerging from cover, Leostic's move was met with a hail of gunfire. Bullets thumped into his body, knocking him to the ground. He lay there, the blood from his wounds seeping into the Cretan dirt. His final words were to call for his mother, before he seemed to breathe his last.

Now reduced to just three, the situation was becoming

increasingly desperate. With his ammunition running out, Mouhot could sense that they were facing long-experienced troops, the enemy appearing well-trained and disciplined. After a while the German troops drew closer to Leostic's bloodied form. Bergé, Mouhot and Sibard watched in horror as the enemy raised their weapons and riddled him with bullets, ensuring the young SAS trooper was well and truly dead.

For an hour the two sides continued to trade fire, as Bergé and his men eked out their last magazines of ammunition. Bullets whistled past their heads, throwing up spouts of dirt, and spraying sharp shards of rock from where they struck the low wall. Nightfall was still an hour away and they were down to their last rounds. Knowing that to stay where they were would mean certain death or capture, Bergé signalled that it was every man for himself.

Sibard was the first to move. He had crawled just thirty yards when he felt the muzzle of a weapon pressed against his forehead. With no other option, he raised his hands in surrender. Bergé fared no better. Moments later, he too was captured while trying to make a break for it.

That left only Mouhot. Finding a hiding place deep in a tangled bramble bush, he lay as still as he could. But finally, he too was spotted. A German officer pointed his pistol at the SAS fugitive and ordered him to his feet. Reluctantly, Mouhot stood up and raised his arms. Glancing over to where Leostic's corpse lay in the dying light, he was filled with an enormous sense of loss. He was just seventeen years old. What a waste of a life.

But the Germans hadn't caught every man who had formed Bergé's raiding party. Two of their number, the mission's second in command, Captain George Jellicoe, and their Cretan guide, Lieutenant Kostis Petrakis, were away, making contact with the

British Secret Intelligence Service (SIS) agent who was supposed to organise their getaway. Thus, by sheer good fortune they had managed to avoid capture.

Somehow, the German commander knew Bergé's patrol was supposed to be six-strong. He demanded to know where the other two were, losing his temper and ranting and raving at his three stubborn captives. Regardless, they remained mute and resolute. There was no way they were going to give up their comrades, no matter how dire the German officer's threats became. Eventually, their inquisitor was forced to give up on his demands and the threats. Instead, he ordered the three prisoners be restrained . . . and marched away.

As their hands were roughly bound behind their backs, Mouhot felt an immense sense of frustration. They had come so close. They were a mere six kilometres from their intended rendezvous with the SIS agent and their point of evacuation from Crete.

Against all odds, their mission had proved a huge success. Operation Number 10 (D) had comprised of a series of attacks on Axis airbases throughout the Mediterranean and North African desert, to be carried out by the SAS and elements of the SBS – the Special Boat Squadron. The collective aim was to destroy as many aircraft on the ground as possible – those enemy warplanes that had been attacking the besieged island of Malta and the convoys that were trying to break through with desperately needed supplies. Dropped ashore by the submarine HMS *Triton* on 10 June 1942, the Heraklion attack had been commanded by Bergé, with the redoubtable Jellicoe serving as his number two. Those chosen for the raid had been handpicked by Bergé, for they were the best he had gathered at Kabrit, the SAS training base set 'deep in the Egyptian desert'.

The six raiders had managed to sneak onto Heraklion airbase under the very noses of the enemy. At one point, while cutting through the wire, they'd been spotted by a German patrol. Thinking on his feet, Mouhot had saved the day by pretending to be seriously the worse for alcohol. Fortunately, the paratrooper-overalls they were wearing helped give the impression that they were some kind of airbase maintenance party, who were seemingly sozzled after a night out on the town. Believing them to be harmless drunks returning to the base, the German guards had walked away, leaving the SAS troopers to go about their deadly business. In short order they'd planted incendiary bombs on the wings of over twenty enemy aircraft. While Mouhot and the others were carrying out that task, Jellicoe had moved further onto the airfield, lacing fuel dumps, trucks and ammunition stores with charges.

Their work done, the raiders had jogged across the base in full view of the enemy, who were caught up in the mayhem caused by an RAF bombing raid. Once out of the gates, they'd made good their escape, heading south towards their rendezvous with the SIS agent and their planned getaway. As they had melted into the shadows, a series of explosions had lit up the night sky, their bombs doing sterling work, blasting to pieces German planes, trucks, ammo dumps and fuel.

The enemy commanders were incensed by the success of such a bold, audacious raid. News of the attack reached Reichsmarschall Herman Göring, the most senior commander in the whole German military, who demanded that heads should roll. Ultimately, it would lead to the resignations of two German generals. In the interim, a series of savage reprisals was undertaken by German troops, who were hell-bent on hunting down the SAS raiders. Twenty 'hostages' – local villagers – were murdered, as they sought to deter the Cretans from aiding the fugitives in their getaway. More killings followed, as scores of innocent civilians were butchered in acts of vengeance and spite. Despite this, the Cretans never wavered. They aided the SAS raiders during their long escape, supplying food, water, shelter and intelligence wherever they could.

But then, in a rare case of Cretan betrayal, a local innkeeper apparently befriended Bergé and his men, as they neared Krotos, just six kilometres from Crete's southern coastline. At first Bergé was suspicious of his 'faux-brotherly countenance', fearing that it was all an act. But subterfuge and treachery was unheard of among the locals, so the SAS commander let it go.

Promising to bring them wine, the innkeeper left, telling them he would be back shortly. Instead, a few hours later, their hideout had been encircled by German troops, but not before Jellicoe and Petrakis had slipped away, seeking out their SIS contact, thus saving them from capture or death.

Bound and disarmed, the three captives, Bergé, Mouhot and Sibard, were to be taken back to the very place where they had conducted their 14 June raid – Heraklion airbase. After an almost pleasant interview with a polite young lieutenant, the mood darkened when another German officer entered the interrogation room. This man, 'small, red-faced, senior in rank', was furious, threatening Bergé, a French SAS commander, thus: 'You are saboteurs, you will be shot.' They were to be executed the following morning, he declared.

Calmly, Bergé retorted that they were 'regular soldiers, fighting in uniform', who should 'benefit from prisoner of war status'.

Then he added, in a tone laced with menace, 'If you shoot us, the German officers who are our prisoners in Cairo will answer with their lives.' In other words, if the three SAS captives were shot out of hand, the British would answer in kind, for they were holding thousands of German POWs in North Africa.

Those last words seemed to hit home. Rather than being executed, the three captives was thrown into solitary confinement. For the next few weeks they 'were continually interrogated . . . but we were reasonably treated and given sufficient to eat and drink', Mouhot would report. Certainly, no one faced a firing squad. Eventually, they were told they were being transported to Germany, where they were to spend the rest of the war in a POW camp. Sure enough, the three captives were driven to the nearby Luftwaffe base at Maleme and flown from there to southern Italy, 'stopping first at a P/W camp . . . and continuing thence by train to Rome and Frankfurt. Our journey took three to four days,' Mouhot noted.

Their destination was Dulag Luft, a prison camp at Oberursel, a town lying to the north-west of Frankfurt. Built on the site of an old poultry farm, Dulag Luft had opened in December 1939, with a small contingent of British and French servicemen being the first prisoners. It consisted of a few wooden barrack-style structures, plus a main building known as the 'stonehouse', which was used as an interrogation centre. It was into the stonehouse that the three SAS captives were placed, again in solitary confinement, and 'given very little to eat' while being 'interrogated on several occasions'.

From the off Mouhot was looking for ways to execute a breakout. The fact that he was incarcerated in the very heart of Germany, with the nearest friendly forces being many hundreds of miles away, didn't seem to faze him in the slightest. Where escape was concerned, Mouhot had previous form. He had already completed one epic getaway, which had led him to join the Free French forces in Britain, and, ultimately, the ranks of the Special Air Service.

Jacques Alexis Edouard Marie Mouhot was born in Cherbourg on 19 October 1911. The eighth of ten children, he and his nine siblings had led a wandering existence, following after the various postings of their father, a career officer in the French army.

Growing into a 'big-boned, square-jawed', handsome young man, and becoming something of 'a darling with the girls', Mouhot had followed in his father's footsteps, joining the French Army. But in 1938 he'd terminated his military contract, to become a ski salesman. At war's outbreak he was called back into the army, being assigned to the 1st Colonial Artillery Regiment, an anti-tank unit which saw fierce action after the German invasion of France.

On 20 June 1940 his unit was overrun by German forces, Mouhot and many comrades being taken prisoner. Shipped to a prison camp near Mirecourt, 280 kilometres to the east of Paris, Mouhot was determined to get back into the war as soon as humanly possible. He wasn't prepared to rot in a prison camp while his country was occupied by the Nazi oppressor. Only one thought was foremost in his mind: escape.

From his German captors, Mouhot learned of General Charles de Gaulle's escape to Britain, from where he began to organise a French government in exile, as the focal point for any Frenchman or woman willing to fight the Nazi invaders. Of course, Mouhot's

German captors accused de Gaulle of being a traitor, but Mouhot thought differently, vowing to join the French leader and take up arms against those who had invaded his native land.

With few of his comrades willing to risk breaking out of the POW camp, Mouhot found himself very much on his own. Regardless, he settled upon a plan of escape so utterly ridiculous that he figured he might just pull it off.

Each day a group of Senegalese prisoners would deliver soup, in huge clay pots. Studying those vessels, Mouhot figured that if he curled into a ball he could quite possibly squeeze himself inside one. Persuading the Senegalese to help him, on 14 July 1940 he clambered inside. With Mouhot safely tucked within, an accomplice placed the lid on top. The pot was then lifted onto a truck and a tarpaulin thrown over the lot. In that extraordinary manner Mouhot was driven out of the camp gates.

Once free of the camp Mouhot crawled out of the pot, jumped down from the truck and swam across a canal, before stealing some civilian clothes from an abandoned farm. With the country in disarray, he was able to mingle with the hordes of refugees who thronged the roads and packed the trains that criss-crossed France.

In that manner he made his way to Paris. Heading for his parents' place he found it to be deserted. So, he caught another train south, to Bandol, a small town on the French Riviera, 33 kilometres to the east of Marseilles, where his parents had an apartment. Reunited with his family, he became a company commander with the newly formed *Compagnons de France*, a youth movement founded by the Vichy government – the collaborationist regime set up following the fall of France. But such a role left Mouhot restless and unsettled.

Upon hearing a series of rousing speeches from General de Gaulle, broadcast on the BBC from London, Mouhot's hunger to fight was spurred. He found that he had a 'fiery impatience' to join de Gaulle. Realising the best route to Britain was via Gibraltar, in December 1940 he set out, departing from Marseilles and seeking passage across the Mediterranean to North Africa, and onwards to the British outpost.

Blagging his way onto a ship bound for Algiers, Mouhot left France with a deep sadness and a heavy heart. His dear family and his beloved country; he was leaving all behind. He wondered if he would ever see France or his loved ones again.

By fair means and foul – Mouhot possessed no papers – he made his way to Tangiers, the North African city that lies directly across the Mediterranean from Gibraltar. There, he paid a visit to the British consul, explaining that he was a French national and an ex-soldier who was looking to join his countrymen in Britain. The consular official proved most unsympathetic, warning Mouhot that if he tried to stowaway on any ship he would have him arrested.

Such threats did little to dampen Mouhot's spirits. He was determined more than ever to carry out his plan. Spying a tugboat flying the British flag, Mouhot decided to ignore the consul's hostility. That night he headed to the beach, stripped naked, buried his clothes in the sand and set out swimming. With a Herculean effort he scaled the vessel's side and made it to the deck. Having discovered the soaked and naked Frenchman hiding among some coils of rope, the tugboat captain, a friendly sort, offered Mouhot food, whiskey and dry clothes. Upon hearing his tale, he promised to speak to the British consul.

Shortly, the tugboat pulled out of harbour, spiriting Mouhot the

50 kilometres to Gibraltar. From there he sailed on the steamer the *Aguila*, to arrive in Liverpool in February 1941. Finally in the United Kingdom, he presumed that joining his compatriots in de Gaulle's Free French would be a simple task. Far from it. Instead, he was taken to the euphemistically named 'Patriotic School', at which he was interrogated incessantly. The line of questioning struck Mouhot as being 'hostile, mean, suspicious'. But at the same time a part of him appreciated what his British hosts were doing. They had every right to be cautious, lest enemy spies might manage to infiltrate the country.

Finally, the inquisition came to an end. Mouhot was duly dispatched to London, to meet with de Gaulle, who congratulated him on his epic escape. There, on 21 February 1941 he signed his enlistment papers. He was now officially a soldier in the Free French Forces. But assigned to a training unit in Camberley, his impatience at the lack of action began to grate. Had he escaped a prison camp in eastern France and made it all the way to Britain, only to be sat around in Surrey twiddling his thumbs?

Fortunately, Captain Georges Bergé happened to be on the hunt for men of a certain calibre, seeking recruits for a new Free French unit, the *1ère Compagnie de l'infanterie de l'air* – the 1st Air Infantry Company (1 AIC). Standing at only five foot six inches tall, with 'deep-set brilliant-green eyes and a shock of unruly dark hair', Bergé had been wounded twice in the defence of France, being decorated with the French Croix de Guerre, plus a British Military Cross. In early 1941 he'd parachuted back into France, on Operation Savanna, one of the first ever special operations missions into occupied Europe. The aim was to wipe out the Luftwaffe's Pathfinder squadron, those who steered the nigh-time bombing formations onto targets in Britain. Faulty intelligence had frustrated the mission, but Bergé had still managed to achieve great things in France.

In short, Bergé impressed Mouhot with his military record, plus his forceful, no-nonsense attitude. Mouhot volunteered on the spot, and was accepted, Bergé recognising in Mouhot all the attributes he sought for the unit he was forming. Dispatched to undergo airborne training at RAF Ringway, in Manchester, the British military's parachute training school, plus further specialist courses in Scotland, in July 1941 Bergé's unit sailed for North Africa. After short spells in Damascus and Beirut, they had headed for Kabrit, to undergo training with the recently formed British SAS. David Stirling, the SAS's founder, was hungry for fresh recruits, and Bergé and his men were battle-experienced from the defence of France, and parachute-trained. Stirling welcomed them with open arms.

Not long after reaching Kabrit, the 1st AIC was formally integrated into the ranks of the SAS, becoming known as the 'French Squadron', and with Bergé as its commander. As their country was occupied by the forces of Nazi Germany, they had 'quite literally everything to fight for'. By now the SAS tally was well in excess of one hundred enemy warplanes destroyed on the ground. The lion's share – some eighty-plus fighters and bombers – had fallen to Blair 'Paddy' Mayne, the man who would go on to command 1 SAS for much of the war. As Bergé warned his fellows, pointedly: 'We have a terrible challenge to live up to. They have already a hundred planes to their name. We will have to work double time to catch up.' Bergé urged his recruits to aim for the stars: 'We must not only catch up with, but overtake Stirling's men.'

The Heraklion raid had been Bergé and Mouhot's chance to make such urgings a reality. Their inaugural operation with the

SAS, it had proven spectacularly successful, but at the same time it had led to their capture and dispatch to a POW camp in Nazi Germany.

The 'stonehouse' lay at the very edge of the Dulag Luft camp. To its rear there was no wire fence, just 'a concrete path' that was patrolled by German sentries. Beyond the path lay 'a small stream and beyond that a field and trees', as Mouhot would report. A searchlight on a raised platform completed the security measures.

Mouhot, Bergé and Sibard were imprisoned in adjoining cells that backed onto the path. Provided with little to eat and interrogated relentlessly, the three gave little away, even when a German parachutist came to sit with them, trying to garner any intelligence he could by dint of their 'shared airborne brotherhood'. But the threat of execution still hung over them. As they were French nationals, the Germans were trying to deny them the legal protections extended to bona fide prisoners of war, arguing that they were illegal combatants. 'We waited for death every day,' Mouhot observed.

Despite being in separate cells, he was able to converse with Bergé through the bars. Discovering that he could squeeze his head through, he informed Bergé, who let him know that he could do the same. If they could wriggle out after nightfall, they could make off into the countryside beyond. Maybe this offered a way out? Surely it was worth a try. By now, Sibard had been taken to the camp infirmary, for he was suffering from an attack of malaria. That meant that any escape attempt would have to be executed by the two of them only.

'Commandant Bergé and I agreed to try to escape,' Mouhot

would note of the moment. Come nightfall, Mouhot would go first, and wait in the trees for Bergé, who would follow. At the agreed hour he made his move. Checking first that the guard was nowhere to be seen, he wormed his head and body through the bars, then clambered up to an unshuttered window and pushed it open. Carefully, he poked his head through, looking for any signs of the guards. The coast seemed clear; not a soul was visible and for some reason the searchlight hadn't yet been switched on. The conditions couldn't be better.

But as Mouhot tried to wriggle out of the narrow window, he realised he faced a problem. Although his head could fit through, the rest of his thickset body was proving a real impediment. There was nothing for it – if he was going to slip away he would have to strip off his uniform.

Once down to his underwear, he tied his clothes into a bundle. Forcing his almost naked form through the small opening, he dropped quietly to the path outside, pulling his clothes out after him. Straining his ears for any signs of the camp guards, he dressed, then 'ran across the field and hid under the trees' to await Bergé. But his elation soon turned to frustration, for as the minutes ticked by there was no sign of his commander. Fully an hour passed, and Mouhot was none the wiser as to what might have happened. He now faced a tough dilemma. Should he make himself scarce, leaving his comrade and commander behind?

In the end his loyalty to Bergé proved too great. Cautiously, his senses on high alert, he crept back to the stonehouse. When he was happy that the coast was clear, he crept up to his commander's cell. 'I . . . tapped gently at his window several times, but got no response. I dared not speak for fear of being overheard.' With no reply forthcoming, Mouhot realised he had no choice:

he would have to go it alone. Figuring he could do no more for Bergé, he set off, heading as fast as he could into the dark wall of trees that lay beyond the camp.

For the remainder of the night Mouhot kept up a stiff pace, pushing south-east. But he was ill-prepared for an escape across Germany. He was wearing British Army uniform and had no food, money, map or compass. In truth, he'd not given too much thought as to what he would do once out of the cell, merely hoping that between them, he and Bergé would figure it out. Now he was alone, deprived of his commander to act as a sounding board.

Regardless, he pressed on. He trekked over fields and through woods, making a wide berth of any settlements. Being summer, the weather caused him no issues. The skies were clear, allowing him to move without hindrance. At dusk the following day he found himself on the edge of a forest. As he sought somewhere to hide, he heard movement behind him. It was a German guard on a bicycle. Strapped over his shoulder was a Mauser rifle. Immediately suspicious, the man started to question Mouhot. Who was he? What was he doing there?

Deciding to try and bluff his way out of it, Mouhot argued that he was 'a French worker' taking a break in the 'beautiful forest', so as to 'enjoy the fresh air'. Thousands of Frenchmen had been shipped to Nazi Germany, as part of the forced-labour pro-gramme imposed on occupied France. Mouhot was attempting to pass himself off as one of their number.

The German guard remained suspicious. Mouhot's story did not add up. Here was a furtive-looking individual, dressed in the uniform of the enemy, wandering about the German countryside. With his rifle in one hand and pointed directly at

Mouhot, and wheeling his bicycle with the other, he forced the Frenchman to move. Eventually, they reached a small settlement that lies between the cities of Wiesbaden and Mainz, some 30 kilometres from the prison camp. There, Mouhot was steered to the police station. Forced to admit that he was an escaped prisoner of war, a telephone call was put through to the office at Dulag Luft. The following morning camp guards arrived to return him to captivity.

Once back in the camp Mouhot was interrogated relentlessly. Just how had he managed to escape? Who had helped him? Again, just as he had done before, the SAS man kept his mouth clamped firmly shut. He wasn't going to reveal a thing. If the guards wanted to know how he had got away, then they would have to figure it out for themselves.

On being returned to his cell, Mouhot was overjoyed to find Bergé still in the adjoining one. He was now able to quiz his commander on just what had happened. Why had he not climbed out of the window, as Mouhot had done? The answer was simple – Bergé hadn't been able to fit his head through the bars.

The very next day, the two men were on the move. Bergé had managed to convince their captors that Mouhot was an officer, and that he should be treated with the respect his rank conferred. Accordingly, the two men were transported some 440 kilometres further north, to Oflag X-C, at Lübeck, a POW camp close to the Baltic coast. They were now about as far away from Allied lines as it was possible to get.

While the Germans had accepted that Mouhot was an officer, they hadn't believed Bergé's claims about their comrade, Sibard. In due course he would be moved to an *Arbeitskommando*, a labour camp, from where he would eventually make good his escape in February 1943, slipping away from his work detail.

An officers' camp, Oflag X-C was home to some high-profile prisoners. As well as Robert Blum, the son of the three-time French president, Léon Blum, and two Polish Olympic athletes, another prized captive was incarcerated within its walls. Yakov Dzhugashvili was also held there. Captured at the Battle of Smolensk in July 1941, he was the son of the Soviet leader, Joseph Stalin. As Mouhot would recall, Dzhugashvili was held in a heavily fortified barracks, with a round-the-clock guard.

No sooner had Mouhot set foot in the camp, than he was placed in solitary confinement, as punishment for his previous escape attempt. Undeterred, upon his release he sought out the Oflag X-C escape committee, which was run by a group of Poles. Shrugging off his earlier failure, that short-lived taste of freedom only served to heighten his desire to be free. That in turn made him immensely popular with the escape committee.

Somehow, even the camp guards seemed to find Mouhot's mysterious (near-naked) escape attempt endearing, nicknaming the robust, charming Frenchman 'the big trickster'. But they were by no means lackadaisical or slapdash in their duties. They kept a watchful eye on Mouhot and would not allow him to join any of the camp's work parties, which were commonly viewed as offering the best opportunities to escape.

Over time, as the guard force was rotated in and out of the camp, his notoriety lessened. Bit by bit, the close surveillance began to relax, until Mouhot found that he was being treated very much like all the other prisoners. By October 1942, four months after his capture, Mouhot was desperate to make another bid for freedom. He figured the time was ripe. Able to volunteer for a small working party – 'four Frenchmen, four Poles and two guards' – he was sent to a siding on the nearby railway line 'to load and unload potatoes'.

While busy doing so, an idea came to him. Gaining the friendship and trust of one of the Frenchmen in the group, Mouhot discovered the man had been a doctor in civilian life. His name was Oscar Lievain, and his story was inspiring. In Lievain, Mouhot sensed that he had met a fellow die-hard escapee, someone who would make a perfect partner for any future attempt.

Born to a French mother in Kyiv, Ukraine, in July 1911, Lievain was just three months older than Mouhot. When hostilities broke out, he enrolled into the medical cadre of the 22nd Infantry Regiment, part of the French Army. Captured in June 1940 in the Somme area, he'd been sent to Stalag VII-A in Moosburg, Germany, and assigned to the camp infirmary. There, he'd become popular with the prisoners, due to his renown for 'protecting the weakest'. Finally, he'd been expelled from the infirmary, for the camp guards had grown antagonistic towards his unbending humanitarian attitude.

Undaunted, he'd volunteered to replace a sick prisoner on a working party. From there, in December 1941, he'd escaped, only to be recaptured a few days later. He'd been sent to Stalag 325 – at Rawa-Ruska, Ukraine, a notorious punishment camp – accused of a litany of misdemeanours, including 'escape, inciting the escape of prisoners, sabotage, enemy of Germany for having organised a resistance group in the camps'. At Stalag 325 he was to witness some of the worst predations of the Nazi regime, for the prisoners were kept in shockingly inhuman conditions. Doing all he could as a medical doctor, Lievain's incarceration at Rawa-Ruska was to prove short-lived. Soon he was transferred to

Oflag X-C. There, instead of his medical skills being made use of in the infirmary, he was detailed to the working parties.

Kindred spirits, Lievain and Mouhot came up with a plan to put before the escape committee. Learning from the mistakes of their previous attempts, both men vowed to be more prepared. With the help of the committee, they were able to manufacture civilian-looking clothing. 'From our bed covers we made ourselves trousers – mine were grey and Lievain's . . . dark green,' Mouhot would report. 'I had also made myself a waistcoat of black material and Lievain had obtained a similar garment in leather.'

They'd need more than just clothing, if they were to make it across Nazi Germany and into France, from where they hoped to link up with the French Resistance. The escape committee agreed to furnish false papers, using 'stamps made from potatoes', plus a supply of German money. Thus equipped, Mouhot felt that he was more than ready.

There remained several hurdles that the two prisoners faced. The guards were supposed to check the working parties as they exited the camp, to see if they had anything hidden under their uniforms. Somehow, they would have to evade such scrutiny.

The day came for Mouhot and Lievain to try to slip away. Donning their makeshift civilian clothes beneath their uniforms, they joined the work party and headed towards the gate. This was the point at which it could all go so badly wrong. Trying to appear as relaxed as possible, they sauntered towards the camp exit. They were in luck. For some reason the guards appeared unusually lax, letting the workers pass without so much as a perfunctory check. The first part of the breakout had gone perfectly. If their luck held, they would be free and clear of their captors very shortly.

The next stage of the escape relied upon the help of their fellow workers. As Mouhot would report: 'We had told a Pole and two of our French friends of our intentions, and they had agreed to do all they could on a given signal . . . to distract the attention of the guards . . .'

On reaching the railway yard the group began unloading the carriages. Frustratingly, the guards were keeping a close watch, giving little opportunity for Mouhot and Lievain to slip away. Mouhot spoke to one of his fellow prisoners, urging him to pass around his family photos, in an effort to attract the guards' attention for as long as possible.

Nodding his head in agreement, that individual pulled out his wallet and began showing off his snaps of his loved ones. The rest of the prisoners reciprocated, before calling over the guards, who 'allowed themselves to be surrounded, squeezed in the middle of our friends', as Mouhot would recall.

Screened from view, he and Lievain slipped beneath a railway carriage and removed their prison clothes. Fortunately, they 'were completely hidden from view by another train on the next track'. Quickly they broke away, their hearts pounding as they dashed across the lines and made for the station. At any point they feared the guards would realise what was going on, knowing they had just a few minutes at best to make their getaway.

Spying a rank of bicycles in the station car park, they seized one each and rode away. Fighting the urge to go faster, they at first cycled gently, conscious not to attract attention. Once they were well out of sight they picked up speed, pedalling as fast as they could. No doubt by now the guards would have realised that two of their working party had vanished, and would have raised the alarm.

After twenty minutes they found themselves deep in the countryside. Reasoning that the enemy would be on the hunt, and that it would be along this very road that they would come, they figured it was time to go to ground. Ahead, Mouhot noticed some woodland, which seemed like the perfect spot to lie up. Wheeling their bicycles, they reached a spot where the undergrowth was thick enough to conceal two men and their steeds, but which also offered a good view of the road.

It was not long before a search party mounted on bicycles sped by in one direction, before a few minutes later they raced past in the other. They were clearly on the hunt for the two fugitives, and having not seen them, were heading back towards the railway station.

Sensing the coast was clear, Mouhot and Lievain emerged from their hiding place and picked up the bicycles. As they were about to pedal away, Lievain discovered he had a problem. His bike had a puncture, and as he was unable to repair it, they had no option but to abandon both machines. After hiding them carefully, the two intrepid escapees set off by the only means now available to them, moving on foot.

Their goal was to make for the border with France. If they could cross that, they would be a lot less conspicuous, and being swallowed up into the wider population would be a whole lot easier. All through the night they trudged, heading south-west towards the city of Hamburg – the first major impediment on their line of march.

By early morning they'd made it to the city outskirts. Since escaping the previous day, they had managed to cover 50 kilometres. As they strolled into Hamburg, the whole place started to come alive, people setting out to begin their working day.

Some even greeted the two fugitives with cries of 'Heil Hitler' as they passed. As yet, nobody was showing either of them any abnormal interest.

Feeling confident, they decided to stop at a café, purchasing two cups of coffee from the money they had been given by the escape committee. The hot drink warmed their weary bodies, doing wonders for their morale. They seemed to be blending in – no one showed them a jot of curiosity. As they left the building, Mouhot leaned over and stole from an unsuspecting customer a 'balaclava-type hat', which was a popular type of local headwear. Pulling it on, he now looked, and felt, just like one of the thousands of others commuting to work.

They made for the nearby railway station, buying tickets for the express train to Frankfurt, which lay just over 130 kilometres from the French border. After a short wait, the train pulled in. Finding a suitable carriage, the two escapees settled down for the four-hour journey. But as the train thundered through Germany, Mouhot began to feel uneasy. They were beginning to draw unwelcome attention, and especially since they were forced to sit there in an uncomfortable silence. Rather than continue to suffer the scrutiny of their fellow travellers, they decided to move to the corridor outside.

But before they had a chance to do so, a ticket inspector stepped into the carriage. He had with him a German policeman, decked out in his distinctive uniform, and boasting an 'impressive stature', as Mouhot described him. The inspector asked to see their tickets. Once they had been thoroughly scrutinised, Mouhot stood up and made as if to leave the compartment. But again he was stopped, and asked to produce his papers. 'I made a pretence of searching for them, first in one pocket and then in another.' While Mouhot was busy doing this, Lievain managed to slip him and make it into the corridor.

Eventually, Mouhot handed his forged documents to the officials. The inspector 'realised they were not genuine as soon as I showed them him', Mouhot observed, for they were crudely done, and would never pass a close inspection. With no chance of making a break for it, Mouhot was arrested on the spot. As for Lievain, he had made it along the corridor and was nowhere to be seen. Mouhot would never see him again, hearing later – erroneously, as it turned out – that Lievain had been caught and shot.

Dragged off the train, Mouhot was taken to a military prison at Kassel, 150 kilometres short of Frankfurt. Mouhot knew that 'once again I failed. I admitted at once that I was an escaper, realising that it was useless to pretend otherwise.' He was held for three days before being moved, by stages, to the horribly familiar surroundings of Oflag X-C, at Lübeck. On arrival, he was brought before the camp commander, who assaulted him with questions. Where had his false papers come from? How had he got hold of the money? What was the source of his civilian clothing?'

The forged papers? He'd made them himself, Mouhot lied. The money? He'd found it 'in a bag at the Lübeck station'. The clothes? He'd made them from a stolen blanket. And so on.

Knowing he was being lied to, the camp commandant was not impressed. 'You stole bikes, stole blankets,' he countered, icily. 'You will pay for the bikes, you will pay for the blankets . . . and you will go to the cell!'

Mouhot was sentenced to fifteen days in solitary confinement. To make his stay in 'the fridge' as it was known, even less palatable, he was fed only bread and water 'with a bowl of soup every other day'. But his spirits remained undimmed. No matter how much his captors made life unpleasant for him, he would seek to escape again, just as soon as the opportunity arose. And should no opportunity arise, then he would make one.

Once released from the fridge, Mouhot discovered that his commander, Georges Bergé, had been moved. Realising they had a prize prisoner in Bergé – the commander of the French Squadron of the SAS – the Germans had transferred him to an even more secure camp, Oflag IV-C, the infamous and supposedly escape-proof Colditz castle. Upon learning of this, Mouhot was distraught. He'd lost his commander, his comrade, and his close friend. But it only made him more determined than ever. His focus remained 'always the same: to escape!'

By February 1943, four months after his failed attempt with Oscar Lievain, Mouhot was ready to try once again. This time he had a new accomplice, a French private by the name of Robert Grangemange. Grangemange hailed from the Vosges area, in eastern France, and he was desperate to return there. His determination to break free, and his readiness to undertake a lengthy journey in hostile country endeared him to Mouhot, making him his chosen escape companion.

Even as Mouhot was preparing for his next attempt, others in the Lübeck camp were busy. Over the last months various prisoners had tried to break out, some being more successful than others. With shears stolen by Mouhot himself, and handed to the escape committee, a hole had been cut in the barbed wire that encircled the camp. Fifteen men had made it through before the Germans had noticed anything. But in less than an hour all had been rounded up, many suffering horrible injuries from the dogs the guards had unleashed upon them.

In another scheme, Polish prisoners had been working on a tunnel, entailing months of secretive, painstaking work, and the surreptitious distribution of the excess soil around the camp. The route ran under the barrack building that housed Stalin's son, Yakov Dzhugashvili. But when German guards had begun strengthening Dzhugashvili's security by surrounding the barracks with a network of barbed wire structures, the work had caused the tunnel roof to collapse. Believing it to be an attempt by so-called 'terrorists' to spring Dzhugashvili, the Germans had him transferred elsewhere.

By contrast to the elaborate tunnel plan, Mouhot and Grangemange's scheme was simplicity itself. In fact, the idea was almost a carbon copy of Mouhot's previous attempt. After all, it had worked, he argued to the escape committee. He had made it out of the camp, and was caught only because his paperwork didn't pass muster. If he and Grangemange could be provided with better ID documents, then there was no reason why they shouldn't make a successful getaway. The committee agreed to do whatever they could.

This time they came up trumps, furnishing identification papers that were infinitely more authentic looking. He and Grangemange were also able to obtain 'a pair of workmen's dark overalls', plus caps fashioned from their bedclothes, and 'some biscuits, chocolate and sugar'. Not only this, Mouhot was given 150 Reichsmarks, plus he was able to secure 'a German map of the district from one of the camp guards, in exchange for some chocolate and cigarettes'. Last but not least, he carried a compass that he had made for himself.

The trouble now was how to get Mouhot – who was doubly notorious; doubly 'the big trickster' – onto a suitable work detail.

He simply couldn't be trusted, and was banned from all such activities, especially those that involved venturing outside the camp gates. He would have to come up with a plan to blag his way onto one such detail, if he and Grangemange were to have a chance of breaking out.

Mouhot approached a French sergeant, who headed an eight-man group. They were taken out daily to peel potatoes in the German barracks, which lay to one side of the prison camp. Mouhot explained his idea to the sergeant. His party left the camp at around eight o'clock each morning, before returning at one o'clock for lunch. Following this, they would resume their duties until early evening, when they would be brought back again. With only one guard to oversee them, it was the perfect group to try to join, and Mouhot reasoned it might just be possible to fool him.

If two of the sergeant's party could feign illness upon their return for lunch, then Mouhot and Grangemange could volunteer to take their places. 'We were to write our names on the list and go out in their place,' Mouhot would later explain. With all the key security checks taking place at the start of the morning shift, 'it seemed probable that my name would not be noticed by the German guard.'

And so, on 26 February 1943, and wearing their dark overalls beneath their uniforms, the two Frenchmen prepared for action. With two prisoners pretending they were sick, just as planned, the German guard sought volunteers to take their place. Not realising that Mouhot was prohibited from such work parties, he and Grangemange were accepted, and marched out of the camp along with the others.

They were led to a room within the German barracks and set

to work. After a while, Mouhot asked their chaperone if he could go to the lavatory. The guard, who had a kindly demeanour, readily agreed. Mouhot left the others to their chores and sauntered over to a small outhouse that served as the toilet.

Once inside, he shed his uniform and stuffed it behind the toilet. A minute later, he was joined by Grangemange, who had also been given permission to relieve himself. They now had to find a way of getting out of the barracks without attracting any suspicion. Dressed in their workmen's overalls, the two men stepped out of the toilet cabin and made for a nearby shed. Inside, they found a 'carboy', a large, two-handled glass container encased in a stout wicker basket, which was used for carrying wine.

Grabbing a handle each, they left the shed and began to walk towards the main exit. Luckily, only a handful of German soldiers could be seen, none of whom showed the slightest bit of interest in what appeared to be two civilian workers going about their business. With the adrenalin surging, the two men proceeded as confidently as they could, resisting the urge to run. At the same time, they knew they had to be quick. It wouldn't be long before the guard would get suspicious as to why they were taking so long on the loo.

Slipping through the main gate without so much as a second glance from the sentry, they found themselves on the small road that ran around the camp perimeter. By now it was around six o'clock in the evening and the sun had set. The lack of light, combined with their dark overalls, provided a degree of cover. After a short while they joined a road that was under construction. Near by, in the half-light, shadowy, wraith-like figures could be seen. These were the exhausted, skeletal forms of Russian prisoners, who were forced to carry out heavy, backbreaking work, while watched over by the most menacing-looking guards. Again, trying to appear as though they were supposed to be there, the two fugitives trudged through their midst, the odd guard casting an indifferent glance in their direction, before turning back to the Russian slaves.

Once they were past, Mouhot and Grangemange increased their pace. Eventually they dumped the carboy in a field and hurried into a nearby orchard. They were some three kilometres from the camp, but it was now that the discovery of their escape became apparent, as the wailing of klaxons began to reverberate throughout the air. Hidden among the trees, they watched fearfully as German soldiers appeared, clearly on the hunt. Their torches cut sharp swathes of light as they swept the area, the beams jerking from side to side, searching for any signs of the two fugitives. Some of the search party had large dogs on leads, and their ferocious barking blended with the blaring of the camp sirens to form a hellish racket.

Mouhot and Grangemange watched aghast as the searchers headed in their direction. Just as they were about to make a break for it, dashing deeper into the orchard, the search-party suddenly halted. One of their team had found the abandoned carboy. As the dogs sniffed around the glass container, Mouhot and Grangemange fully expected the guards to press on into the trees, where surely the two of them would be discovered. But even as they watched, the dog handlers turned away, making towards a patch of woodland which they presumably thought offered the best place of concealment. Having found nothing, they put the carboy to the noses of their dogs, hoping for them to pick up the scent, but they seemed to get little response.

Eventually the searchers seemed to give up the chase and headed back towards the camp.

There was no doubting that Mouhot and Grangemange had ridden their luck. If they were going to make it count, then they had to make a move now. Using Mouhot's rudimentary compass and the map to guide their way, they set off south-west, moving in the same direction that Mouhot had taken, when escaping with Oscar Lievain five months earlier. He and Grangemange would have to cover as much ground as possible during the dark hours, so as to get as far away from the hunters as they could.

By the following morning they had covered almost 50 kilometres, reaching as far as the outskirts of Hamburg. Their intention was to get out of Germany as fast as possible, where 'every inhabitant constituted a danger for us,' Mouhot noted. Again, much like before, the two fugitives greeted anyone in the city who caught their eye with a 'Heil Hitler'. But this was making them nervous. At any moment they could be discovered for what they were. They simply had to get out of Germany. With Holland being the closest neighbouring country, it was there that they decided to head.

Passing through Hamburg, they headed due west, making for Bremen, which lay 95 kilometres away. At one stage they managed to catch a ride on a bus with a large body of French workers. With no checks being carried out they rumbled on unnoticed, and managed to reach Bremen without incident. Deciding to continue on foot, they set out directly for the Dutch border. Relying upon his 'SAS skills', Mouhout proceeded to navigate by the stars, pushing ever westwards. Resting up in cover during the day, he and Grangemange moved only at night, sticking to minor paths and roads.

Living off their meagre rations and any water they came across, the two intrepid escapers eventually made it to the River Ems, a hundred kilometres to the west of Bremen, and only thirteen short of the Dutch border. If they could just get across the frontier, then they would have marked a significant milestone in their escape.

But, once across the Ems they found that the terrain beyond became increasingly marshy and wet, being cut through with canals and small streams. There seemed to be no alternative route, so they would have to trudge on through. As the freezing water seemed to rise around them, Mouhot realised that unless they got out of such terrain and onto dry land, they were very likely going to freeze to death, and especially as the wintry night thickened. Spying a lone grassy knoll rising from the water, they made for that. For the remainder of that night they huddled together on that hummock, soaked to the skin, frozen to the bone, and trying to share each other's body heat. All the time their teeth were chattering, their bodies shivering violently.

Come sunrise, they sensed that somebody was watching them. From the bank of a nearby canal two men in uniform were observing them curiously, Mauser rifles slung over their shoulders. As the dawn brightened, they unslung their weapons and beckoned for Mouhot and Grangemange to cross over to them. Menaced by those weapons, they had little option but to comply. Feeling sad and embittered at having been caught 'so stupidly close to the goal', they proceeded 'in silence, heads bowed . . .'

Taken to a nearby farm, they discovered that it was 'the German headquarters of the frontier officials'. They couldn't have been more unlucky. At the last moment, they had walked straight into the hands of the enemy. It was 12 March 1943, and still Mouhot was no closer to freedom than when he had been captured with Bergé and Sibard on Crete, nine months earlier.

Once it was established that they were escaped prisoners of war, the two Frenchmen were returned to captivity, this time being moved to Stalag VI-C at Bathorn, a few dozen kilometres from their place of capture. Fearing a transfer back to the distant Lübeck camp, and knowing that Bathorn lay very close to the Dutch border, Mouhot 'went to see the Senior French Officer of the camp and told him of my intention to escape. I asked him if he could give me any help or advice.' If Mouhot was making a break for it, then Grangemange was determined to go with him.

The French officer proved hugely helpful, supplying them with overalls and a rough plan of the frontier, pointing out a good place to attempt to cross. He was also able to give them two addresses in the Dutch border towns of Weerselo and Hengelo, where they should expect help. To aid in their escape, he promised to get Mouhot and Grangemange onto a working party that was carrying out construction duties outside the camp grounds. The detachment consisted of eight prisoners and one guard, and 'it was customary for this party to be away for two days at a time.'

At 8 a.m. on 20 March 1943, the small group of prisoners and their guard took the short train journey to their work area. On arrival, they set to their backbreaking task, lumping stone and sand onto goods wagons. With the eight prisoners working in a row, the guard was able to stand at one end, where he had a good view of each of them. Making a break for it would be far from easy, with such a sentry keeping close watch.

Mouhot studied his surroundings. 'Ahead of us was a stretch of sandy ground with some widely spaced fir trees, and behind this a fairly dense wood.' If he could divert the guard's attention, even for a short while, then there was good cover in which to make a break for it.

At noon, the working party took a lunch break. Mouhot now had a chance to speak to Grangemange. As they discussed their plan of action, the sentry came to sit with the prisoners. While the guard had his back turned, Mouhot and Grangemange stuffed their pockets with as much food as they could 'from the provisions given us for the two days we were away. We also had with us a good supply of chocolate and biscuits,' essential energy food for the trek ahead.

That done, Mouhot raised a paper towel and indicated to the guard that he needed to relieve himself. Nodding, the German gave his permission. Mouhot stood up and walked towards a nearby fir tree, slipping behind it. Just as they had done at Lübeck, a minute later Grangemange joined him.

Ensuring they could not be seen, the two Frenchmen slipped from tree to tree, edging further into the forest. Having covered a good distance, and with the guard not yet aware of their intentions, they finally broke into a run, sprinting deeper into the trees.

Seconds later there came shouts from behind, as the guard began yelling for the prisoners to return. Ignoring his increasingly wild cries, Mouhot and Grangemange ran on and on, pumping their arms hard, as they leapt over fallen tree trunks in their bid to get away. Soon enough the guard gave chase, but burdened with his weapon, and being somewhat older than his quarry, he faced a dilemma. If he continued, then the others in the work party could also make a break for it. Stopping, he unslung his rifle and leaned against a tree. Chambering a round, he took aim and fired at the two escapees, who were by now some distance away, slaloming between the trees. The bullet flew harmlessly high and wide.

Unable to continue with the pursuit, or to nail such elusive targets, the guard was forced to turn away and return to the other prisoners.

After they'd covered a good kilometre, Mouhot and Grangemange discarded their uniforms, to reveal the overalls they wore beneath. They sensed that the escape was very much back on, for they knew they were close to the Dutch border. Heading deeper into the woods, they found a spot to wait until dark. With nightfall, they moved out, pushing west until they reached a small river. Suddenly, they heard the barking of dogs. For a long moment they feared it was a patrol in pursuit, before they realised it was a group of German customs officers on the far side of the water.

Once they had passed by, Mouhot and Grangemange forded the river and continued towards the Dutch frontier. Eventually they came to a road-block. This was the border post, and beside it lay a small cabin. Inside, they spied a group of German soldiers huddled around a stove, their focus very much on the playing cards each was holding. As quickly as they could, and being careful not to make a sound, the two fugitives slipped past and flitted away into the dark of the night.

They had done it. Incredible tenacity and perseverance had paid off. They were finally off German soil and had made it into the Netherlands.

But they were still far from safe.

Since the *Blitzkrieg* of May 1940, the Netherlands had been occupied by the forces of Nazi Germany. As with all occupied territories, the invaders had ruled with an iron fist. Two un-accompanied Frenchmen, neither of whom could speak Dutch or had any proper identification papers, would stick out like a sore thumb. As both men appreciated, they could not last long without the help of the locals.

Armed with the two addresses given them by the Senior French Officer at Bathorn, they made for the nearby town of Weerselo. By the morning of the third day of their escape they'd found the first house. After knocking at the door, they were greeted by a nervous maid who informed them the master of the place was not in. 'She did not seem at all willing to help us,' Mouhot would report. With nothing else for it, they hurried away.

Deciding to try again later that evening, when hopefully their contact might have returned, they again found only the maid at home. But this time she seemed more welcoming, inviting them in and giving them a drink and something to eat. She also gave them 'several thick sandwiches to take away'.

Having little luck at Weerselo, they decided to head for the second address on the list, at the nearby city of Hengelo. Hurrying their way there, they arrived later that same evening. Unable to locate the address and aware that their presence on the streets might attract unwelcome attention, they decided to look for somewhere to bed down for the night.

Taking a path that would avoid the city centre, they turned down a side street only to reach a dead end. Outside one of the properties was a small group of young people, who glanced at the two fugitives curiously. The pair became nervous, as all eyes were now upon them. Turning around, they went to leave, but not before one or two shouted over to them in Dutch, using words neither of them could understand.

Not wanting to attract any more attention, Mouhot warned his companion not to look back. 'Let's keep our pace normal.'

Seconds later they heard running feet and turned to see two figures dashing towards them. Rather than appearing hostile, they seemed genuinely concerned. As the strangers mouthed away at the two fugitives in Dutch, Mouhot could think of no other response than to blurt out the one word that all might understand: '*Français*'. He was taking a huge gamble in revealing that much, but what else was he to do? They were lost in a foreign city with nowhere to go. He had to put his trust in someone.

Motioning for the two fugitives to follow him, one of the young men declared in English: 'Come, we'll hide you.'

With nothing to lose, Mouhot and Grangemange followed, as the mystery figure took them to a nearby house. More young men were gathered inside. Mouhot and Grangemange could bed down there for the night, they were told, while arrangements would be made to move them on. Their hosts proceeded to rustle up a meal. By a stroke of good fortune, it seemed they had fallen in with a group of youngsters who had contact with the Dutch Resistance. If so, these people should be able to help them get to France, and hopefully find a route to Britain and back to the war.

An hour or so after they had eaten, a mysterious Frenchman turned up. 'This man took our numbers, names and regiments and told us he would call for us the following evening,' Mouhot recounted. Given civilian clothes and 50 Reichsmarks by their new friends, to assist them on their journey, the next day, as promised, the Frenchman returned with two bicycles.

They set forth, with Grangemange and their French helper riding the bikes, and Mouhot following on foot. After stopping at a second house, the occupants of which had 'sheltered other evaders', they were on the move again, arriving at a third property where they were to spend the night. Here they bathed, were given razors to shave, handed new clothes and enjoyed a delicious hot meal. For the first time in an age they felt almost normal again, as if they had rejoined the real world. They now looked very much like your average Dutch citizen, and not like POWs on the run. But still they had no papers, no knowledge of the language, and there was a long way to go before they reached home ground – France.

At noon the following day, 25 March 1943, their French chaperone took them to the nearest railway station, buying tickets for the journey to the small town of Valkenswaard, 135 kilometres to the south-west. There, they would change trains for Maastricht, a further 60 kilometres south, on the Dutch–Belgian border. Reaching Valkenswaard without incident, their new friend left them. Having shaken hands and wished them good luck, he gave them the address of a contact in the Belgian city of Liège who would assist them with their onward journey. Later that day the train pulled into the railway station at Maastricht, from where they had to cross into Belgium and cover the 20 kilometres to Liège.

Getting into Belgium would prove easy enough. Under cover of darkness they followed 'a main road and after walking several kilometres we saw a large farm', Mouhot would recall. By this time the two travellers were tired and hungry. They needed food and somewhere to stay the night. Hoping to beg a meal and a dry place to sleep, they approached the farmhouse. Shocked to see the two men, the farmer was immediately nervous, fearing what price he would pay if caught harbouring them.

After a little persuading he finally relented, giving them food and allowing them to sleep in his barn. The next morning, the farmer's son, 'who was a student at the university', agreed to guide them into Liège. Once there, the two went in search of the address of the contact who was supposed to guide them on the next stage of their escape.

Despite hours trudging around the city, the mystery address was nowhere to be found. Their situation was looking increasingly dire. With no place to stay and the city crawling with German troops, they decided to head west, making for the town of Mons, which lay a short distance from the French border. There was a reason that Mouhot argued for Mons as the point from where to cross the border into France. In 1939, when serving with the 1st Colonial Artillery Regiment, he had been billeted with a family that lived in the small hamlet of Ferrière-la-Grande, just across the border from Mons.

That family, the Merciers, had accommodated Mouhot and his fellow troops in one of their barns. One day, after a particularly punishing march, Mouhot had ended up with bruised and bloodied feet. Seeing this, the family had taken him into their home and, with great solicitude, had patched him up royally. Over time, a warm friendship had been kindled. If he and Grangemange could make it to the Merciers' small farm, then Mouhot was certain they would be properly looked after.

Using buses and trains wherever it seemed safe, the two fugitives finally made it to Mons. With their newly acquired clothes they blended in with the population, nobody giving them so much as a second look. 'Although we frequently followed the main roads, we were never stopped by any officials, nor were we asked to produce papers.'

Taking a bus to within spitting distance of the French border, they stopped off at a small café to take stock. Deciding to put their trust in the proprietor, they revealed to him that they needed to cross into France. Again, they were in luck. The café owner advised them that there were no German patrols about right then, so the border crossing should prove relatively easy. This was music to their ears. They had come so far and were so close now. It was three years since Mouhot had last been on French soil. Despite France being occupied by the Nazis, the fact he was almost home boosted his spirits hugely.

The proprietor proved exceptionally helpful, changing their Reichsmarks for French francs and offering the escapees a bed for the night, to rest their weary feet, which by now were swollen and blistered from all the time spent on the road. Hoping that the following morning they would cross into France, they both slept well.

At dawn they thanked their courageous host for his hospitality and set off. Using minor roads and tracks, in no time they had flitted across the border, having come across not a soul who sought to challenge them. As Mouhot led his friend onwards his spirits were high. He was in familiar territory and felt certain that assistance was close at hand. It took a couple of hours to reach Ferrière-la-Grande, where he headed directly to the Merciers' farm.

Immediately, his old friends took the two men in, being delighted to see Mouhot again. In the rough and ready surrounding of their humble farm they plied both men with food and drink. Seeing the pitiful state of their bloodied and swollen legs and heavily blistered feet, Madame Mercier bathed and bandaged them as best she could. But for Mouhot, this reunion with old and faithful friends was to lead to a parting with a more recent and highly valued companion.

While Mouhot planned to head for Paris, where he aimed to find those who would help spirit him to Britain, Grangemange had different ideas. He would set out to join his family at Gérardmer, a township set on the edge of a lake in the Vosges mountains, some 320 kilometres to the south-east. When the time came for their parting, they wished each other good luck, Robert Grangemange being the first to set forth, disappearing into the night and bound for the Vosges.

With his fellow escapee gone, Mouhot was deprived of a companion whose company he had enjoyed, and with whom he'd discussed each stage of their escape, as they had endeavoured to overcome each and every obstacle. But it did not greatly faze him. After all, three years earlier he had made a similar epic trip alone, crossing the length and breadth of France and much of North Africa, in his bid to join de Gaulle's Free French. Right now, he would simply have to execute a repeat performance.

The next morning, Mme Mercier sallied forth to purchase for Mouhot a single rail ticket to Paris. Thanking his old friends for their courage, generosity and hospitality, Mouhot took the ticket and set out. At eight o'clock that night, after a seamless journey, the train pulled into the French capital, and Mouhot alighted onto the streets of yet another occupied city.

At first, he did not know quite what to do. All around, the presence of the occupation forces was evident. From buildings adorned with swastika flags to the military vehicles speeding along the roads, to the German troops on the streets, and their commanders in their glistening uniforms – at every turn the occupiers seemed to be dominant. They sat at Paris's famous pavement cafés, sipping coffee and cognac as though they owned the city. It struck Mouhot that the native Parisians moved along almost in subjugated silence. And here he was, an escaped French POW, and a soldier of the British SAS, bereft of ID papers of any kind.

All it would take was for one of those German soldiers to ask for his identification, and his goose would well and truly be cooked. Rather than risk drawing any attention to himself, he made use of his intimate knowledge of the city to disappear, making his way to a hotel in an area of Paris that he described as 'a district of low repute . . . where I did not have to produce papers. It was by now the end of April 1943 and I spent the next eight to ten days staying in hotels of the lowest type.'

He 'ate very badly' and soon the few francs he had managed to procure were running low. Of course, this could not last. He had to do something to further his escape. With family living in Paris, Mouhot figured he had no option but to risk making contact and to seek help.

One of Mouhot's five sisters, Germaine, lived alone in the 11th Arrondissement, a stone's throw from Notre-Dame. She had married into French nobility, her husband, Comte Claude de Choiseul Praslin, being a hereditary count whose ancestors had held prominent positions in French society. Sadly, the count had died from tuberculosis in 1938, leaving her widowed. But in the hope that Germaine could help him, Mouhot decided to head for the place where he had last known her to live.

He was in luck. She had not seen her younger brother for a number of years and his sudden arrival at her Paris door came as a total shock and surprise. Since leaving France he had not been in contact with any of his family, for fear that doing so might cause them real problems. Coming face to face with Germaine, it was now that Mouhot realised just how much he had missed them. They were a huge part of his reason for wanting to evict the forces of Nazi Germany from his homeland, so they could live together in peace, like normal folk.

Germaine still had the kind of contacts that Mouhot sought. Shortly, she had arranged an appointment with the local mayor, and together they had cooked up a credible cover story. Mouhot duly told the mayor that he was 'a demobilised soldier who had been sent back from Germany as being unsuitable for labour', and asked for his 'official demobilisation papers'. Apparently believing Mouhot's story, the mayor was able to provide all the necessary documentation, including 'an identity card, food coupons and all the other papers necessary for a civilian'.

Overnight almost, Mouhot's fortunes had been transformed. He now had all the proof he needed to live out the remaining days of the war as a free man in Paris, should he so desire. Learning he was there, his mother, Charlotte, made the journey to visit him. Mouhot was tempted to settle down with his family to wait for hostilities to end. But he was still a French soldier and an SAS trooper. He had signed a document pledging to fight the Nazis until they were defeated, 'committing to serve with Honour, Loyalty and Discipline . . . for the duration of the war currently underway'.

By mid-July he was becoming more than a little restless. At every turn he saw the forces of the enemy dominating all walks of life. He was becoming increasingly tense whenever he came across German troops. The desire to get back to his unit was starting to burn inside him. Matters were made all the worse in that he couldn't discuss this with his sister and his mother, for fear they would become worried and upset. But with the behaviour of the average Parisians starting to really grate on his nerves, he simply couldn't comprehend their passivity in the face of the occupiers.

The people of Paris seemed to have been reduced to dumb animals, concerned only with where to find food or how to keep warm. Where was their pride, Mouhot wondered? Where was their patriotism? Why did their anger not flare up against their tormentors? Such thoughts and his growing sense of anger made Mouhot determined to 'rejoin my comrades and resume the fight'.

Of course, there was another side to France. Mouhot knew there was a very active Resistance network. He would read in newspapers of the arrest of '"terrorists" and "bandits" in the pay of the English', and of sabotage against factories manufacturing armaments for the German military. He would find leaflets and underground newspapers espousing French patriotism and denouncing the Nazi occupiers. The challenge was how to contact such people.

Feeling 'more exiled than in a foreign land', Mouhot knew he had to abandon his easy life in Paris. Somehow, he had to cross the Channel, get to Britain, and rejoin his comrades in the SAS. At that very moment they were engaged in fierce combat operations in the Mediterranean. Operation Husky – the Allied invasion of Sicily – was well under way, the SAS spearheading the battle for the heavily defended island, as they would the coming assault on mainland Italy. And here Mouhot was, stuck in Paris, getting more and more frustrated by the day.

With little other option, Mouhot finally confessed his angst to his mother and sister. Sensing that trying to persuade him to stay was pointless, they made the difficult decision to assist him. As luck would have it, his mother knew of a woman who might be able to help her son get to the south of France, and from there into neutral Spain. Known simply as 'Madame Fontaine', this patriotic Frenchwoman was said to be part of a Resistance network that had already aided escapees bound for Britain, including downed Allied pilots looking for a way to get home.

After Mouhot had made contact with Madame Fontaine, she secured a rail ticket for him to travel south towards the Spanish border, as her network took him under their wing. Linking up with the agent known only as The Architect, Mouhot had made his way into the dark patch of forest lying at the fringes of the foothills of the Pyrenees. But hunkering down there in cover, he had become convinced that the shadowy undergrowth to all sides was thick with concealed enemy troops, on the lookout for individuals just like him.

He could hear figures hidden in the dark bush, the greenery rustling every now and then as they shifted about. He was certain of it. But alone in that woodland, what other option did he have than to wait, to remain hidden, and to hope that he could avoid discovery.

Eventually, he heard the sound of a vehicle. A few moments later, a truck pulled up and a man got out. Shortly, there was a bustling in the trees all about, as, one by one, figures emerged from their places of hiding. With a sigh of relief, Mouhot realised that these had been the 'suspicious noises' that had so spooked him. A number of fellow fugitives had been hidden on all sides, each hell-bent on escaping across the mountains. There were 'about seven or eight' and all were 'waiting to be taken into Spain', he would report.

Quickly, all those gathered – Mouhot included – were ushered onto the truck and a tarpaulin pulled over to hide them. After driving for some twenty minutes, they ground to a halt and all were ordered out. Ahead of them, the mountains that form the border between France and Spain towered high, their snow-capped peaks reflecting the rays of the setting sun, which hung low in the western sky.

With a pair of guides leading, the group of evaders set out, heading south through the thickly forested landscape, following the course of the Ariège river towards Tarascon, a small village lying 20 kilometres short of the border. As the sun sank below the horizon, taking with it all warmth and light, the group pressed on through the shadows and the gathering chill. Moving upon well-worn paths that snaked through the trees and forded fast-flowing streams, the route seemed selected to bypass any villages and to avoid roads.

Clearly, the guides knew the area intimately. They strode confidently forward, urging their charges to remain as silent as possible as they pushed south. They warned them that German patrols were known to frequent the area, and it was crucial that none of the escapees made any undue noise that might betray their presence.

As they tramped onwards, Mouhot found himself beginning to enjoy the experience. It was a beautiful part of the world, the whole area being a stunning example of nature at its finest. He was fit enough and well fed, after his long sojourn in Paris, and he didn't find the trek particularly arduous.

As he climbed towards the mountain passes, scaled slopes of rocky scree, traced goat trails that ran through the region, and plunged into the depths of ravines wherein clean, fresh rivers roared, he found himself enjoying the spectacle of natural beauty. 'I slept under the stars . . . I admired the landscape . . . the trip was transformed into a beautiful walk.'

For seventy-two hours they pressed ahead, the border drawing ever closer. Resting during the daylight hours, they continued come nightfall. As it was summertime, the weather was firmly on their side, but it meant that the hours of darkness were short. They ate from food left in caches along the way, as Mouhot would recall.

Upon nearing Andorra – the tiny, independent state, sandwiched between France and Spain – their guides wished them good luck and left. Another pair would take the escapees on from there. But the closer they got to the border, the more vigilant they needed to be, for here was where the German patrols were concentrated. Many escapees had made this trip before, only to be caught at the final hurdle. Often, their guides were murdered, their bodies left to rot. Clearly, the brave men steering their way across the mountains were doing so at very great risk. Armed to the teeth, they would not hesitate to engage in a firefight if the need arose. After all, capture for them would mean certain death.

Nearing the outskirts of Andorra, Mouhot and his fellow escapees were taken to a farm. A short walk was all that was needed to spirit them across the border into Spain, they were told. For a while they rested, awaiting the right opportunity to make their move. Gradually the group parted ways, as, in ones and twos, escapees crept across the border. Finally, a man arrived driving a truck. He was a greengrocer hailing from Barcelona and he had come for Mouhot. Climbing into the back, Mouhot hid among the many crates of fresh produce and they set off.

As the truck trundled along the road, Mouhot realised that he was entering Spain. After so many escape attempts, he had finally made it to comparative freedom. Crete seemed so long ago, now. It had been over a year since the firefight near Krotos that had ended with the death of young Leostic, and the capture of those who had survived. From there Mouhot had travelled thousands of kilometres and been incarcerated in innumerable prisons and POW camps, and made so many frustrated escape attempts.

But at no point had he ever given up. His desire to rejoin the ranks of the SAS had been all-consuming. Now, all he had to do was to find the right officials who could get him to Britain and he would be back into the fight.

Once safely in Barcelona, Mouhot headed for the British consulate. But in a repeat performance of his meeting with the British consul, back in North Africa, the man he spoke to here seemed equally reluctant to believe him, or to offer any help. After Mouhot had relayed his tale, the consul's response was that his story seemed 'so improbable that I am allowed to wonder if it's a true story or an adventure novel'. Told that he would have to wait while it was all verified, Mouhot was ordered to return in a week.

With little money or means of shelter, the great escapee would have to survive on his wits. Seven days later he was back. By then his identity had been verified, and the consul himself was the first to shake Mouhot's hand. Learning of the SAS man's lack of funds, he was given money, and a room was booked at a top-class hotel, where for the next seven days he 'lived like a prince', reasoning he'd more than earned it.

From there Mouhot was driven to Madrid, where he caught a train for Gibraltar, reaching the British Overseas Territory on 9 September 1943. Upon arrival he was to learn some extraordinary news. His close friend and SAS comrade Jack Sibard, whom he'd last seen in captivity at Oberursel over a year ago, had also managed to escape, passing through Gibraltar just recently.

Shortly, Mouhot boarded an RAF transport aircraft and was flown to Bristol, arriving there on 11 September.

A few days later, after a full debriefing, Jacques Mouhot was dispatched to Camberley to rejoin the Free French, and was soon reunited with his comrades in the SAS. After undergoing training in Scotland, on 7 June 1944, the day after D-Day, Mouhot was parachuted into Brittany as part of Operation Samwest, a behind-the-lines mission designed to prevent German forces from heading to the Normandy beaches, to assault the Allied bridgehead.

While in the field Mouhot was informed by telegram about the birth of his first child, a son. He'd married an English woman, Freda Edwards, whom he'd met while in Camberley, and was now a father. The missive, penned by Brigadier Roderick McLeod, recently appointed as the overall commander of the SAS, was addressed to 'the valiant fighter of Crete'.

For his breakout from Germany and his epic escape, Mouhot was awarded the French Croix de Guerre on 25 February 1946. He was demobilised after the war and settled into civilian life in Surrey, together with his wife Freda. They went on to have four children. Jacques Mouhot died aged seventy-four in Cambo-les-Bains, Aquitaine, France, in December 1985, and he was buried in Paris. Of his wartime service, Mouhot was to write simply: 'I felt I had done my duty.'

After being transferred to Oflag IV-C, Colditz Castle, Major Georges Bergé, the leader of the Crete mission, linked up with Lieutenant Colonel David Stirling, the founder of the SAS, who was also being held there. Freed from Colditz when it was liberated by the Americans in April 1945, Bergé stayed in the French

Army until 1962, rising to the rank of Brigadier General. During his service he was to receive many military honours and accolades. He died aged eighty-eight in Mimizan, France, on 15 September 1997.

Following the successful raid on the Heraklion airfield, Captain Lord Jellicoe escaped from Crete with Lieutenant Petrakis, both men returning safely to British lines. Awarded the DSO, in April 1943 Jellicoe was promoted to the rank of lieutenant colonel and became commander of the Special Boat Squadron, the water-borne special operations force, seeing action in the Mediterranean, Dodecanese Islands and Greece. After the war he moved into politics, taking a seat in the House of Lords and later working for the Foreign Office. Jellicoe received many decorations, including the Distinguished Service Order, Military Cross and French Croix de Guerre. He died in February 2007, aged eighty-eight.

Corporal Jack Sibard, captured on Crete with Mouhot and Bergé, escaped from Stalag VI-C, the POW camp at Bathorn, Germany. He reached Britain in May 1943, via Gibraltar, and resumed operations with the Free French forces.

Oscar Lievain, the doctor with whom Mouhot had made his first escape attempt from Lübeck, had not been shot, as Mouhot had feared he had. Following his escape from the train while en route to Frankfurt, Lievain was recaptured and returned to Stalag 325, at Rawa-Ruska, Ukraine. From there he was transferred to Stalag XX-A in Thorn (now Toruń), in Poland, until it was liberated by the Red Army in January 1945. After the war Lievain continued working as a doctor. Between 1961 to 1965 he was president of the Association of Stalag 325, a group set up for those who had been incarcerated at Rawa-Ruska. He was to live a long life, dying in Paris in 2016 at the age of 105.

After leaving Mouhot with the Merciers in Ferrière-la-Grande, Robert Grangemange made it back to his village in the Vosges, where he would join the French Resistance.

For men such as Jacques Mouhot, the war was very personal. After the fall of France many such Frenchmen could not settle to a life under the Nazi yoke. Their country had been occupied by brute force and they felt compelled to continue the fight. Thousands of such men made their way across the sea to Britain, seeking to strike back at the German occupiers. Over a thousand of them, like Mouhot, joined the ranks of what became the 3rd and 4th Regiments of the Special Air Service, training with their British counterparts for behind-the-lines operations that would support the Allied landings in Normandy in June 1944.

Mouhot, Bergé and Sibard epitomised what it was to be members of the SAS. Resolute, free-thinking, empathetic, unbreakable – but most of all, brave and daring in the extreme. High-risk, high-reward – those qualities had embodied their missions and the escapes and evasions that had followed.

Such attributes would be epitomised by our next great escapers, as they crept through darkened enemy terrain with chaos and mayhem in mind.

Chapter Three

THE ITALIAN JOB

July 1943, Sardinia

The German soldier strolled up the rocky, dust-dry hillside. Ahead of him, on a distant knoll, two low bushes swayed in the breeze blowing off the Mediterranean, some 50 kilometres to the east. The roar of Junkers Ju 88s – twin-engine, multi-role aircraft, today configured as torpedo bombers – broke the peace of the hot summer's day, as they took off from the twin runways behind. Ottana airfield, situated in the centre of the Italian island of Sardinia, was home to a rich assortment of 'fighters, ground attack and reconnaissance aircraft'. That in turn made it a prime target for Britain's elite forces, and especially since Operation Husky, the Allied invasion of Sicily – and mainland Italy to follow – had been launched that very morning.

Tasked with guarding a section of the airfield perimeter, the guard had wandered up the rocky hillside seeking 'to take the air'. After a few minutes, he turned and headed back to his duties.

Had he been just a little taller, or had he proceeded just a little further, he would have been able to see over those bushes that swayed in the breeze. On the far side he'd very likely have seen three men, each trying to remain as still as possible, their hands gripping their pistols, cocked and ready, so they could spring into action should they be discovered.

As the German sentry turned away, twenty-nine-year-old Captain John Verney, formerly of the North Somerset Yeomanry and the Royal Armoured Corps, and now serving as an officer with Britain's Special Forces let out a sigh of relief. He glanced to his left, where three more of his men, including his good friend Captain Edward Imbert-Terry, lay behind a similar bush, equally alert to the danger. They'd arrived the previous night and it was only when the sun had risen that they'd realised just how close they were to an enemy guard tent. It lay less than 200 yards down the hillside.

Verney studied the airfield, their target for what was code-named Operation Hawthorn, a mission undertaken by the men of the SBS detachment, plus those of 1 SAS Regiment. He decided that tonight would be when he and his men would strike. No sense in remaining there any longer, he reasoned, and especially with the danger that they might be discovered. The sooner they completed their mission, the sooner they could begin the long trek to their rendezvous on Sardinia's east coast, where a sister patrol, led by SAS Lieutenant John Cochrane, had set up a base from which to evacuate Verney and his men, plus a number of other patrols then engaged in similar sabotage operations across the island.

As the group of six men lay in hiding, Verney's mind drifted back to how the fates had conspired to bring them here, to the very middle of enemy-occupied Sardinia – for Ottana had not been their original target at all.

With Operation Husky set for a launch date of 10 July 1943, dozens of associated Special Forces missions had been planned throughout the Mediterranean. As German torpedo-bombers operated from the airfields scattered across Sardinia, it was critical that they be sabotaged, to prevent them from attacking an Allied invasion fleet which would be carrying just short of half a million troops. As Verney would write of their Sardinia missions: 'The RAF had attacked . . . those airfields but, to supplement this vital work, a submarine would put three parties . . . ashore on the west coast . . . on the nights of 30 June, 1 July and 2 July. At the same time a second submarine would land a fourth party on the east coast to form a base, on which the others would converge and from which they would be evacuated on 24 July.'

The official Operation Hawthorn report noted, 'A detachment of 1st SAS Regiment under the command of Major Lord Jellicoe, DSO, was detailed for the operation.' But as Jellicoe was strictly forbidden from landing on Sardinia for 'security reasons . . . the command had passed to Captain Verney'. The initial targets were the airfields at Villacidro, on the south of the island, Milis further north, plus Alghero, on the north-west coast, and it made perfect sense for the highly experienced and respected Verney to lead the missions on the ground.

Born in 1913 in India, John Verney's father was Lieutenant Colonel Sir Ralph Verney, the 1st Baronet of Eaton Square. A veteran of the Second Boer and First World Wars, he'd served as the Military Secretary to the Viceroy of India until 1921, before returning to Britain. Having spent much of his childhood in India, the young Verney had been educated at Eton, before going to Christ Church, Oxford University, to study Modern History. After graduating he started a career in the film industry, working with the likes of Ronald Colman, Charles Laughton and Robert Donat, famous actors of the age. But being drawn to the kind of military life that his father had enjoyed, Verney signed up with the North Somerset Yeomanry, a part-time cavalry regiment, in 1936.

Military life, although enjoyable, irritated Verney. 'I disliked from the start marching in step, calling people "sir", and being called "sir", saluting and being saluted,' he would recall. 'Nor could I reconcile my egalitarian principles with the glaringly un-equal privileges and comforts enjoyed by officers.' Verney believed he was no better than any of the men, just because he happened to have been born on the sunnier side of the street. Viewing the privileges of officer status as being distasteful, he was tailor-made for the Special Air Service, where individual merit mattered far above rank, class or breeding – though of course, Verney didn't know that yet.

When war beckoned, he found himself on a ship sailing for the Middle East. Before departure he made sure to marry his sweetheart, Lucinda Musgrave, and it was while he was serving abroad that he would find out that she was expecting their first child. In June 1941 he was to see real action, for his unit was to take part in the invasion of Syria, a nation which was allied with Vichy France. As Vichy had granted permission for German aircraft to use Syrian airbases, from where they were attacking Allied shipping in the Mediterranean, the British had decided the time had come to hit back hard.

That July, Verney and his men had found themselves providing cover from a ridge in Syria, as a large-scale British infantry attack went in against enemy positions. Their role was to draw fire from a nearby fort and the surrounding hills. With enemy troops holding the high ground, it wasn't long before Verney and his men found themselves pinned down. Though this was his first taste of proper action, Verney soon realised that 'darting about among rocks dodging bullets was . . . quite good fun and quite unreal'. He was equally surprised to see how relaxed many of his troops were. 'I saw men sleeping, literally sleeping, with bullets spattering around them.'

Shortly, Verney's parent unit, the North Somerset Yeomanry, were absorbed into the Royal Armoured Corps, swopping horses for tanks. Verney went on to see sustained action in North Africa, taking part in the Battle of El Alamein in October 1941, the engagement that Churchill would describe as the 'end of the beginning' in terms of turning the tide of the Second World War. By then, Verney had grown used to the horrors of the battlefield, witnessing combat in all its brutal and bloody reality. As he would later reflect, 'The charred faceless corpses in the burned-out tanks would have cured me, had I needed curing, of any romantic illusions about war.'

With the conflict in North Africa heading towards Allied victory, Verney was duly recruited into the ranks of Britain's Special Forces. His experience in battle, coupled with his egalitarian attitude and ability to act decisively under pressure, made him the perfect fit. Undergoing harsh training at the SAS/SBS desert base, Verney was to 'learn several new things about myself . . . as well as learning how to plant a limpet mine underwater or shoot a German in the stomach'. He came to understand the value of self-discipline, and that as a volunteer he was free to withdraw himself, should he ever come to think that the unit was not for him. 'We were there at all by our own fervent wish, and were free to leave any time we chose.'

But Verney had no intention of quitting this elite fraternity. Joining had awakened in him a sense of purpose, offering a real chance to make a positive contribution to the war effort – a war he wanted over as soon as possible, so he could return to his wife and young son. In short, he was exactly the kind of material that the regiment's founders were looking for.

On 22 June 1943 those selected for the Sardinia raids moved from their training base, in Algeria, to the port of Algiers, to board the waiting submarines. But with conditions inside HMS *Severn* being cramped in the extreme, many of Verney's men fell ill. They were unused to this claustrophobic, pressure-cooker-style means of travel. As the submarine's captain, Lieutenant Commander Andrew Campbell, would report of his raider-passengers, 'the majority suffered from constipation and lack of appetite' with 'cases of temperature (and) headache'. Verney would characterise their malaise as being psychological – 'a result of mental fatigue rather than a physical reaction to the enclosed space and lack of oxygen'. Or, as he'd later observe, 'We attributed their headaches, difficulty in breathing and lack of appetite to their conditions' aboard the cramped submarine.

Eleven days after setting sail the first raiding party, led by Lieutenant John Duggan, was dropped 'a considerable distance from the shore', meaning they had 'three and a half miles to paddle to the land'. Even so, the men were overjoyed to be free of the submarine's cramped confines and to be out in the open air, and were eager to get on with the job. The second raiding group, consisting of captains Brinkworth and Thomas's patrol, were dropped the following night, and they were equally relieved to be free of the submarine's steely embrace.

But as Lieutenant Commander Campbell edged his vessel northwards, in preparation for dropping Verney and his men, an unexpected issue forced him to abort the mission. A problem developed with the vessel's all-important air compressor, forcing Campbell to make an about-turn and steam for his home port of Algiers. Of course, for Verney, Imbert-Terry and the four men they commanded, this was a huge disappointment, especially as they were going to have to endure many more days cooped up in the submarine, heading for home.

It was 4 July by the time HMS *Severn* docked in Algiers, which meant that Operation Husky's launch date was scheduled for just six days hence. Unwilling to give up on their part in the planned Sardinia raids, Verney sought some means by which to continue. Only one viable option remained, in terms of their means to deploy: they would have to use the more tried and tested method of entry for the SAS – going in by parachute.

Fresh plans were drawn up and the target changed. Instead of attacking the coastal airfield at Alghero, Verney and Imbert-Terry would go for gold. They would drop into the heart of Sardinia, seeking to hit as many warplanes as possible, targeting the main Luftwaffe base at Ottana. From there, they would attempt to trek 130 kilometres to the hills near Capo Sferracavallo, on the island's east coast – the rendezvous point from which the various raiding parties would execute their escape. They'd have to maintain a punishing schedule, for an Allied submarine was scheduled to pick them all up on the night of 24 July. If they failed to make that rendezvous, they were on their own.

On the night of 7 July, just three days before the Husky invasion forces were to go ashore, a single Halifax bomber took to the skies. Officially, its mission was to 'drop leaflets' over Sardinia containing Allied propaganda, but after that it was to 'continue to do another job'. The leaflet-drop was designed to furnish 'cover' for the raiders riding aboard the aircraft, those heading in to destroy German aircraft on the ground – a trademark mission of such special forces.

As the four-engine heavy bomber thundered north across the Mediterranean, Verney studied the five men who made up his stick – a single patrol of paratroopers. He could not have picked a better bunch. His good friend, Edward Imbert-Terry, had been in the Coldstream Guards before joining the elite forces and he was a formidable soldier. Beside Imbert-Terry, typically, the implacable Sergeant John Scott appeared to be asleep: 'his eyes were shut, his very fair skin was a chalky white, his features rigid, purposeful.' The other three raiders stared dead ahead, each lost in his own thoughts, while steeling themselves for whatever was to come.

Having lost so many days due to the aborted submarine insertion, they would need to move light and fast. With 'the night of 10/11 July . . . agreed as . . . the latest possible date for the attack, owing to moonlight', and the fact that Husky would by then be in full swing, each man was carrying just 25 pounds of equipment. They'd abandoned their American-made M1 carbines, each raider being armed with only a pistol, plus five incendiary bombs, and rations for just a few days. All kit and equipment would be secured to their bodies, including their sleeping bags, which were 'worn between harness and backside (providing an admirable protection)', as Verney would describe it. The sparseness of weaponry and kit suited their new mission objective, for they were 'more than enough encumbered already for a parachute jump . . . Mobility and stealth were better weapons for our purpose.'

Not having had the time to study the target area closely, Verney left it up to the pilot to select a suitable drop zone. They just needed to get on the ground as close as possible to the airbase and without being spotted. Once down, he'd work it out from there.

With the time approaching 2300 hours the Halifax began to lose altitude, dropping down to 900 feet, the pilot preparing to offload his charges. He'd chosen an area for the jump 'three miles west of Ottana . . . near the west bank of River Tirso'. As the pilot circled the intended drop zone, he passed the coordinates to Verney, so he would know exactly where they were on the map. The raiders checked the straps on their parachutes and tightened their American-made cork para-helmets, while ensuring their sleeping bags were firmly tucked in place at their backsides. Then, beckoning them all forward, the RAF dispatcher lifted the lid from the Halifax's drop-hole, which was sunk into the aircraft's belly like a bathtub.

Verney was to be the lead jumper, with Imbert-Terry bringing up the rear. This was their first exit by way of a drop-hole, for they'd always trained by leaping out of an aircraft's side-door. With a rush of nerves Verney perched on the edge of the dark aperture, his legs hanging into the void. Suddenly the red light above his head flickered on, signalling 'Action Stations'; make ready to jump. With little time to think the lamp flashed to green, and the dispatcher yelled 'Go!', slapping Verney on the shoulder. Shaking off his anxiety, Verney edged forwards and dropped through the hole, slipping vertically into the moonlit night.

One by one the others followed, dropping out behind him, their silk 'chutes snapping open sharply above their heads. Gradually the oscillating parachutes stabilized, and, almost serenely, the line of six paratroopers floated down towards the ground. Meanwhile, the Halifax, its mission complete, powered away, the sound of its four engines fading to nothing as it slipped from view.

Drifting towards earth, Verney took stock of where they'd been dropped. It seemed as if the pilot had chosen well. The ground below looked devoid of any life, of any watchers. To Verney it appeared like 'a completely deserted area . . . flat, but very rocky and hard . . . We were on a plain, but parched . . . barren, stretching away in all directions.' Fortunately, he and his men all made good landings, and without the slightest hint that they had been detected. In short order they rallied, hiding their parachutes in some bushes, before hefting their loads and setting off.

Verney steered a course north, threading their way through the moonlit landscape in the direction he knew the airfield to lie. After a mile or so they reached the Tirso river, 'a wide shallow pebbly bed between steep bush banks'. Fortunately, its flow was nothing more than a trickle, making it easy-enough to ford. But the riverbed was open and exposed, and as they flitted across the six men strained their ears, alert for the slightest sign of life, and on the lookout for any locals who might alert the enemy.

Having successfully navigated the river, Verney reckoned their target lay no more than five miles to the north. He figured they'd find a suitable place to hide up for the remainder of the night.

Come sunrise, they could better assess their whereabouts, and that of the target. Finding a thick patch of thorny scrub, the six men burrowed their way deep inside. It was approaching dawn on Thursday 8 July 1943.

All that day the sound of farmers working in their fields drifted to their ears, but they seemed oblivious to the fact that a group of British soldiers were lying in hiding close by. Verney and his men could hear enemy aircraft buzzing through the skies, as they flew in and out of Ottana airbase. With darkness encroaching, they set out again, pushing ever north. Once they'd reached a position that Verney reckoned lay close to the airbase, he gave the order to hide up for the remainder of the night. The following evening, even as the vanguard of the Operation Husky invasion force would be steaming in to hit Italian shores, he and his men would strike.

That, at least, was the plan.

But as dawn broke, Verney began to suspect he had misjudged their position, fearing that the airfield lay a greater distance away. After a day spent lying low, they set forth once more, hurrying across the dark terrain. Shortly, they heard barking and, as if from nowhere, a figure loomed out of the night. He had the appearance of an Italian farmer, and disconcertingly, he brandished a shotgun, the muzzle of which was pointed directly at Verney and his men.

Fortunately, Verney just happened to be fluent in German, which he'd learned in Vienna, when visiting during his teens. He began to engage the man in that language, now and again switching to the few words of Italian that he knew. Maybe they could bluff their way out if it, he figured, and especially if their accoster believed them to be German troops.

'*Tedeschi*,' he called out. '*Buona sera . . . Soldati Tedeschi. Noi vostri amici*' – Good evening. We are German soldiers. We are your friends.

Gradually the man lowered his shotgun. Verney's bluff seemed to be working. As the six raiders filed past, each gave the farmer a grin and bade him '*Buona sera*'. None had fancied their chances – pistols against a shotgun – but Verney's cool-headedness seemed to have won the day. His boldness, combined with the fact that the American para-helmets they wore resembled German head-gear, must have fooled the man into believing they were indeed '*Tedeschi*'. Over the coming days this brush with the shotgun-wielding farmer would give Verney the confidence to bluff others in a similar way, to the immense benefit of them all.

Pressing on, they almost stumbled upon their target. Cresting a ridge, they discovered the airbase lying just below them, stretched across the night-dark plain. Finding a clump of bushes positioned on a rocky outcrop, which offered a good view of the airfield, they settled down in cover. It was 2 a.m. on 10 July. As Verney would subsequently report, 'It was too dark to see where the planes were,' so they decided to lie low and observe, identify and mark out their exact targets.

Shortly after the raiders settled into cover, Allied soldiers would hit the southern beaches of Sicily, some 650 kilometres to the south-east of Sardinia, as the Operation Husky forces stormed onto Italian shores.

Come daybreak, Verney was surprised to spy the enemy guard tent, which lay barely 200 yards away. They'd missed it when taking cover in the dead of night. To make matters worse, it soon became clear that those stationed there were in the habit of wandering up to the bushes, either to answer the call of nature or to smoke. With German guards strolling about just a few feet away, these moments became tense in the extreme. Even so, Verney still had to wake one of his men, Private Rogers, from his slumber each time a German came too near, fearing that Rogers's snores would give them away. He seemed able to sleep through anything.

Eventually, the sun slipped below the horizon. It was time for action. The six raiders roused themselves, breaking cover with the utmost caution as they prepared to hit the airfield. Imbert-Terry and Verney went into a huddle, making any final refinements to the plan as a result of what they'd observed that day. Splitting into two groups of three, they would wait until the moon had set before making their move, giving them the cover of complete darkness.

Imbert-Terry, along with Lance Corporal Brown and Private Hand, would head to the northern end of the airfield, lacing the planes positioned there with bombs, and concentrating on the Junkers Ju 88 torpedo-bombers. Verney would press south, along with Sergeant Scott and Private Rogers – the arch-snorer – seeking to do the same. Moving light – leaving their backpacks at their place of hiding – they'd set the bombs to detonate at 0400 hours, then rendezvous back at the bushes at 0300. That would give them an hour's head start, for an intense manhunt was sure to follow the blowing apart of that German airbase. Between them they carried thirty charges, so at least that many enemy warplanes could be destroyed, if all went well; hopefully the blasts and the resulting fires would spread quickly, taking out further airframes.

Imbert-Terry and Verney agreed that they'd wait for the other party only until 0315 hours, before setting off. Should they get split up, they'd seek to meet again at the distant escape base camp.

With the plan set, it was 0145 by the time Verney considered it dark enough to move. Laden only with their pistols, their incendiary bombs plus their 'timer pencils' – thin, acid-activated detonators – the raiders flitted downslope, making towards the airfield, ensuring they gave the nearby guard tent the widest possible berth. As they pressed on Verney was dismayed to discover that a 'stretch of dead ground lay at the foot of the hill', which he'd not been able to see from the bush. This 'upset navigation . . . and caused serious delay in reaching the Landing Ground'. By the time they'd cut their way through the perimeter fence and slipped onto the airfield, it was 0230. They would have to move silently and fast, if they were to plant their bombs and make it safely away.

Imbert-Terry and his men peeled away to the north. They were soon swallowed into the gloom of the night. Verney led Scott and Rogers southwards, going at the double, knowing there to be at least twenty warplanes in their section of the airbase. But the targets proved difficult to locate. A thick mist settled over the airbase, and that, coupled with the pitch black, made navigation a nightmare. It was quite by chance that they stumbled across the first plane. Working quickly, the men pulled out their bombs and attached them to the nearest Junkers, pushing the timer pencils deep into the dough-like explosives. That done, they moved on to seek other targets, all the while their senses on high alert for any sentries that might be lurking thereabouts.

Locating another Junkers, Verney pulled out a bomb. But as he fixed it to the aircraft, he noticed with surprise that another charge had already been attached. It could only be Imbert-Terry and his party's work. Operating in the mist-shrouded darkness, it seemed they were targeting the same planes! Locating just one more Junkers on which to plant their charges, Verney realised it was already 0300 hours, the very time they had agreed to rendezvous back at the bushes. He faced a tough decision. The remaining warplanes were such tempting targets, but if they were to stand any chance of getting away then they had to leave now. Reluctantly, he gave the order to pull out. Time being of the essence, they dashed away from the airbase 'regardless of the noise'.

Fifteen minutes later they reached the rendezvous. All the knapsacks were still there, meaning that Imbert-Terry, Hand and Brown must still be on the airfield. By 0330 Verney decided he could wait no longer. They were well over a hundred kilometres from their escape base camp, and if they were to stand a chance of evading capture they needed to be on their way. With a heavy heart he grabbed his kit, ordered Scott and Rogers to do the same, and the three set off, trying to put as much distance as they could between themselves and the airfield, which was about to be transformed into an inferno.

They'd not gone far when a voice called out to them, stopping them dead in their tracks. Verney glanced to one side. A German sentry was standing on a nearby track. It was clear he'd mistaken them for his comrades; in the dim light their American para-helmets had to give the impression that they were friendly troops. In fluent German Verney responded, although he attempted to adopt what he hoped was a slight Italian accent. They were Italian troops on a night march, he explained. Still, the German sentry 'seemed puzzled and then suspicious'. For a brief moment Verney was tempted to raise his pistol and shoot the man, but then their cover would be well and truly blown. Instead, he bade the sentry a 'friendly' goodnight, and he and his men strolled away, only increasing their pace and changing direction when they were out of sight.

On they hurried, scrambling over rocks and bushes in their haste to get as far away as possible. They'd been moving for around an hour when a series of deafening explosions ripped through the night, as all hell let loose on the airfield. Turning around, the three fugitives observed the sky above the airstrip seeming to turn into dazzling daylight. As Verney would later report, 'We watched explosions . . . all within a few minutes and I counted eight. What with the fires and ammunition going off and later Very lights, I think there must have been a very satisfactory turmoil on the Landing Ground.'

Firing Very lights – pistol-launched flares – the Germans were illuminating the airfield, in an attempt to locate the saboteurs. But in Verney and his men's case at least, they had made good their escape, even as the aircraft burned furiously. Of course, Verney was worried about his three comrades, chief among them his good friend Imbert-Terry. Had the sounds they'd taken for exploding ammunition actually been the noise of a firefight, he wondered? Had the detonations been grenades exploding? Had the flares that had been fired exposed Imbert-Terry and his men to enemy attack?

'I began to picture them staying too late on the landing ground, cut off, fighting a desperate last battle with grenades,' Verney would reflect. A feeling of guilt overcame him – guilt for not having remained on the airfield longer seeking out more targets, just as he supposed Imbert-Terry must have done. Instead, he had bugged out, heading for the safety of the Sardinian hills, while he feared his friend was down there fighting for his life. Imbert-Terry 'had done the right thing, had been a hero', he would remark. 'And we were here, un-heroically safe.'

Forcing his doubts and his worries to the back of his mind, Verney focused on his driving priority right now – getting his comrades to Capo Sferracavallo by the 24th, so they could be picked up by the Allied submarine. Pressing on, the going became tough, as the three men scaled steep, rocky hillsides, going as fast as they were able. With dawn the enemy were bound to launch a manhunt. The Germans were renowned for being masters of efficiency. It would not be long before they were on the prowl for the British raiders.

As the sun cast its first rays over the barren moonscape of central Sardinia, Verney spied a suitable bush near the summit of a low hill. As had now become almost routine, the men wormed their way inside, to await nightfall.

Verney must have drifted off, for he was shaken awake by Scott. The sergeant held his fingers to his lips and pointed. Standing not ten yards away were two Italian soldiers who were clearly searching for the British raiders. Slowly Verney and his men drew their pistols, ready to start blazing away should they be spotted. But the Italians seemed decidedly lackadaisical in their duties, as they nattered away and glanced 'vaguely in all directions'. After fifteen minutes they moved on. Had they at any time searched the bush properly, Verney and his men would surely have been discovered.

Alarmingly, the sound of rifle fire rang out, as the search parties 'stopped and fired into bushes'. Unable to change position,

Verney and his men had no choice but to remain stock still and endure a tense and fretful day. At one point they spied three carabinieri – Italian police serving with the military – on horseback, racing past in the valley below, heading for the airbase, which was still very much within the fugitives' line of sight. Enemy warplanes still came and went, and Verney worried about just how many he and his men might have destroyed. But then the words of Major Jellicoe, who had overseen the planning of the mission, came to him. 'Each bomber is potentially capable of sinking a troop carrier, that is of putting perhaps 2,000 men out of action . . . If, between us, we succeed in destroying only one German bomber, then the operation will have been worth attempting.'

With the sun setting, Verney decided it was safe enough to light a small fire and brew up some tea. Shielding the flames as best they could and wafting the ensuing smoke away with a map, the hot drink gave them a much-needed boost for the journey ahead. With their backpacks slung across their shoulders they set forth. As moonlight bathed the surrounding area, they stuck to the shadows, their senses on high alert. Heading eastwards over the rocky hills, they recrossed the trickle that was the Tirso river. 'My nerves were jumpy,' Verney would reflect, cowbells and other noises setting him on edge.

Then, from the surrounding darkness, he heard a challenge ring out.

Without waiting to see who it was, Verney broke into a run, Scott and Rogers following his lead. On they dashed, scrambling up the nearest hillside, sprinting ahead for all they were worth. Finding what looked like good cover, the three men fell to the ground, gasping for breath. It was only then that they were able to take stock of what had happened. Nobody, it appeared, had come after them. There had been no pursuit, and no weapons were fired. Verney was confused. It was all very odd. Then he began to ponder just who it was who had called out? What exactly had the voice in the shadows said? Was it possible that it had been Imbert-Terry and his men?

Scott and Rogers argued that it very likely was them, Scott believing that he'd heard a voice crying out Verney's name. Grabbing his binoculars, Verney trained them on the valley below. After scanning the area for a while he spotted three figures walking along in single file. Was it Imbert-Terry, Brown and Hand? With the light being so bad, he just couldn't be sure. But after a while he figured it had to be, for their attire appeared to be khaki, while their headgear seemed to be the American cork helmets that all were wearing.

Quickly Verney led his men on a mad scramble back down the hillside. By the time they'd got to where they'd sighted the three mystery figures, they were nowhere to be seen. Verney was convinced that he'd missed a golden opportunity to link up with the rest of his team. He was tortured by the realisation. 'I nursed an awful sense of guilt and self-loathing,' he would reflect.

With heavy hearts Verney and his men pushed on, pausing only to drink from the streams and brooks they occasionally came across. Carrying minimal rations, they were running short of food, a problem that needed to be rectified as soon as possible. On the evening of 12 July, two days into their march, they approached the small village of Sarule, east of Ottana. Spying a farmhouse, Verney decided to see if they could buy some food with the money he had been given before deploying.

Pretending that they were German soldiers whose truck had

broken down, he was able to buy 'eggs, cheese and large flat biscuits in lieu of bread'. Having nothing smaller than a 500 lire note, he had to leave that with the farmer, promising to return the following day with notes of a lesser value. This worried Verney. It was small details such as these that would get talked about by the locals, and that might get them all captured. In a report he was to write, he'd argue: '500 lire notes too big, must have small change as well . . . obviously arousing suspicion.'

Needing to get as far away from the farmhouse as possible, by 0200 hours on the morning of the 13 July Verney and his men had entered the outskirts of Gavoi village. They decided to slake their thirsts at a nearby water trough. As they did, they realised they were being watched. Two Italian youths were regarding them with a degree of curiosity. After a few moments the young-sters approached, asking for cigarettes. Verney retorted that none of them smoked. Deciding again to brazen it out, he casually asked if they knew where the nearest German troops might be, to reinforce the impression that 'we were Germans'.

The two youngsters invited Verney and his comrades to join them for a glass of wine. Scott and Rogers argued that they should leave, but, as Verney was to later admit, 'I was seduced by the idea of wine,' and so he followed them into a dark alley. By the time he realised that the Italians had led them, instead, to the local police station, it was too late. Once again, he would have to rely on bluff and front to get them out of a sticky situation.

Even as the youths knocked on the police station door, Verney announced: 'It's late and I think we ought to be getting on, after all.'

One of the youths clung to his arm, 'insisting that a glass of wine would take no time'. Breaking free, Verney and his men started to walk away. A few moments later, two well-armed carabinieri caught up with them, demanding to know just who the three mystery figures might be.

Adopting a haughty demeanour, Verney asked if any of them spoke German. When one responded that he spoke French, Verney replied in that language, demanding to know why they had stopped a German officer and his men, and what all the fuss was about? Immediately the policemen became apologetic, asking if Verney could wait a minute while their marshal came – the chief of the town's police. A few moments later, a 'fat, elderly little man' appeared, together with some Italian soldiers. Now heavily outnumbered, the only hope was that Verney might convince the enemy that they were what they claimed to be – German troops. Seeming impatient, Verney argued that he had 'wagered with my Colonel that I could walk in the night from Orani to Fonni', and that he was now being inconveniently delayed.

The marshal wavered, clearly not wanting to upset a supposed German officer. With a fierce 'Satisfied now? Good night!' Verney strode away, quickly followed by Scott and Rogers. Behind them, one or two of the Italians responded in similar kind, wishing them goodnight.

Once out of sight, the three fugitives ran for all they were worth, heading off the roadway and into the hills. They were well aware how narrow had been their escape. Verney realised he would have to be far more careful. They still had over a hundred kilometres to cover, moving over rough terrain and passing towns and villages, before they reached Lieutenant Cochrane's base – their escape camp.

Finding a suitable place to lie up, they waited for dawn. For Verney sleep did not come easily. His nerves were frayed. When he dozed, it was only for a short while, before the sound of distant cowbells would jerk him awake. Eating the eggs and cheese they had purchased from the farmer, Verney and his men decided to skirt around the town of Fonni, which lay a little to the south, for it was garrisoned by enemy troops. Forced back into the hills, they came across a potato field, and were able to augment their meagre rations. The few peasants they came across seemed to pay them little heed. With those who did show any interest, Verney was able to use the tried and tested bluff – that they were German soldiers on patrol.

By the night of 15 July Verney and his men had pushed into the high, barren, rocky hills of Sardinia's Gennargentu range – just 45 kilometres short of their rendezvous point on the east coast. By 0200 hours they'd reached a high mountain pass that cut through the peaks, taking to a track on the far side, which snaked down towards the town of Villanova. With their submarine pick-up scheduled for nine days hence, Verney decided to find some good cover in which to enjoy an extended rest. They were sorely in need of it, the long slog and lack of sleep proving exhausting. There was little sense in tiring themselves still further, and especially since they had plenty of time to make the rendezvous.

Feeling relatively well-rested, the following night they set off once more, reaching a point well to the south of Villanova, some 30 kilometres short of their rendezvous. 'The moon had only just risen and the light was obscure,' Verney noted, when they spied a group of Italian soldiers resting by the roadside. Again, acting as if they had every right to be there, they strode confidently ahead. As they pressed on, more and more enemy troops appeared out of the darkness. There looked to be at least a company-strength party, complete with baggage carts. Most appeared to be sleeping, but some raised their heads curiously as Verney and his men marched by. Doggedly, the three pressed on, now and again raising a hand in greeting and calling out 'Buona sera' to any who caught their eye.

Though it felt like an age, at last they seemed to have run the gauntlet and were through the Italian position. All seemed well until, after they had made a further fifty yards or so, they heard a shout from behind. Someone was ordering them to halt. Undecided at first whether to make a run for it or not, Verney decided to use the trusted tactic of talking their way out of it.

Two soldiers approached. Who were Verney and his men, they demanded, and what were they doing on such a road at such an hour? Adopting his tried and tested 'superior' attitude, Verney explained that they were German soldiers on a training march. Flexing his arms to show off his biceps, he went on to declare, 'We Germans believe in keeping fit . . . we make a practice of marching long distances at night over mountains.' Unsure whether the ruse was really working, he wished their inquisitors goodnight and the three pushed on, their hearts beating ten to the dozen as they went.

Then, on the road ahead, 'a stream of straggling foot soldiers and a lorry containing more troops appeared'. With their nerves just about shot, Verney and his men turned off the road and headed down a grassy hillside, hoping the dark of the night would shield them from view. Without risking a backwards glance and unable to contain themselves any longer, they broke into a run and sprinted for the nearest cover.

Expecting to hear the sound of pursuit and the crack of rifle shots, they were amazed when neither materialised. Once again,

Verney's brazenness seemed to have won the day. But as all appreciated, things could not go on like this for much longer. It seemed that the closer they got to their goal the more nerve-racking it all became. Sooner or later their luck was bound to run out. Finding another good hiding spot, they decided to spend the remainder of the night and all the next day there, maintaining as low a profile as possible.

At one point they were disturbed by an old woman, forcing them to move to higher ground, but there they managed to find a small cave that offered better concealment. At dusk they moved out, heading for the coast road, which would take them the last few kilometres to the rendezvous at Capo Sferracavallo and the pick-up by submarine. The going proved tough, the rocky terrain exhausting. To make matters worse they were running low on water, finding no springs or streams from which to replenish their supplies.

It was now the night of 18/19 July. Across the sea, the battle for Sicily was raging, as Allied forces pushed north to take the entirety of the island. Members of the SAS and SBS were playing a crucial role, carrying out hair-raising missions at the vanguard of the Allied advance. But all that was of no matter to Verney and his men. If they were going to get off Sardinia and join the coming battle for Italy, they needed to keep pushing onwards towards their rendezvous. Now on the seventh day of their flight, thirst was becoming a real problem – they needed to find water fast.

Coming to a road that snaked towards Tertenia, the final town lying between them and their goal, they kept a close eye out for any possible sources of water. It was not long before they came across an old man. Verney asked him where the nearest spring might be. He was relieved to be told that it was close, the kindly Italian giving him directions. Minutes later, the three soldiers were filling their helmets with the clear, life-giving liquid, before pouring it down their throats until their bellies were full. After replenishing their bottles, and feeling thus reinvigorated, they pressed on.

In the early hours they found themselves on the road just south of Tertenia, moving ever closer to their goal. As they strode on, they spied an ox cart up ahead. Verney considered bypassing it by heading into the nearby bush, but decided they would simply overtake it. Their luck had held good, so what trouble could a few civilians with an ox cart give them?

As they drew level, Verney could see a man 'sitting up, half awake, on the tailboard'. A number of others were asleep inside the cart. Asking the bleary-eyed Italian if there was water ahead, the man responded that it was a mile further on. Thanking him, Verney and his comrades pressed on.

But after fifteen minutes, Sergeant Scott whispered a warning: 'We are being followed.'

'Are you sure?' Verney demanded.

'Three men,' replied Scott. 'About a hundred yards behind.'

Verney had to think fast. Unlike their previous encounters with the enemy, this was the first time they seemed to have aroused enough suspicion to be pursued.

'We'll walk faster,' Verney declared. 'Don't look round yet, but when I say, glance back casually and see if they've dropped behind.'

It soon became clear that their pursuers were not to be shaken off so easily. Despite Verney and his men upping their pace, they began to close the gap. With no other option, Verney decided to stop by the roadside, as if taking a rest break. Their pursuers approached, turning out to be Italian troops. At first they appeared friendly, smiling even. But then the questions began: Who were Verney and his men? Why were they on this road at such an hour? Where were they going?

By now used to this line of interrogation, Verney responded casually. They were German soldiers on their way to Villaputzu, a small village a few kilometres to the south. There was nothing for the Italians to be concerned about. Worryingly, the cart they had overtaken earlier was nowhere to be seen. Surely, it should have caught them up by now? Had it turned back? If so, why? To raise the alarm? A feeling of dread came over Verney.

Trying to act naturally, he asked where the nearest fresh water might be. The Italians led them to it, and waited as they replenished their bottles. Suddenly, the sound of the ox cart could be heard and a moment later it trundled into view. The Italian soldiers asked Verney and his men to join them at the cart for some wine. Verney was starting to feel most uncomfortable. But with the Italian soldiers showing no sign of moving on, he thought it best to humour them. Offering to buy a bottle of wine off the carters, he handed over a 500 lire note, at which the occupants whooped with joy. Selling a bottle of cheap plonk for such a hefty sum was clearly a cause for celebration.

Crowing about their new-found riches, the Italians – carters and soldiers alike – set off, leaving Verney and his men alone on the roadway. That had been far too close for comfort. As soon as the enemy were out of sight, Verney and his comrades hurried off the road. Dawn was fast approaching, meaning their main focus now was to find somewhere to hide, 'but the landscape on all sides was barren and open'. Scott whispered another warning that they were being followed. 'I was not really surprised,' Verney would later reflect. 'I just felt rather sicker at heart than before.'

Stopping to allow the man to pass, Verney recognised him as one of those from the ox cart. Something was clearly amiss. Once the figure was out of sight, they made their move, dashing up a low hillside, seeking any place that would give them a chance at concealment. As they made for some cover, the sound of galloping hooves filled their ears. It was coming from the direction of Tertenia, which lay some two kilometres to their rear.

The carabinieri, it had to be.

Realising that they could be searching for no one but the British fugitives, Verney and his men dropped their packs and sprinted up the slope. Choosing a thick bush near the summit, they flung themselves down almost on top of each other, making themselves as small as possible.

It was not long before the terrain below was thick with carabinieri and Italian civilians, all on the hunt. So tightly were Verney and his fellows crammed together, they could barely pull out their pistols or grenades and put up any kind of a fight. As the searchers passed and re-passed their patch of bush, apparently not detecting the fugitives, Verney began to entertain a hope that they could still pull through. But inwardly he was chastising himself. 'I wondered whether we should have thrown grenades when the carabinieri were on the road, instead of bolting and hiding.'

Finally, Verney's sense of optimism was to prove misplaced. With a policeman standing only five yards away, they were spotted. Raising his rifle and yelling wildly, he fired a round into the air. Immediately more carabinieri and civilians converged on his position, the crowd grabbing at the three British soldiers and dragging them from cover. More rounds were fired skywards in joyful celebration, the reports echoing around the hillside.

The saboteurs had been caught.

Feeling utterly despondent, the three captives were hauled towards the road. As Verney would recall, 'We were the centre of an excited mob, shouting, firing their rifles in the air, pulling us by the limbs, seizing our arms and possessions, screaming orders at each other and at us – an experience which might have seemed almost amusing if we had not felt so bitterly humiliated.' A feeling of shame and embarrassment overwhelmed him. Relieved to be 'alive, fear of what might await us, disappointment, despair; those were all there too, but humiliation at first predominated'.

With the Italians whooping for joy, they searched the three captives, confiscating anything of use or value, before marching them towards Tertenia. 'On the way they tried to chain us together, but Captain Verney would not allow it,' Sergeant Scott would report. Verney argued vehemently that they were 'soldiers, not convicts'. And so, as the day broke, the three disheartened men, although not yet held in chains, trudged into enemy captivity.

Having offered up only their names, ranks and service numbers, Verney and his comrades were placed on a truck and driven 25 kilometres north to the town of Gairo. On arrival, they were questioned briefly by an Italian Army colonel, again giving only the information required under the Geneva convention. They were allowed to sleep until the following morning, whereupon they were driven to Silanus village, passing through the very areas that they had spent the last few days traversing on foot. The journey proved immensely disheartening, for Silanus lay just a few kilometres from Ottana airbase, the target of their raid ten days before.

Upon arrival the captives were split up. Scott and Rogers were placed in the town jail, while Verney was taken west to the nearby town of Bortigali. After spending so long in the company of his comrades, the parting was a bitter blow. 'The past two weeks had drawn us as close to one another, almost, as men can be,' Verney would reflect. 'And we said goodbye now as though we would meet again on Monday morning, after weekend leave.' Scott and Rogers had made sterling soldier-companions. 'I should like to record the unflagging cheerfulness and determination shown by Sgt Scott and Parachutist Rogers,' Verney would later report of his comrades.

But one separation would lead to an unexpected reunion. Upon arrival at Bortigali, Verney was shocked to see that his second-in-command from the Ottana raid, his good friend Edward Imbert-Terry, was there, together with captains Brinkworth and Duggan, who had led the other raids against enemy airfields. He was dismayed to discover that Brinkworth and Duggan's mission had been unsuccessful, for they'd been captured shortly after making landfall. Worse still, there was heavy suspicion of betrayal.

One of the men, an Italian-American private by the name of Louis Temperano, had been recruited last minute as an interpreter. Unaccountably, he had disappeared from Captain Brinkworth's patrol shortly after landing. The suspicion was that he had told the enemy everything, compromising the whole operation. Even Lieutenant John Cochrane's base party, camped out at the escape rendezvous, had been rounded up by enemy troops. Of course, there was no way that Temperano could have given away Verney's patrol, for he'd have had no knowledge of their change of plan, following HMS *Severn*'s forced return to Algiers.

But either way, Verney and his men's arduous trek to the rendezvous had been completely in vain. Reunited with Imbert-Terry, Verney was finally able to ask whether it had been him and his men that they'd seen in the middle of the night, a few days earlier.

'Yes, of course,' Imbert-Terry confirmed. 'Why did you go rushing off? We searched for you for hours.'

Before Verney could offer any kind of a proper explanation he was called for interrogation. Flanked by sentries he was led up a dark staircase to what appeared to be 'the drawing room of a private house', complete with 'carpets, curtains and ornate furniture'. Seated at a desk was an Italian Intelligence officer, 'middle-aged, rotund', as Verney would describe him. It was clear from the off that the man was pursuing his own agenda, his questions quickly turning from gaining anything of military value, towards a seemingly nostalgic conversation about his previous job, selling 'silk stockings in Alexandria', and how he 'longed to be back there'.

Knowing Verney's party to have been dropped by parachute, he wanted to know exactly where his men had stashed their 'chutes, seeking to retrieve the silk for his own ends. As Verney would recall, 'He was charmingly ineffective in his efforts to persuade us to tell him where they were.' At various points he made threats, warning Verney that the Germans would very much like to speak to him. As he was a 'saboteur', they would be most displeased with his activities. Had the Italian carried out such a threat, then Verney and his comrades would have very likely fallen victim to Hitler's 1942 'Commando Order', an illegal

After SAS founder David Stirling was captured in February 1943, Blair 'Paddy' Mayne (above centre, with his men) took over command of the SAS. Stirling and Mayne founded a unit of equals, recruiting freethinking, self-sufficient men. Intensive survival, escape and evasion training (pictured below) prepared the men for what their unit would very likely face – being hunted remorselessly, and facing the risk of capture behind enemy lines, and the escapes that would follow.

In July 1943, Captain Roy Bridgeman-Evans (above, second from left) led a patrol of SAS on Operation Chestnut, parachuting into Sicily. The drop went disastrously wrong, with the aircraft releasing at the wrong altitude, their containers packed with weapons and explosives being scattered far and wide. One aircraft would never return, legendary operator Major Geoffrey Appleyard (below right) being killed. What followed for Bridgeman-Evans and his men would be one of the most epic escape and evasions of the war.

In a daredevil operation, a patrol of French SAS were dropped into Nazi-occupied Crete by submarine, the Jolly Roger denoting the sub's successful missions. After carrying out a devastating raid on a Luftwaffe airbase, the raiders were hunted remorselessly, all bar one being killed or captured. What followed was one of the most die-hard escapes of the war, as thirty-two-year-old Sergeant Jacques Mouhot repeatedly slipped his captors' clutches, crossing the length and breadth of Nazi-occupied Europe before finally reaching Great Britain.

Amongst the many who would be incarcerated alongside Sergeant Mouhot (above left) was Yakov Dzhugashvili (above right), Soviet leader Joseph Stalin's son. Held at Oflag X-C they were 'guarded by armed sentries, who patrol all around, non-stop, night and day'. Mouhot refused to give up, and his incredible serial escapes were celebrated in the press. Fittingly, he rejoined the SAS in time for the D-Day operations to liberate Nazi-occupied France.

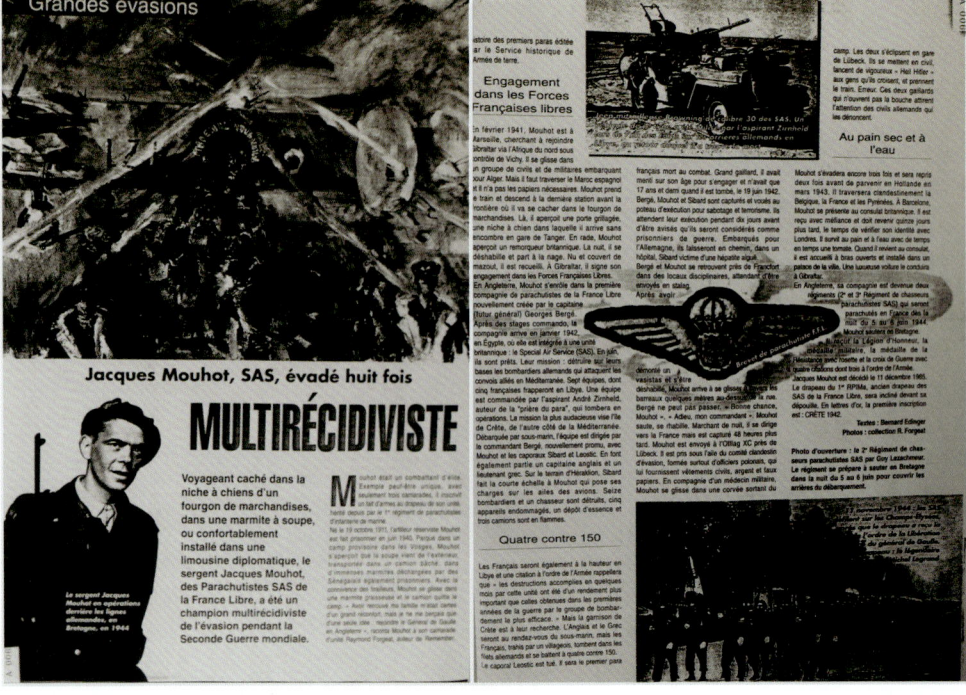

In July 1943, Captain John Verney (left) led an SAS patrol to raid Ottana Airbase, on Sardinia. After executing a daring night assault, Verney and his men were betrayed and captured. From the outset Verney was determined to escape, his hunger to make it back to Britain fuelled by his love for his wife, Lucinda, and infant son, Julian. Teaming up with Captain Martin Gibbs, (below, fourth from left, front row), a veteran of the Long Range Desert Group, they executed an incredible getaway.

Another veteran of the Long Range Desert Group (above left), Captain Lewis 'Archie' Gibson (above right) would be recruited by SAS founder David Stirling as his driver (below, Stirling, centre, in hat with pipe, Gibson in hat far left). Gibson's skill at desert navigation and at evading the enemy was legendary. During a series of hit-n'-run operations in North Africa Gibson would save the SAS founder's life, being awarded a Military Medal (MM).

Months later, Gibson would find himself in war-torn Yugoslavia, leading a battle-hardened patrol to link up with the Yugoslav partisans. By boat, mule train, on horseback, but mostly on foot, Gibson (below centre, bare-headed) and his men would spread havoc behind enemy lines. As their presence became known to the enemy they were hunted remorselessly.

In September 1944, Sergeant John Alcock parachuted into Nazi-occupied France, on Operation Pistol. Alcock (right of photo above, with elder brother, Charles), blew up locomotives and sabotaged enemy positions, but he and his men soon became the hunted. Their escape route lay across the fiercely contested frontline, where American forces, commanded by General Bruce C Clarke (below left), faced the enemy.

instruction that all Allied soldiers operating behind the lines be handed over to the Gestapo for interrogation, after which they were to be shot out of hand; in short, murdered.

But in truth Verney's inquisitor had no intention of carrying out such a threat. He fully suspected that Italy would soon be out of the war. The invasion of Sicily was going very much in the Allies' favour. What was to say that Sardinia wouldn't follow shortly? If so, he might be subject to whatever punishment the Allies saw fit, especially if he had handed over British para-troopers to be killed by the forces of Nazi Germany.

Instead, on 22 July 1943 – three days after his capture – Verney and his fellow officers were trucked 55 kilometres north to the town of Sassari, close to the island's northern coastline. En route they picked up Lieutenant Cochrane and Captain Thomson, who were being held in the town jail. Now, all of the officers of Operation Hawthorn had been reunited, albeit in enemy cap-tivity.

For three weeks they were 'imprisoned . . . in a farm', Verney would report. 'Conditions were reasonable, we had been allowed to keep 1,500 lire each and . . . bought quantities of cheese, milk, grapes, watermelons and cigarettes.' Each day a medical officer would visit, to treat the malaria several of them had contracted, plus one or two other ailments. But this somewhat easy existence came to an end on 14 August, when they were taken by rail to the port of Palau, where a ferry shipped them to La Maddalena, a small island just off the north-east coast of Sardinia, which served as an Italian naval base. From there, they were told, they were to be shipped to the Italian mainland.

Presently Verney's thoughts turned to escape. He had been away from home for three years and had not seen his wife,

Lucinda, in all that time. He had never, as yet, clapped eyes on his son, Julian, and he was growing increasingly desperate to do so. He had no intention of spending the rest of the war confined within a POW camp. Together with Imbert-Terry he looked for a means of breaking away. If they could pilfer one of the small boats they'd spotted in the harbour, surely they might be able to cross the 25 kilometres of sea separating La Maddalena from the French island of Corsica to the north. Large tracts of Corsica were controlled by the French Resistance, with whom Verney and Imbert-Terry could attempt to link up.

After pestering the Italian captain responsible for them – 'a small, wizened man who in peacetime had been a schoolmaster' – the six officers were allowed to stay in La Maddalena's naval barracks, under guard, and to use the mess for their meals. The place was 'surrounded by a high wall . . . grouped round a courtyard with one building planted in the centre', plus the windows in their rooms were barred. It would take a large amount of guile, luck and boldness if they were to execute a successful breakout. Irrespective of the difficulties, Verney and Imbert-Terry were determined to try. To do so, they would need the help of their fellow officers.

On their fourth day at La Maddalena, an Italian destroyer steamed into harbour, charged to transport the prisoners to the mainland. It was now or never, if they were to get away. As Verney would note: 'Our plan was to escape after dinner, always a sociable meal, when friendly sailors showed photographs of their families and when, afterwards, we gossiped in the doorway before walking back across the yard to our room.' The guards tended to allow their prisoners a few moments' relaxation, before escorting them back to their quarters. This privilege was something the two British officers hoped to exploit.

Stuffing their pockets with as much food as they could, they put their plan into action. With dinner finishing at 9.30 p.m., they were counting on their brother officers to play their part to perfection. Brinkworth, Duggan and the others stood chatting with the sailors, drawing the guards into their conversation. Having caused no trouble so far, their Italian captors thought little of such apparently friendly behaviour. Seizing the moment, Verney and Imbert-Terry slipped away, walking purposefully around the barracks searching for a way out, and acting as if they had every right to be there.

Finally, they spotted the main exit some fifty yards away. 'The gate was open,' Verney would recall. 'We could see the harbour outside. There was no silhouette of a sentry visible . . . Casually we walked across. We kept outside the circle of light from the mess door.' Glancing behind, they could see their brother officers talking animatedly to the guards, their part in the escape being played to perfection. With the sun hanging low in the west, the two men simply strolled through the gates and out of the camp.

Immediately they made for the waterside. Finding no suitable boat in which to make their getaway, they trekked inland, heading for the north-east coast. The island being so small, it was just an hour before they reached the sea. Spying a small rowing boat with a sail, 'as if placed for us at that exact spot by Providence', they quickly hauled it out into deeper water and clambered aboard. Placing the oars into their metal housings, they began to row. This was the critical point. With so many enemy vessels anchored in and around the island, they had to move as stealthily as they could. The sun had set and a bright, waning moon reflected off the surface of the water. Slowly they pulled away from the shore, their senses on high alert, their hearts pounding.

Shortly they were nosing out of a small inlet, slipping between two headlands that led to the open sea. Silently they heaved at the oars, moving ever closer towards freedom. And then they saw movement on one of the shorelines. It was a sentry. As yet, fortune seemed to favour them, for the man had his back to the water. But if he should turn around he was bound to see them and a challenge was sure to follow.

Suddenly, a voice rang out from the opposite headland. Verney turned and called back cheerily, hoping they might be mistaken for Italians. Instead, a shot rang out, the bullet cutting between the two British officers. It had been dangerously close. Throwing caution to the wind they dragged at the oars for all they were worth, desperate to reach the open sea. Within seconds more figures had appeared, rifles blasting hot lead towards the boat. The escapees were now in mortal danger, as bullets slammed into the wooden sides and threw up angry spouts of water all around.

With every impulse telling them to jump into the sea to save themselves, they kept at it, determined to get free of the cross-fire churning up the waves. But then they sensed that all hope was lost. Joining in with the crackle of rifle fire, there came the unmistakable rat-a-tat-tat of a machine gun. It would be only a matter of seconds before the gunner found his aim and they were both killed. With no other option, Verney and Imbert-Terry stopped rowing and raised their hands. To continue would only lead to one outcome – the death of the pair of them.

As the fire abated, they did as they were ordered – taking to the oars again and turning inland. Once back at the shore, they were hauled out by Italian soldiers. Verney, ever the one to try a ruse, attempted to argue that far from being escaped British prisoners, they were Germans out for a spot of night fishing. But this latest lie was to prove futile. An officer arrived who knew exactly who they were.

By the time they were returned to the naval barracks it was three o'clock in the morning. The 'wizened' Italian captain was furious. He was joined by another officer, a Lieutenant Scioca, the man responsible for escorting them to mainland Italy. He seemed equally incensed. They had been made to look like idiots and they were having none of it, Scioca declared. Described by Imbert-Terry as '5 feet, 8 inches tall, thin, rat-faced, dark, with sunken eyes, slight in build', Scioca approached them menacingly. In full view of everyone he spat viciously into each of their faces, ordering the two captives to be taken to a nearby room. Inside were a number of carabinieri and Italian soldiers. Oddly, some curious civilians were also in attendance.

Ordering everyone out except a pair of carabinieri and two soldiers, Scioca had some mattresses brought into the room. With a nasty grin, the Italian lieutenant left, accompanied by the wizened captain. No sooner had they exited than Verney and Imbert-Terry were ordered to lie on the mattresses. While two of the Italians kept them covered with their weapons, 'the other two began kicking and hitting us and beating us with rifles. They continued to do this for a quarter of an hour,' Imbert-Terry would report.

The onslaught was horrendous, as the Italians beat the defenceless men. Imbert-Terry had been suffering from dysentery and, having swallowed a few mouthfuls of seawater during their escape attempt, Verney's bladder was playing up. After the initial beating, he asked if they could go to the lavatory and started to raise himself to do so. Instead, one of the soldiers punched him violently in the face, knocking him back down. This heralded a second assault, Verney being kicked 'in his private parts' and 'repeatedly . . . about his legs and body'. After telling the two captives they would be shot in the morning, they were left to nurse their wounds. Luckily, they had managed to ward off the worst of it, receiving mainly cuts and heavy bruising.

But their torture did not end there. The following morning Scioca returned, 'apparently to gloat, for he paid no attention to our request to be allowed to go and clean ourselves up'. Left in the room with no food or water for fourteen hours, by the time they were finally dragged outside Verney and Imbert-Terry were in a desperate state, their bodies battered, and their clothes soiled by being denied the toilet. They were also desperately hungry and thirsty, having been deprived of any food or water.

Scioca and the captain were nowhere to be seen. As Verney and Imbert-Terry were to learn, they had been sacked from their positions due to the fugitives' escape attempt. Shocked at the disgusting state of the two British officers, the Italian naval commander ordered them to be cleaned up at a nearby water trough. A couple of hours later, battered, bruised and with their spirits at their lowest ebb, Verney and Imbert-Terry boarded a launch to take them to the waiting destroyer and the journey to the mainland.

Sulmona POW camp, known as Campo 78, lay in the foothills of the Apennine mountains, 120 kilometres east of Rome and some 50 kilometres from the Adriatic coast. By late September 1943 the Germans were using it as a transit camp for Allied prisoners being shipped north to Germany. But on 8 September the Italians had surrendered, and thousands of Allied POWs had taken to the mountains, making a bid for freedom. Many would be rounded up by German troops and their Italian Fascist comrades, and forced back into captivity. Italian civilians found to be harbouring an Allied escapee were shot, and their homes burned to the ground.

On Thursday 23 September, a group of Allied prisoners arrived at Sulmona for processing and onward transport to Germany. Among them were captains John Verney and Edward Imbert-Terry, along with twenty-seven-year-old Captain Martin Gibbs, originally of the Coldstream Guards, and a good friend of Imbert-Terry's from before the war. In Gibbs, Verney and Imbert-Terry could hardly have found a better man with whom to try to engineer their next escape, for Gibbs had already had an extra-ordinary war.

Serving with the Coldstream Guards, in December 1940 Gibbs had been recruited into the original desert reconnaissance and intelligence gathering specialists, the Long Range Desert Group (LRDG). Predating the SAS by a year, the LRDG had specialised in deep desert penetration missions, seeking to gather crucial intelligence on the enemy in North Africa, and to execute the odd, opportune raid while at it. Indeed, the SAS owed much of its early success to the legacy forged before them by the men of the LRDG – never more than a few hundred-strong – for initially it was LRDG patrols that had ferried the SAS raiders to and from their targets.

While serving with the LRDG, and traversing the desert sands in their two-wheel-drive Chevrolet pick-ups, Gibbs had discovered deep desert caves adorned with rock art and carvings of animals, from an ancient time when the desert had bloomed.

On one occasion a terrible *khamsin* – dust storm – had blown up, and Gibbs had been forced to radio headquarters that his patrol was in real distress, and heading back to base. He and his men returned plagued by heat exhaustion and dehydration. Their water rations had proved woefully insufficient, and some of his men were going 'right off their head'.

Gibbs and several others were evacuated to hospital in Cairo, but it was fully two months before he was fit enough to return to war. Even so, Gibbs spent many 'arduous months' with the LRDG, and when pulled back to his parent unit it was to his desert patrol's detriment. Gibbs went on to be captured in the June 1942 fall of Tobruk, but would subsequently escape twice, although each time he was recaptured. In short, Gibbs had buckets of experience operating deep behind enemy lines, and had shown himself game for any attempted breakout, no matter the risk involved. He'd also played a vital role on the escape committee of his previous POW camp. All of this made him a kindred spirit to Verney and Imbert-Terry.

As matters transpired their stay in Sulmona was destined to be a short one. At one o'clock in the afternoon of 30 September 1943, just a week after their arrival, all officers were ordered to the parade ground. They were to be shipped to camps in Germany that very night. Frantically, the three friends searched for somewhere to hide, but with the German guards threatening to machine-gun ceilings and burn down the buildings, to deter soldiers from hiding out, Verney, Imbert-Terry and Gibbs were forced to join the hundreds being trucked to Sulmona railway station. There, they were to board a train steaming northwards for Germany.

Frustrating though this was, they were not to be put off, vowing to take the first opportunity that presented itself to escape. The fact that he had not seen his family for so long was preying on Verney's mind. 'I wanted to see my son. Moreover, I knew my wife would be getting anxious,' he stated, simply. Determined to be the masters of their own destiny, the three men just needed the right opportunity to make a break for it.

This would come sooner than any expected.

Transporting the prisoners to the railway station proved a laborious process, and by that evening barely half the British officers had been taken away Those already on the train had to endure hours waiting in the sidings, as the trucks went back and forth to the camp to collect more men. Eventually, well after dark, the train was declared full, with hundreds of POWs crammed into dirty and cramped cattle trucks for what was bound to be an unbearable journey.

It was then that Verney noticed a familiar face. Crammed in close by was Lieutenant John Cochrane, the SAS officer who had been tasked with setting up the escape camp during Operation Hawthorn. Cochrane was freezing cold and soaked to the skin, for he'd just attempted a getaway, leaping off a truck on route to the station, after which he'd hidden in a waterlogged ditch. Eventually he was found by some Italian peasants, who had handed him over to the Germans. As Cochrane told Verney, he was convinced he would have made it, but for the Italians giving him away.

Cochrane's story gave Verney a boost, for he'd shown that he was prepared to go it alone, displaying the never-say-die attitude that was the bedrock of those who served in Britain's Special Forces. His mind full of thoughts of escape, Verney dozed off, but at eleven o'clock he was shaken awake by Imbert-Terry. The train had started to move, yet it seemed it was merely being shunted between sidings and was still only a short distance from the station. If they were going to escape their opportunity was now, Imbert-Terry argued, before the locomotive made it to the main track and gathered speed, for after that any leap would likely prove fatal. First they would have to find a means of breaking out of the wooden carriage.

Imbert-Terry pointed to a small aperture near the ceiling – what looked like a ventilator. Quickly, he hauled himself up and peered through. From what he could see of the outside, the carriage seemed to be in a narrow cutting, with a German sentry posted right beside them. As Imbert-Terry watched, the German soldier turned away and strode up the line of carriages, being swallowed into the night. Sensing their opportunity, Imbert-Terry argued that if they could squeeze through the ventilator and drop to the tracks, they could hide in the bush until the train steamed away.

The aperture looked just about big enough for a man to wriggle through. Recruiting Captain Gibbs to their cause – the LRDG veteran and good friend of Imbert-Terry's – the three would-be escapees made their move, as the other officers around them dozed. Sadly, the soaking wet Cochrane was simply too exhausted to join their breakout. Hauling their bodies up to the narrow ventilator, one by one they wormed through and lowered themselves onto the gravel beside the track. Their hearts pounded, the crunching of the stones beneath their boots seeming to reverberate alarmingly around the Sulmona hills. Of course, this was merely their heightened senses magnifying everything, for there was little sign that the sentries had heard anything untoward.

Moving with stealth they dropped to their stomachs and

crawled for the bushes, each of them barely daring to breathe. Seconds later they were burrowing their way into the thickest, most inhospitable scrub. Gazing out from cover they could make out the forms of the nearest sentries, moving along the train and looking out for anyone trying to escape. How they had not been spotted was anyone's guess, but, for now, they seemed to be relatively safe.

A few minutes later the train began to move, chugging slowly at first as the carriages passed by only a few feet away. Gradually it picked up speed, before it was lost from view, the sound of the snorting locomotive fading into the night.

So far, so good. Verney, Imbert-Terry and Gibbs had managed to slip away. They would not be going to any camp in Nazi Germany any time soon. Instead, they would be starting out for Allied lines, wherever they might be.

Verney looked to the south. The lights of the town of Sulmona showed about a mile away, with the Montagne del Morrone mountain range lying to the east. Beyond that there appeared to be a second, higher range silhouetted by the light of the stars. Using a secret wireless set hidden in the Sulmona camp, they'd been able to tune into BBC news reports, from which they'd learned of the last known position of British troops. Armed with that knowledge they formulated a plan: they'd head west into the hills, then hook southwards, making for the British lines, which were around Benevento, roughly a hundred miles distant. All they needed to do was cover that distance undetected, and without being taken prisoner again.

It was only as the three men readied themselves to move that Verney realised the date was hugely significant. It was 30 September 1943 – his thirtieth birthday. He had never envisaged spending a birthday celebration quite like this. With the train now well out of sight the three men stole away, moving west through the night towards the distant mountain range. And so Verney commenced a second epic trek through enemy territory seeking to escape, but determined that this time he would succeed.

As the trio trudged across muddy fields, the 7,000-foot-high mass of the snow-capped Monte Genzana cut the horizon. Conscious of Cochrane's recent experiences, they decided they couldn't afford to trust anyone, regarding every Italian as being potentially treacherous. They would steer clear of all locals, plus any villages or farms they came across. Believing the Allied advance would be swift, they figured they would only need to trek for a week at most, before they'd be able to link up with their comrades. With precious few rations – a couple of bread rolls, a handful of raisins and one tin of meat – they planned to live off the land, stealing vegetables or fruit along the way.

With the sun about to rise, they discovered a thicket of bamboo set beside a stream – a perfect hideout. Using Imbert-Terry's greatcoat as a groundsheet, they settled down as best they could on the cold, damp ground, seeking to last out the day hidden within the bamboo's shadowed depths. But it would prove difficult to do so, for a group of locals began working near by, collecting walnuts. By nightfall, the three fugitives had managed to avoid discovery, and they picked themselves up to continue their journey west into the mountains.

Skirting around any settlements, they crossed a railway line and a couple of roads, before arriving at the foothills. Seeking to reach the high ground before daylight, they forced tired legs to keep moving, clambering up the hillside, but the going became increasingly tough. Eventually, they emerged above the line of cultivated land, reaching a woodland of stunted oaks, beyond which reared slopes of barren rock. If they pushed ahead too far, they feared sunrise would find them exposed on the bare heights. Instead, the three fugitives decided to wait out the day hidden amid the thick oak woodland, which seemed to offer great cover.

But their confidence in their place of hiding was to prove misplaced.

Morning brought a fine but persistent drizzle. Soon, they were soaked to the skin, and were forced to huddle together for warmth, shivering on the forested hillside. All of a sudden a stranger hove into view, seemingly as surprised at catching sight of them as they were of him. Disconcertingly, he'd approached to close quarters, unseen amid the thick forest and the dank, moisture-laden air. Even more worryingly, he brandished a shotgun.

Verney had lingering memories of the Italian farmer who had accosted them during their mission to Ottana airbase, shotgun at the ready. But before he could launch into his standard act – 'we're German soldiers out trekking the hills' – the stranger cut him short. In reasonable English he explained exactly who he was. No enemy, he was in truth a former Italian Air Force officer, and he had no doubt that the trio were Allied escapees. More to the point, he would be delighted to help them in any way that he could. With Italy having signed the Armistice with the Allies, they were now on the same side, united against a common enemy – Nazi Germany.

Most Italians, especially in the rural areas, would be only too pleased to assist Allied escapees, he explained. The time to throw off the yoke of German occupation was now. The escapees should go down to one of the farms, he added, where the locals would provide food and shelter. But with Cochrane's experiences fresh in their minds, Verney, Gibbs and Imbert-Terry declined. The former Air Force officer's response was to declare that he would go and fetch them some provisions from his home, which lay a mile or so away. Deciding to trust him – they were unarmed, and with his shotgun he could easily have overpowered them – Verney and his comrades settled down to wait. But cautious as ever, they remained ready to run should anyone return with the carabinieri or German troops.

In reality they had nothing to fear. The Italian officer returned just before sunset, bearing a giant bowl of delectable bean and macaroni soup. As he had proved as good as his word, they decided to put their faith in him. Gathering what few belongings they had, they followed him deeper into the hills, for he'd promised to lead them to others who could assist with their escape.

Shortly, they came across an isolated stone hut. Inside was a group of young men, each of whom carried a weapon of some sort. They were known as 'giovanotti' – those who had come to live in the hills, to avoid being shipped to Nazi Germany as forced labour. With them were four escaped British soldiers dressed in civilian clothes. They'd been on the run for weeks, they explained, and were planning to move south the following morning. What they revealed gave the escapees cause for hope, for they'd met with nothing but kindness. In this region at least, Verney, Imbert-Terry and Gibbs should have nothing to fear by putting their trust in the locals, they explained. It was all most heartening.

At dawn the following morning, the four British soldiers set out. Verney and his companions had decided to stay with the *giovanotti*, gathering their strength, and in the hope that the Allied advance would catch up with them. But this band of *giovanotti* would do little to impress. While they willingly shared food and shelter, their boastful and reckless behaviour – they would shoot off their guns for no reason at all – started to grate. But equally, the trio were reluctant to abandon the sanctuary they offered. The one thing they needed more than anything was accurate information. Just how far away was the frontline? Did it make sense to stay and wait? Or was it more prudent to follow the four British soldiers, and take their chances crossing the lines?

In a nearby hut they discovered a pair of Italian officers, whose attitude seemed more akin to their own. They had access to a secret radio in Introdacqua – a village not far away – and the information they had garnered was encouraging. They were convinced that British troops would reach the area in two weeks, or even less. But with no sounds of battle anywhere within hearing, Verney refused to accept the Italian officers' words at face value. Driven to discover the truth for himself, he persuaded them to take him to their hidden radio set that very evening.

At dusk they set out, with Verney now dressed in civilian clothes instead of his British uniform. Flitting through the darkness, he crossed 'vineyards and olives to the outskirts of the village, a honeycomb of stone-tiled roofs and cobbled alleyways'. Entering, Verney found himself on a narrow, twisting street with a church lying at the far end. The place was dimly lit, the only light filtering out of the windows and open doorways of the houses they passed. The two Italians seemed to know almost everyone, and they stopped to chat at every turn, making the going slow. It all added to Verney's nervousness. Despite his civilian disguise Verney felt glaringly conspicuous, and as he soon realised, in truth all the townsfolk seemed to know exactly who he was.

Eventually, they arrived at the house with the hidden radio. Frustratingly, that night's news broadcast contained nothing of any value regarding the Italian front, focusing instead on a report in French about the dire state of German morale. Other than having confirmed for himself that the locals were very much on their side, the trip into Introdacqua had taught Verney nothing about where the frontline might lie.

For the next few days he and his comrades were visited by locals, bringing water and hot meals, but sadly little of note about the Allied advance. The bad news was to reach them on the fifth day. Without warning, German troops had marched into Introdacqua looking for billets, and many more were to follow. The escapees' position in the hut on the hillside above had become untenable. It was time to move. Verney, at least, would not be discomfited at having to leave the *giovanotti*. He suspected the feeling was mutual. Their dislike for each other – *giovanotti* for British escapees, and vice versa – was threatening to boil over. It was best for all if they went their separate ways.

On the night of 7 October 1943 – a week after they'd jumped from the train that would have shipped them to Germany – Verney, Imbert-Terry and Gibbs were guided away from the hut by the two Italian officers. 'We crept in single file down the hill past Introdacqua and worked our way round the shoulder of Genzana – the 7,000 foot high mountain to the south of Introdacqua – skirting the highest fringe of cultivation,' Verney noted. Eventually they arrived at a farmyard, where they were greeted by 'a cheerful, youngish peasant called Gabriele'. After sharing a glass of brandy with their new host and his young wife, they bedded down for the night in his pigsty, which was all the accommodation that Gabriele could offer.

Still, beggars – or fugitives – couldn't be choosers.

With German troops thick on the ground, the threat of dire reprisals hung over any locals caught helping Allied troops. The following morning the escapees were led up the mountain to a secluded cave. Their guide was Gabriele's nephew, Dionino, who proudly showed off his American leather pilot's style jacket. Here, they settled into something of a routine: days would be spent hiding in the cave, while at night they would head down to Gabriele's farm to eat, and to sleep in the warmth of the pigsty. They remained desperate for accurate information about the Allied advance, hoping that somehow it would find its way to them.

Life in the cave became increasingly monotonous. Outside the ground was open, offering a good view of the valley below and the Strada Nazionale – the main road heading south from Sulmona. In an effort to kill the boredom, the trio began counting the number of military vehicles moving along the highway. Presuming the Germans were falling back using one of their main avenues of retreat, they kept a count of every vehicle that passed, hoping that might help them gauge the fortunes of the war. On the first day they recorded 150 trucks heading north, with only a third of that number travelling south, which had to reflect how rapidly the Germans were withdrawing. But when a massive convoy appeared that evening, heading south, boasting too many vehicles to count, their optimism was quickly dispelled.

It was dispiriting. So too was the knowledge that many of the locals knew exactly where they were hiding out. The fugitives began to feel uneasy, sensing that they needed to move to somewhere more secluded. Eventually, Gabriele and Dionino agreed to take them to another cave, one that they had heard was occupied by a British general and a fellow escaped POW. The following day they returned with a donkey laden with supplies, and all set forth across the mountain. Edging through thick expanses of beech forest, the going was slow. When finally they reached their destination they found it deserted. If the cramped cave had ever harboured a senior British officer, he was long gone.

After showing the escapees where the nearest water source was, Gabriele and Dionino left, promising to return in a few days with more supplies. Verney, Imbert-Terry and Gibbs named their tiny hideout 'Little Ease', after a cramped, 1.2-metre-square torture chamber that lies beneath the Tower of London. Likewise, their mountainside cavern was no more than five feet in height and depth, and it left just enough floor room for the three of them to lie down side by side.

For days they waited, shivering in their cramped hideaway. Though winter was approaching, the fugitives felt unable to maintain a proper fire, for fear it might betray their position. With threadbare blankets and with their boots full of holes, keeping warm and dry was proving a nightmare. Finally, there was noise outside the cave. Dionino had returned bearing more supplies. With him was an older man, Antonio, his cousin – a middle-aged farmer who rarely spoke, but seemed possessed of a kind heart – plus two girls, who turned out to be his daughters. They were ill-equipped to cope with the weather, but seemed accustomed to it, and they carried a huge pot brimming with macaroni, which was steaming hot still.

Antonio, who had once visited America, spoke a good smattering of English. He brought disturbing news. In recent days farms had been raided by German troops, on the hunt for escaped Allied prisoners of war. Regardless, Antonio had volunteered to take the lead looking after the British fugitives. Remaining at Little Ease was impossible, he argued, especially with bad weather closing in. Instead, he suggested, Verney and his comrades should come back down the mountain and stay in the hayloft of a neighbour's farm. He assured them it would be safe. In truth, life at Little Ease had become unbearable, and the promise of warm food and shelter was too much to refuse.

The fugitives' spirits were raised by a letter that Antonio bore. Written by one Frank del Signore, an Anglo-Italian who had been interned at the outbreak of war, due to his pro-British leanings, it read:

Dear Sirs, I am a British subject in hiding from the Germans. It is both my duty and my desire to render you assistance. I am in touch with two British generals, living in the valley, who are anxious to have your names . . .
 God save the King! Rule Britannia,
 Your humble servant, Frank Del Signore.

P.S. The glorious Eighth Army has taken Campobasso, is advancing rapidly on Isernia and should be in Sulmona shortly.

This was truly a godsend. If Frank del Signore's information was accurate, then the Allies were approaching Isernia, which lay a mere 48 kilometres to the south. Maybe hiding out in these hills had been a wise move after all. With darkness approaching the trio packed up their possessions and set off on the long trek, eager to link up with Del Signore and discover all they could about the British advance.

By the time they reached Antonio's house it was well after nightfall. Once he'd checked that the coast was clear, they were led through the darkness to a 'wide stone staircase, into an attic, its windows heavily shuttered'. By the dim light of a single candle that sat upon a small wooden table, they discovered 'a debonair Bertie Wooster-ish young man of perhaps thirty, smartly dressed in a plus-four suit of dark brown tweed and wearing a trilby hat of palest fawn', as Verney would describe their first sighting of Frank del Signore.

The Anglo-Italian proved eager to talk, being excited at the opportunity of helping these British officers. He explained that over the years he'd been pressured to join the Italian armed forces, but had steadfastly refused, remaining 'loyal to the British Crown'. As a result he'd been interned and ill-treated. With his health deteriorating, he had been released, moving in with his sister, who lived on a nearby farm. From there he had started to help any Allied escapees who had come his way.

'We English must stick together,' he reassured Verney and his comrades.

More importantly, Del Signore had access to a radio, which meant that he was privy to the latest news from the BBC. Joining Del Signore, the escapees based themselves at a farm owned by Sinibaldo Amatangelo, known to all simply as 'Sam'. He was to leave a lasting impression on Verney. Sam had spent time in America and spoke reasonable English. Aged around forty, short and compact, with his striking blue eyes he struck Verney as resembling a typical English farmer, more than any local. Sam could not do enough for the fugitives, providing them with food and shelter, even giving them a haircut and shave, of which they were all in dire need.

Settled in to enjoy Sam's hospitality, they slept in his hayloft and enjoyed regular updates from Del Signore, via the radio. All seemed set for British troops to roll through this region, at which point Verney, Imbert-Terry and Gibbs – plus Del Signore – could link up with the victorious Allies.

But just when all seemed to be going so well, misfortune struck.

Forty-eight hours after linking up with Del Signore and Sam, Imbert-Terry fell ill. His high temperature and violent, trembling fevers gave the sickness away for what it was – malaria. It was common enough among those soldiers who had spent any time at their Philippeville training camp, in Algeria. Sam provided blankets and overcoats to keep the feverish Imbert-Terry warm, as they attempted to nurse him back to good health. But the following morning, things were to take a turn for the worse.

At dawn, Sam entered the hayloft in a state of consternation. German soldiers were combing the area, searching the farms, hunting for escaped Allied POWs and the *giovanotti*. The trio had to leave immediately, he warned. With Imbert-Terry being too sick to move, a compromise was reached. While Sam would hide Imbert-Terry as best he could, Verney and Gibbs would slip away. Minutes later, they hurried into the hills, following a well-worn track pointed out by their host. Around them, the mountain paths were crammed with fleeing *giovanotti*, taking with them all they could carry and followed by their womenfolk.

Verney and Gibbs were forced to revert to their cavemen-like existence, as Frank del Signore took on the role of bringing them provisions, news reports, plus word of their ailing comrade. He would announce his presence by whistling 'The British Grenadiers', a centuries-old military song and his signature tune, highlighting his somewhat eccentric persona. From him they learned how villages had been raided, German troops rounding up hundreds of *giovanotti* and stealing the locals' cattle. With the enemy on all sides, Verney made the only decision he felt he could: they needed to move to more isolated ground, taking the feverish Imbert-Terry with them.

Having packed provisions, the trio set out, heading for a large cave set in the foothills of the snow-capped Mount Genzana. 'It lay in a dell on the steepest part of the hill,' Verney noted, 'well screened by trees, which did not prevent a view of the Strada Nazionale several hundred feet below.' It seemed like the perfect spot in which to remain hidden, while keeping watch on the valley.

It was 20 October 1943 by the time they reached their new redoubt. The trio had been on the run for twenty days and were not a great deal nearer to freedom than when they'd jumped from the train. From their new vantage point they spotted flights of RAF fighters strafing the road, but while it was heartening to see, it did little to bring any relief. Each day either Sam or Antonio would appear, bearing food and wine, their devotion to the three escapees proving unshakeable and resolute.

On their sixth day at their Mount Genzana hideout, the now familiar tune of 'The British Grenadiers' was heard on the path below. Moments later, the distinctive figure of del Signore appeared. He bore worrying news. German troops had occupied the neighbours' house, forcing him into hiding. The enemy were flooding into the area, in an effort to counter the British advance.

'The next week or two . . . would be critical in the valley,' del Signore warned. 'The Germans would seize whatever food they could . . . ransack every farm, and behave altogether with calculated frightfulness.'

Local villagers were massing in the hills, bringing their cattle and anything else of value. Not wanting to be a burden on their Italian friends, Verney and his comrades reached a difficult decision. Despite Imbert-Terry's weakened condition, they would attempt the long trek to the inhospitable cavern they'd nicknamed Little Ease. While the prospect of returning there was dire, they figured it would be bearable for a while, and they hoped it would buy them enough time for Allied forces to break through.

As the trio trudged up the snow-covered hillside, with Imbert-Terry supported between Verney and Gibbs, their spirits were given a sudden and much needed boost. From the valley below the roar of aircraft engines filled their ears. A flight of British fighter aircraft swooped over Sulmona, diving to attack targets on the road. The noise of their gunfire reached the watchers clearly. Somehow, it seemed to bring the war materially closer, and served to lift their spirits.

But in truth, Verney and his comrades had little idea how long their grim sojourn at Little Ease would last. With little sign of an Allied breakthrough, they were forced to endure the privations of that tiny, freezing cleft in the rock for weeks on end. Amazingly, during all of that time Sam or Antonio, or their children, would visit, making the six-hour round trip to supply the fugitives with food, despite the huge risks they ran in doing so.

Sam did little to hide his anger and exasperation, upon spying the dire state of the escapees. He seemed visibly moved by how his

British friends were forced to live, blaming it upon the Germans, who he cursed and then cursed some more.

Being unable to wash and shave, their appearances were becoming ever more wild, as Verney noted. Their hair grew longer and tangled, like bird's nests, their beards ever more voluminous. To make matters worse, Imbert-Terry's malaria kept flaring up, forcing him to stay in the cramped confines of the cave for days on end, while his friends kept a small fire going to ward off the chills.

More and more villagers began to appear on the mountainside – locals fleeing from the enemy. German troops were rounding up everyone they could and shipping them out, while robbing their valuables and stealing their cattle. Eventually, two British army sergeants appeared at Little Ease. They had escaped from Sulmona prison camp some weeks earlier. Unburdened by a malaria-ridden comrade, they attempted to make a break for British lines, which they believed to be 'about 30 miles away in a straight line'. Maddeningly, they were forced to return the very next day, for they had blundered into German troops who were positioned throughout the woods. It was impossible to get through, they argued.

Even so, Verney knew that if he was to see his wife and young son anytime soon, then they would have to make a break for it, and before the winter weather really kicked in. With this in mind, he and Gibbs decided to execute a reconnaissance of the area they would have to cross. By now it was early November and it was a constant struggle to keep warm, as flurries of snow and sleet whirled across the hillsides.

Climbing into the heights, Verney and Gibbs reached a vantage point offering a fine view south, to where Monte Genzana merged into a further range. From that elevated position they could see Monte Greco, a 7,500-foot peak lying to the west of Castel di Sangro, where British lines were supposed to be. To them, it didn't look so far away. For the briefest of moments, Verney wondered whether they should abandon their good friend, Imbert-Terry, and make a break for it. Without the burden of their sickly companion, doubtless they could make it. His desperation to see his family was overwhelming. But in his heart he knew he could never desert his comrade, who even then was huddled up in Little Ease wrestling with another bout of malaria.

On their return to the tiny cave, bad weather closed in. For the next forty-eight hours the storm raged, forcing them to stay within Little Ease's claustrophobic confines. Despite the appalling conditions, Sam fought his way doggedly through the near-blizzard, bringing food and information. Writing of him years later, Verney would declare that there were no words to encapsulate Sam's innate goodness, nor the esteem and affection they felt for each other.

By now, the trio had been at Little Ease for approaching a month. More Italians kept joining them on the remote hillside. As the menfolk built makeshift huts hewn from the forest, their families moved in, bearing whatever meagre possessions they'd managed to salvage from the marauding enemy. The enemy round-ups were intensifying, the only means of escape being to flee into the most inhospitable highlands, but that just drew the enemy after them.

It was 27 November when their situation looked at its most desperate. While chatting inside a nearby cave occupied by some villagers, a woman glanced out of the entrance and hissed a warning: '*Tedeschi*'. German troops were just a few yards away.

Quick as they could Verney and Gibbs crept to the furthest recesses of the cavern, throwing a pile of bedding over themselves. At the same time the women crowded into the entrance, so as to block any view. If the Germans decided to search the place then that was it – Verney and his fellows would be caught, and those who were sheltering them would doubtless be shot.

After what felt like hours, but was in reality a few minutes, the Germans headed off, having questioned the Italian villagers repeatedly. It turned out that they had been on the hunt for cattle, and it was only when the locals agreed to reveal where they had hidden theirs, that the enemy troops moved on. As soon as they were out of sight, the fugitives were hustled back to Little Ease, at which point the villagers implored them to leave. Their continued presence was simply too risky. Knowing this to be true, the desperate trio decided to head back down the mountainside. They would make for Sam's house and take stock once they got there.

Late that night they were reunited with their stalwart helpers and friends. But while Sam and Antonio welcomed them in, it was immediately clear that they simply couldn't stay. German troops were billeted on all sides, some just a few hundred yards away. Learning that the British had overrun Castel di Sangro, and that fierce fighting was taking place at Roccaraso, just 23 kilometres away, the need to make a break for British lines was all-consuming.

Gibbs and Verney had had sight of the new British frontline, due to their earlier reconnaissance from Little Ease. Based upon what they'd seen, they figured the nearest friendly positions were no more than five hours walk away. To his mind, there was no longer any argument not to go.

With little more delay, Verney, Imbert-Terry and Gibbs

made ready to depart. They were unanimous in their convictions – this was the moment. Freedom was so close, the pull too strong to resist. But several factors made even such a short journey daunting. It was well into December by now, the weather becoming increasingly harsh. Snowstorms, rain and sleet brought freezing temperatures – conditions that would prove deadly for anyone caught in the open.

Even so, the need to get moving was pressing. The locals expected snow to fall in even the lowest-lying valleys, which meant that the fugitives' very footsteps might give them away. Moreover, a sustained fall of snow would render the mountain passes impassable. With Verney's desert boots full of holes and Gibbs and Imbert-Terry's equally battered, they asked Sam to find some more durable footwear. Once again, the resourceful Italian came up trumps, handing out boots that looked comparatively pristine. Not only this, but an abundance of food was crammed into a heavy pack.

Thus kitted out, the trio decided to set out that very night. They'd head for the town of Villetta Barrea, less than 20 kilometres away, which was now reported to be in British hands. Once darkness had fallen, they set forth on what they hoped would be the final leg of their journey, using a map from a guidebook that Sam had managed to find them.

Not wanting to leave his British friends, Sam had decided to accompany them on the first stage of their journey. Trudging through deep snow in freezing conditions, after several hours of exhausting slog the familiar sight of the cave where they had spent so much time loomed before them. They were back at Little Ease, the first landmark on their journey. Turning to the diminutive Italian, a man who had kept them alive through countless trials and tribulations, Verney felt an immense sense of sadness mingled with an overwhelming gratitude.

At the last moment, Sam, who was visibly upset at their parting, tried to dissuade the trio from pressing on. 'No good in the mountains. Too cold, too far,' he kept repeating, through tear-filled eyes. Pointing to Imbert-Terry he announced; 'Him bloody sick. Them Germany sons of bitches catch you . . . Come and stay in my loft for the winter 'til your peoples come.'

To quieten his fears the trio promised to turn back if the going were to prove too difficult. Finally, Sam seemed to accept that their minds were made up. Even so, their parting proved heartrending. A distraught Sam asked if he might kiss the three fugitives goodbye. He seemed convinced that they were going to their deaths on the mountain, and begged them to retrace their steps at the first hint of any real danger.

As Verney noted, he and his two fellows were close to tears themselves. They set off, trudging around the snowbound flank of the mountain, occasionally glancing back to see the little Italian standing in the freezing whiteness, watching and waving, until finally he was lost from view.

For the next few hours they pressed on, but progress was at a snail's pace, especially since Imbert-Terry was suffering the ill-effects of repeated bouts of malaria. To add to this, the boots that Sam had provided were ill-fitting, causing their feet to blister. The pack laden with food was heavy and cumbersome, forcing the fugitives to jettison some of the heaviest items. At one point, upon reaching a ridge where the snow had frozen solid, Imbert-Terry lost his footing and fell, 'skidding two hundred feet down on his back. His language, when he regained my level, was unprintable,' Verney would note.

At 2 a.m. on 12 December, many hours after they had set out, the escapees reached the mountain summit. It was shrouded in thick, freezing cloud. As they plunged into the opaque mass, it began to snow heavily, slowing their progress still further. Clearly, there was little chance of reaching the frontline that night. In fact, there was a pressing need to find shelter, lest they freeze to death. They needed a place to hide up for the daylight hours, somewhere they could try to work some warmth back into their bones.

Then, in a moment in which it felt like the gods were watching over them, they spied the distant form of a shepherd's hut, half buried in heavy drifts. Sweeping away the snow, they pushed open the door and stepped inside. Lying on the floor in front of a blazing fire, two *giovanotti* lay fast asleep. Upon hearing Verney, Imbert-Terry and Gibbs enter, they awoke. Shortly, they too revealed that they were making for Allied lines.

The three fugitives decided to spend the day inside the hut, resting and eating as much of their rations as they could, before heading out come nightfall. The *giovanotti* provided some useful information about the route ahead. They believed that German troops were positioned at vantage points all along the mountain heights. It proved immensely worrying, and Verney was able to grab only a few hours' snatched sleep.

Their Italian companions also believed that the village of Villetta Barrea was now in British hands. It lay just a few hours' hike away. As Verney would recall: 'In daylight the snow cleared enough for us to see the valley three miles away across our route. The fir trees were black and menacing as if bristling with Germans, though it should be possible to keep above them along the ridge . . .' By evening, Verney, Gibbs and Imbert-Terry were ready to make their final push to freedom.

They set out, heading for a snowy, cone-like peak that they believed marked their destination. The going was tough, far tougher than they had expected. The snow was piled into thick drifts, as they attempted to by-pass where they feared the Germans had to be. With boots pinching blistered, swollen feet, they forced themselves to keep moving, blanking their minds to the pain. Eventually, they reached a vast plateau of unbroken snow, with the summit, Monte Greco, lying beyond. Ahead lay a high mountain pass and their route to freedom on the far side. It looked to be no more than an hour away.

Passing a few clumps of stunted trees, they spied wolf tracks in the snow. They pressed on, their heads bowed against the cold and wind. 'Our movements became automatic and I don't think I have ever felt more utterly tired and miserable,' Verney would recall. At one point they came across boot prints, evidence of a German patrol that had passed recently, but after scanning the area they could see no obvious sign of the enemy.

At 4 a.m. they reached the pass that they believed led down to Villetta Barrea. Quickly they scrambled onwards, the terrain narrowing into a steep-sided valley. An hour before daybreak they paused to get their bearings, using the map that Sam had provided and comparing it to the lie of the land. Dawn ushered in a bright, sunny day, the change in conditions lifting their spirits. They were so close now. A few miles below the River Sangro tumbled through a gorge, as it made its way from the snowbound heights towards the Adriatic Sea. Running almost parallel to the river was a road, which Verney believed led directly to Villetta Barrea, where British forces were said to be.

The trio wondered whether they might have passed through German lines without realising it. Were they in fact in no-man's-land, the area of a battlefield sandwiched between the two front lines? The very thought proved invigorating, their spirits soaring. Spying a flock of animals further downhill, Gibbs hurried ahead to speak to the shepherd. But as Verney and Imbert-Terry watched him go, the sound of artillery fire tore apart the dawn skies, and a first shell plunged into the hillside a couple of miles away. The barrage was coming from the other side of Castel di Sangro, and therefore had to be from British positions. It could mean only one thing: they were still behind German lines. As if to confirm this, they spotted a patrol moving along the road below. The sound of their voices rose distinctly to the three fugitives. They were unmistakably German!

Verney and Imbert-Terry took cover as they waited for Gibbs to return. When he did, his news was grim. He'd made it as far as a few hundred yards from Villetta Barrea, but found the place to be crawling with German troops. If the Allies had taken it, clearly they had been driven out again. Making it through Villetta Barrea would be risky in the extreme, he warned, and nigh-on impossible during daylight. Somehow, they would have to hide out for one final day, before making a break come night-fall. To give themselves a better chance of getting through, they agreed that each of them should go it alone. They would set out separately, leaving just as soon as it was dark and seeking to rendezvous on the far side.

Throughout the remainder of that day they kept watch on the valley below, as German troops led pack animals to and from the village. Eventually, at dusk they made ready to move. Gibbs was to go first. After bidding his friends farewell and good luck, he set off down the hillside. Verney and Imbert-Terry watched him go, and shortly he was lost to the darkness, only the faint echo of his footfalls betraying his onward progress.

Ten minutes after Gibbs had left, Verney turned to his friend, Imbert-Terry. They had shared so much together, ever since they had boarded that submarine back in Algiers for Operation Hawthorn. That was nearly six months ago. Now, they could afford little more than a quick farewell, before Verney turned and set out into the darkness.

At first he moved slowly, conscious of the clatter of his hob-nailed boots on the rocky ground. Using the pitch darkness as his shield, he decided to head higher up the mountain, seeking to circumnavigate the German positions by climbing above them. After two hours he was where he had hoped to be, the shadowy forms of German soldiers and mules clearly visible just a hundred yards beneath him.

Then the moon began to rise, casting a dim and eerie light across the mountainside. Ahead, German voices broke the silence. Verney couldn't determine just where they were, but he felt horribly vulnerable. 'I had been in pitch darkness hitherto, but was now exposed on the barest of hillsides.' If he were to stand any chance of making it, he would have to change his plan, and fast. With his heart beating so rapidly it felt as if it would burst from his chest, he edged slowly down the slope. He would head for the bottom of the gorge, and the thickest shadows, following it all the way to Allied lines.

After a long and difficult descent he finally reached the guts of the narrow valley. He was, by now, totally exhausted. The tough trek coupled with the fear of being caught had taken a heavy toll on both his nerves and his energy. Above him 'the gorge, a mixture of rock and forest, rose . . . two thousand feet on both sides and the river, thirty yards wide, roared deafeningly between them.' Following the course of the Sangro would take him to British lines, he was certain of that. But fatigue threatened to overcome him, and if he lost his vigilance he was bound to run into the enemy.

After drinking a bellyful of ice-cold river water, he sat down to rest and to think. As he contemplated his next move, exhaustion must have overcome him. By the time he awoke, Verney found that it was 3 a.m. and the moon was now obscured by mist, darkness once again being his friend. Picking himself up, he began to press eastwards along the gorge, moving in the direction of Castel di Sangro. After an hour 'the track ended and a sort of bridge . . . spanned the river'. Crossing it, he found himself on another path, 'a yard wide, between sheer rocks on one side and the river bank . . . on the other'.

Suddenly all seemed lost.

Rounding a corner, he spied movement in the shadows, not five yards away. It was the unmistakable form of a German sentry. Quickly, Verney pressed himself against the sheer wall of rock, praying that he'd not been seen. Slowly, he peered around the edge of the precipice, moving with infinite care. Maybe he'd got lucky, Verney wondered. But almost instantly there were two loud reports, accompanied by blinding flashes from the sentry's rifle muzzle. It took an instant for Verney to realise that the German was actually shooting at him, though how he could have missed from such a short distance was impossible to comprehend.

Dropping to the earth, Verney scrambled for the river. As he did, the German fired again, the bullet whistling past, missing his head by inches. 'I was into the river faster than a snake and worked my way along with only my eyes and nose above water,' he would recall.

This was it. Do or die. He had to get out of the line of fire, and the only way he could do that was via the freezing waters of the Sangro. After a hundred yards of bone-chilling immersion, he crawled out, fully expecting more bullets to come hammering his way. Shivering uncontrollably, he lay for a moment on the icy bank, fighting to get some warmth back into his bones. Luckily, the German sentry seemed to have lost sight of him. Verney appeared to be safe . . . for the moment.

Gritting his teeth, he decided to brave the river once again. For as long as he felt able, he traced its course downstream, before pulling himself onto the bank once more, lest his body shut down with hypothermia. For an hour or more he kept doing this; moving in and out of the water, and proceeding steadily downstream, with each immersion taking him closer to Castel di Sangro. Then he spied something on the south bank. Barbed wire. It could only mean one thing – a minefield. Surely that had to mean that he had reached no-man's-land. If he could make his way through this last obstacle, surely he would find British troops.

With infinite care, Verney hauled his frozen form over the wire and began to trudge south through the minefield. Acutely aware that at any time one of his footfalls might land on an anti-personnel mine, detonating it and blowing himself to pieces, his nerves were in tatters. Shivering violently from the long immersion, and desperate as he was, it was pure adrenalin that propelled him forward, each footstep equating to a deadly game of Russian roulette.

And then he figured he had to be through the worst. Perhaps

this was not to be the day that John Verney would get blasted to pieces. He was approaching what appeared to be a deserted village when something jumped out of the shadows in front of him, bringing him to a stop. And then he let out a sigh of relief. It was a black cat crossing his path. Was it an omen?

By now the sun was beginning to rise, casting faint rays across the mist-blanketed hillsides. Ahead, Verney spied a road. Oddly, there was not the slightest sign of life. Having crawled across the open highway, he inched his way up the hill on the far side, which was pockmarked with shell-holes. On reaching the ridge above he came across three Italian villagers riding donkeys.

'Are there any Germans round here?' Verney blurted out, exhaustedly.

Looking at him with initial suspicion, they trio realised he had to be British, and most likely an escaping POW. Climbing down from their mounts they embraced Verney, ignoring his frozen, soaked and muddied form, before pointing behind them. There were British soldiers in Montenero, they told Verney. All he had to do was continue walking and he would find them.

'*Niente tedeschi, niente tedeschi!*' they laughed, as Verney stumbled off in the direction they had indicated. *No Germans, no Germans!*

Verney forced his frozen limbs to move. He was so close now. He had come so far, endured so much. Braved so much. Surely he had made it, and would soon be home, where he'd be able to see Lucinda, his wife, and finally meet his young son.

And then he laid eyes upon it – the village that the Italians had spoken of. At first the 'much battered buildings appeared deserted'. But as he scanned the ruins, he spotted something utterly distinctive. Parked behind a wall was a British Bren gun carrier – a small troop transporter armed with a single Bren light machine gun. Turning a corner, even as a shell tore overhead, he saw a group of British soldiers gathered in a doorway, chatting and smoking cigarettes.

Catching sight of Verney staggering down the roadway, they took little notice of him, imagining him to be an Italian farmer. For some reason, the Special Forces captain suddenly felt incredibly self-conscious, and embarrassed even. Walking past them, he heard voices in a building further along. Crossing the threshold, he found himself in a small room occupied by two 'half-dressed Privates cooking breakfast'.

'Christ, Nobby, look at what the cat's brought in,' one remarked, as Verney stood there, a huge grin breaking out across his features.

Amazingly, he had done it. After all the months spent on the run, living in caves in the Italian mountains, he had pulled it off. He had made it to Allied lines. He was free.

After due processing, John Verney returned to England and was reunited with his wife, Lucinda, and finally got to meet his young son, Julian. As he would write with great candour regarding his motivation for escaping: 'It is a POW's duty, we had often been told, to escape in order that he may continue to fight for his country. My own reasons for escaping had been entirely different. I had escaped to rejoin Lucinda and Julian, and for nothing else.'

After his epic getaway Verney went on to serve in France and Germany, eventually forming part of SAS Brigade staff, and getting promoted to major. By the end of the war he had been awarded an MC, two Mentions in Despatches and the Légion d'Honneur (Chevalier), a high French honour. But Verney was to suffer the curse of so many who had trained in Algeria. Plagued with malarial attacks, he 'remained the colour of a daffodil' until he was demobilized from the army, in November 1945.

In 1959, upon the death of this father, Verney became the 2nd Baronet of Eaton Square. He was also a successful writer, painter and illustrator and was the author of many children's novels. In time he penned two books based upon his experiences in the Second World War, *Going to the Wars* and *A Dinner of Herbs*. A devoted family man, he would have two sons and five daughters with his beloved wife, Lucinda. Sadly, Julian, his firstborn son, would die at a very young age.

Verney would travel extensively in Italy after the war, returning to Sardinia, among many other of his wartime haunts. While driving around the island with his wife and friends, in his Standard Vanguard car, they were arrested by a 'carabinieri patrol armed to the teeth', for not carrying their ID papers. Suspected of being 'a gang of international dope smugglers', ironically Verney was taken to the very village where he'd been held during the war, to be questioned by the carabinieri chief in the very same police station.

'Ah me, just as I remember it,' was Verney's remark, as he gazed up at the building.

John Verney, 2nd Baronet, would pass away peacefully at his home in Clare, Suffolk on 2 February 1993 at the age of 79.

Edward Imbert-Terry also successfully crossed into British lines on 14 December 1943. As he would later note of his good friend Verney:

As a member of the trio, I feel it strongly as my duty to state that both Capt. Gibbs and myself would have perished from

cold and fatigue in the snow etc., had it not been for the inde-
fatigable leadership and bravery of Capt. Verney in insisting
that at all costs, the party must keep moving ... although
this undoubtedly meant that he himself was delayed ... Capt.
Verney had never failed to inspire all ... with the greatest
confidence and admiration for his continuous powers of lead-
ership, style and bravery, and I as senior officer and soldier
present ... feel it my duty to bring such admirable perfor-
mance of duty before the proper authorities.

Martin Gibbs was unsuccessful in his attempt to cross to Allied
lines with Verney and Imbert-Terry. Having set out before Verney,
he was captured while trying to cross the 'German front line near
Castel di Sangro'. Two days later, he escaped through the window
of the building in which he was being held, and made his way
back to 'his former haunts, where he lived in a cave', and where
once again he was fed and sheltered by the ever-faithful Sam.
On 12 March 1944, he once again set out for the British lines,
crossing the Maiella mountain range in the company of a large
body of British POWs and Italians, plus Sam.

En route they ran into a blizzard. Marooned in such conditions, the escapees were intercepted by German troops who
opened fire on them. Gibbs was recaptured and soon contracted
pneumonia, due to suffering prolonged exposure in such freezing
conditions. After being interrogated in Italy, in July 1944 he was
taken to Oflag IX-A/Z, a POW camp at Rotenburg, in Hesse,
Germany. The camp was liberated by Allied forces in early April
1945, and Gibbs, the serial escaper, was finally free.

For their epic escapes, John Verney and Edward Imbert-Terry
would be awarded the Military Cross. Their citation reads:

Both captured in Sardinia on 16 Jul 43. Sent via Maddalena to Campo 21 (Chieti). While at Maddalena they attempted to escape by rowing boat but were spotted when passing the last headland, fired on, and forced to pull into shore. After recapture they were beaten up by two Carabinieri and were sent the following day to Campo 21. After the Armistice the Germans took over this camp and P/W were taken to Campo 78 (Sulmona) and from there entrained for Germany. Capts. Verney and Imbert-Terry and another officer got out of their cattle truck during a halt and hid on an embankment until the train left. They made their way towards the Allied lines and finally met British troops at Castel di Sangro on 15 Dec 43.

Verney's powers of leadership and the respect his men held for him, both on Operation Hawthorn and during their following captivity, embodied all the attributes required of a Special Forces officer. His devotion to his men endeared him to all with whom he served.

The failure of so many of the Operation Hawthorn missions in Sardinia, in July 1943, was blamed on that one particular soldier – the Italian-American interpreter, Louis Temperano. Whether or not he had betrayed them remains unproven, but it was not long after his disappearance that all the patrols were captured. Many of those men subsequently escaped, including the two troopers who had formed Verney's sabotage team, Sergeant John Scott and Private Rogers. By the time the official Operation Hawthorn report was written, seventeen of the thirty-odd men who had embarked on the mission had either returned to Allied lines or were known to have broken free and were on the run. In Sergeant Scott's case, he managed to rejoin Special Forces, going on to soldier with the unit through to the liberation of France and the push into Nazi Germany, distinguishing himself as one of SAS commander Blair 'Paddy' Mayne's key deputies. This determination to get back into the fight was typical of those who served with the wartime SAS.

Sardinia itself was to fall without a shot being fired. When the Italians surrendered on 8 September 1943, the Germans simply abandoned the island. Lieutenant Scioca, the perpetrator of the assault on Verney and Imbert-Terry following their attempted rowing boat escape, was duly reported to the United Nations War Crimes Commission, both soldiers giving detailed accounts of their ill-treatment at his hands. It is unclear if any punishment was handed down to him.

The final praise regarding this truly epic escape must go to the many Italians who helped Verney, Imbert-Terry and Gibbs during their time on the run. Without their spirited assistance, the intrepid trio would very likely have perished or been recaptured. The Italians did as they did, knowing fully well the consequences should they be caught. Sam, Antonio, Gabriele, Dionino, Frank del Signore and the many others who contributed to Verney's and his comrades' survival, were typical of the many Italians who fought Fascist tyranny. Verney would go on to immortalise them himself, when writing his two books, *Going to the Wars* and *A Dinner of Herbs*.

As Verney and his men had braved the Italian mountains, so another group of SAS soldiers had launched one of the most daring escape and evasions of the war. It would prove to be one of the most audacious in the history of the Regiment.

Chapter Four

LOVE, COURAGE AND GUERRILLA WAR

August 1944, Neretva River, Yugoslavia

The piercing screech of a heavy shell split the morning air, the report from the artillery gun echoing across a valley thick with curtains of driving rain. Instinctively, Captain Lewis 'Archie' Gibson ducked down, turning his head to see just where it had come from. Around him, his men, and their Yugoslav partisan escorts, 'hurled themselves into whatever cover they could find', taking shelter behind the boulders that dotted the hilly, densely wooded landscape. Moments later the next projectile hit, slamming into the slope to their right, the blast lifting earth and rocks high into the air.

As Gibson hunkered down amid the sodden vegetation, more shells began to plaster the area, one smashing into the side of a building in Pasičina, a village that lay on the hillside above. That partisan stronghold looked to be the target of the German heavy guns, which were firing from across the valley. Gibson couldn't tell if his small patrol had been seen, or if they'd been caught in an enemy bombardment unintentionally. They'd been winding their way through the hills towards the headquarters of the local partisan leader, Commandant Tolić Drinko, who had himself taken cover just a few yards away.

The narrow track they'd been following had allowed them to proceed in single file only. It cut through the forest that provided cover from the Germans, and their Ustaše allies – the Ustaše being Yugoslav fascists in league with the forces of Nazi Germany. Had an eagle-eyed German soldier or Ustaše fighter spotted them? Gibson just couldn't be sure.

As the artillery fire continued to tear into the terrain, Gibson decided that they had simply been unlucky. The shells were landing mostly in and around the village. He didn't believe he and his men had been spotted. But to make a move now, when the enemy had all their focus on this area, might well prove fatal. If they broke cover, surely they would be seen and blasted to pieces. It was safer to wait it out until nightfall, he reasoned, and then continue their journey under cover of darkness. As Gibson was fully aware, the Germans had been wise to their presence in Yugoslavia pretty much since the moment they had arrived, so the hunt was on. Knowing that a small band of British Special Forces were operating in the area, enemy commanders were hell-bent on catching them.

Taking cover beside him was his interpreter, Zara Menko, her dark hair plastered to her face by the incessant rain. She was a *drugaritsa* – one of the female couriers used by the partisans to relay messages and to act as spies; brave young women playing a life-or-death game to help drive the Nazis from their homeland. With her hair cut short and 'dressed like a man', from their very first meeting Gibson had found the petite young woman strikingly attractive. There had been an instant connection. And despite her masculine-seeming clothing, 'she still managed to convey her femininity only too well,' he observed. With her near perfect English, she had become an essential member of his team and was never more than a few feet from his side. In the short time they'd been together, they'd formed an inseparable bond.

As the rain lashed down and the relentless bombardment continued, the small band of British soldiers and their Yugoslav comrades resigned themselves to what looked like being a long day under fire.

Gibson and his party of six men had been in the Dalmatia region of Yugoslavia for over five weeks and had already seen plenty of action. Sent in to observe German aircraft movements – enemy warplanes were harrying Allied shipping in the Adriatic – they were to radio warnings to their base at Rodi, on the east coast of Italy, whenever they saw enemy fighters or bombers taking to the skies. That would enable alerts to be signalled to any Allied ships that might be plying the seas. But once on the ground here, and seizing the opportunity to forge a strong partnership with the partisans, their plans had been refined. They were to support the Yugoslav patriots in any way they could, by relaying intelligence, and crucially, by guiding in air drops of weapons, food and ammunition, plus calling for air strikes against key enemy targets.

At first, matters hadn't gone well at all. Upon first reaching Yugoslav shores, Gibson and his team had been treated with a large degree of suspicion. Many of their so-called comrades demanded to know just why they were here, and why the Allies had done so little to support the Yugoslav partisans before now. What had changed? Why should they be trusted?

Matters weren't helped in that Gibson and his men had arrived far later than originally intended. Back at their base in Rodi, Captain Bob Maxwell, their immediate commander, had wanted Gibson and his men to parachute into a drop zone (DZ) adjacent to the German held town of Mostar, site of the greatest concentration of enemy warplanes. But fearing that a parachute drop direct into the Mostar area was fraught with danger, the long-experienced Gibson had argued otherwise.

'What's going to happen when we turn up unannounced, in the middle of a distinctly unfriendly neck of the woods, with no ground support and no contacts?' he'd objected. 'I'd much rather go in by sea with the knowledge and support of the partisans.'

Fortunately, Maxwell had listened to Gibson's reasoning and concluded that he was right. And so, on 14 August 1944, Gibson and six of his most trusted men were sent on their way by sea, for a mission codenamed Operation Behemoth.

Setting out by boat from the island of Vis, off the Dalmatian coast, the seven Special Forces operators had in their possession a document drafted by a senior Yugoslav partisan leader, which should have given them unfettered passage into the territory beyond. Their mission had been approved at a high level, being given the green light by Tito himself, the leader of all communist resistance forces in Yugoslavia.

Confident of their credentials, their small boat had ploughed through the night, slipping between the islands of Hvar and Korčula, and heading for the mouth of the Neretva river, from where they would unload and march the 50 kilometres to Mostar. As dawn broke on the 15th, they had chugged into the tiny harbour. At the quayside was a surly-looking commissar – an official of the Yugoslav Communist Party – who, as far as Gibson was concerned, should have had prior knowledge of their arrival. Their operational order, dated just two days earlier, confirmed that a welcome party would await: 'the recce party will move by sea to a selected landing beach . . . where arrangements will have been made for their reception.'

Gibson handed the commissar the pass he had been given, but the wooden-faced official simply 'looked at it briefly, then handed it back with a dismissive gesture'. No matter what it might say, or who it was signed by, he didn't particularly give a damn. It became clear how unwelcome they were when he ordered them to turn their boat around and return whence they had come. Despite Gibson brandishing his slip of paper, and arguing that they had every right to be there, the commissar was 'having none of it', as Gibson later remarked. 'He was adamant. They had to leave.'

With no other option, Gibson stepped aboard the boat, which promptly set off back to Vis. Even as Gibson's frustration boiled, he was to discover that this particular cloud had something of a silver lining: during the journey back to Vis, Ken Smith, his radio operator, discovered that their wireless set didn't work. Had they managed to land and reach their area of operations, there would have been little they could have done. So maybe their rejection by the commissar had been a blessing in disguise.

Ten days later, with radio repaired, Gibson and his men made another attempt to land. This time they were more successful, choosing to give the ill-natured commissar a wide berth. Rendezvousing with a different reception party, at least they were allowed ashore and with all their equipment. But even here their welcome was less than friendly, as the British soldiers were surrounded by 'shadowy figures . . . their guns cocked and pointing at the group', as Gibson would note. But once a bottle of fiery local liquor had been passed around, each of the British soldiers taking 'the requisite gulp', the partisans seemed to relax a little. From there, the long trek inland had begun.

Now, some five weeks later, Gibson and his men were lying in the cold, wet undergrowth of the Dalmatian hills, enduring this artillery barrage. Even so, Gibson allowed himself a fleeting smile. With each passing day he and his men had endeared themselves to the partisans. They had proved themselves to be committed guerrilla fighters who shared the same objectives – to rid Yugoslavia of the Nazis. They had achieved so much in what was a relatively short period of time. And for Gibson personally, his journey to this rain-soaked hillside had been challenging, yet rewarding, in the extreme.

The second of four children, Lewis Archibald Gibson was born in the market town of Crieff, near Perth, Scotland, on 8 November 1919. His father was a banker, who had served as an officer in the Black Watch during the First World War. After gaining a promotion at work, he had moved the family to Perth, to take charge of the bank branch there. Unfortunately, he was to die suddenly when Gibson was just thirteen years old.

It was pretty clear that 'Archie' would not be following in the family profession, or that of his forebears, many of whom were also bankers. As he would reflect in later life, 'my arithmetic was appalling and I had no interest in accounts.' Gibson knew he was not the type to sit in an office all day, crunching numbers. He was looking for a life of adventure, one spent in the open air where he could feel free and alive.

From an early age he had been obsessed with motor engines

and automobiles. Whether it was cadging rides in trucks with local delivery men, or 'whipping the motor out of his father's mower, fitting it to his bicycle and running around', he understood that whatever path he followed it would have to include motor vehicles in some shape or form.

At school – Morrisons Academy, in Crieff – he was considered 'average' academically, but was a fine rugby and cricket player, appearing many times for the first teams. He was also a keen member of the school's Officer Training Corps (OTC) in which he learned to play the bagpipes. His proficiency was such that at the age of fourteen, it brought him into contact with European royalty. While holidaying with relatives in St Fillans, on the banks of Loch Earn, his pipe playing was overheard by Queen Wilhelmina of the Netherlands, who had rented a house near by. So impressed was she that the young Gibson was asked to perform for her each evening, whereupon he would be rewarded with a glass of 'Dutch liquor'. He was also asked to 'carry the queen's painting gear down to the loch and stay in attendance to keep the flies off her'. At the end of the summer, when it was time for them to part, Gibson was handed an envelope by the queen's aide-de-camp. Expecting some form of financial gift, he was hugely disappointed to see that it was merely a letter expressing her thanks. He was 'disgusted, having expected at least a crisp five pound note'.

Leaving school at age fourteen, Gibson went to work at a large insurance corporation as a clerk. But this wasn't the life for the high-spirited Scotsman. Bored stiff with the work, he was forever getting into trouble with his colleagues. Ever the practical joker, his pranks would land him in hot water, whereupon his charm and likeable manner usually prevented the punishment from being too severe. On one occasion, when sent to the chairman of the corporation, he left the man's office with a pay rise, and not the dismissal he had been expecting. He would write of the encounter: 'This interview had an important psychological effect on me, and since then I have never had any hesitation in approaching the man at the top.'

With the money he was earning he bought himself a motor-cycle, totally against his mother's knowledge, and he rode to work each day, parking it some distance from the family home, lest she find out. Apart from risking her fury, he was also courting trouble with the police, for he was under-age and the motor-cycle was neither taxed nor insured. Discovering his secret steed, his mother flew into a rage and attacked it with a coal shovel, demanding he get rid of it. Reluctantly, the young Gibson hauled the machine away and sold it . . . only to replace it with another model, one he was determined to keep from his mother's prying gaze.

At the age of sixteen Gibson made the decision to join the Territorial Army. After all, his late father had been a major in the Black Watch; maybe he could emulate him. Knowing that he was a year too young, he lied to the recruiter, giving his age as seventeen. It would turn out to be a life-changing decision. Military life suited Gibson. It gave him the outlet he craved. It also gave him access to a wonderful array of motor vehicles. 'The motoring bug had bitten me. All I wanted to do was to ride a motorbike or drive a car,' he remarked. In the summer of 1937 he decided to take the plunge and join the army full-time. When he broached the subject with his mother, she supported it, arguing that the army might give her wayward son 'some direction in life and control his wilder urges'.

Advised to join the Scots Guards by the janitor at Morrison's Academy, who had once been a regimental sergeant major in the regiment, Gibson was soon on his way to the Guards' depot at Caterham, Surrey, to begin his basic training. Four years later, Gibson, just twenty-one years old, would find himself serving with Britain's elite forces deep in the North African desert.

The eight men of what was known as 'L Detachment', Special Air Service (SAS), slipped through the shadows. Gripping their Thompson machine guns, and burdened under the weight of their backpacks laden with incendiary bombs, their senses were on high alert. Ahead of them, looming out of the darkness of this cool January night was the harbour of Bouerat, a port town on the north Libyan coast, their target for what was codenamed 'Operation Number Six'.

The would-be raiders were commanded by Captain David Stirling, the SAS's founder. Their mission was to locate enemy shipping in Bouerat's deepwater harbour and blow them all to hell. With Allied forces on the advance, but still many miles to the east, the Germans and Italians were using Bouerat port to bring in their much needed fuel supplies. If Stirling and his men could destroy those fuel tankers while at anchor, it would strike a heavy blow against General Erwin Rommel, the commander of Axis forces in North Africa, allowing the Allied advance to be redoubled. That was Stirling and his raider's purpose tonight.

Approval for the raid had come from the man at the very top – General Claude Auchinleck. 'The Auk', as he was affectionately known, was a staunch supporter of Stirling and his fledgling band of SAS raiders, especially since their attacks on enemy airfields deep behind the lines had gained them something of a legendary reputation. Here at Bouerat, the Auk 'wanted the SAS to put limpet mines on Axis tankers in the port, and blow up the Panzer's fuel'. With a thirst for action and eager to prove the SAS's worth, Stirling had readily agreed to the plan, opting to lead the raid personally. And so, on 10 January 1942, a small convoy had set out from their base in Jalo oasis, in the southern Libyan desert. Just as with previous missions, they had been ferried to their objective by the trucks of the Long Range Desert Group, the mission scheduled to take place on the night of 24/25 January 1942.

The LRDG – brainchild of Colonel Ralph Bagnold – were the original desert reconnaissance and raiding force. An adventurer before the war, Bagnold had travelled the deserts of North Africa extensively, and he had a vast knowledge of the terrain and how to navigate it. Twice he'd put forward his idea to the top brass to form a small unit which, with suitable vehicles, could penetrate the desert and conduct reconnaissance operations. Repeatedly his ideas had been dismissed out of hand.

Eventually, Bagnold had managed to get a meeting with the then commander-in-chief Middle East, General Archibald Wavell. If such a unit could be formed, Bagnold argued, the information relayed back to headquarters would prove invaluable. It would enable the Royal Air Force to be scrambled, and to bomb enemy supply routes and transport columns. Wavell, recognising the sense in what was being proposed, gave Bagnold the go-ahead to start recruiting. Months later, the LRDG – by then seasoned desert navigators – had teamed up with the SAS to carry their raiding forces to and from target.

As they crept towards Bouerat harbour, it was clear to the SAS raiders that their objective of blowing up German and Italian tanker ships was dead in the water. The port was devoid of any vessels. This 'minor inconvenience' seemed not to worry the tall ex-Guards officer, David Stirling. They would simply have to find other uses for their bombs, he argued. In any case, laying their charges on enemy shipping would have proved somewhat challenging. The folbot, a small collapsible canoe that was supposed to be used to slip across the harbour, 'had been smashed beyond repair'. The LRDG truck carrying it had hit a large pothole, damaging the craft and rendering it unusable.

With no folbot to hand and no enemy shipping to destroy, Stirling began to cast about for alternative targets. Spying a tall radio mast on the high ground overlooking the harbour, he dispatched two men, Captain Duncan and Corporal Barr, to plant their explosives on that. He then split the eight remaining raiders into two four-man parties. He would lead the first, with troopers Johnny Cooper, Reg Seekings and Bob Bennett to hand, while the experienced Sergeant Pat Riley would lead the second. They would search out targets of opportunity, seeking to blow the place sky high.

They moved off on foot, creeping deeper into the port. Slipping between the darkened warehouses that lined the harbourside, the men acted swiftly, placing their bombs against food dumps, machinery and equipment stores, and setting the timers to blow in half an hour. Working fast, all seemed quiet, and there was little sign of any sentries. It appeared that security was lax, the enemy never expecting to encounter British soldiers so far behind the front line. On one occasion, disaster almost struck as the two teams converged on each other, both groups raising their weapons to fire, until, at the last moment, they realised their mistake.

When it seemed that all the 'obvious targets were covered', Stirling ordered the men to move out, heading back to the LRDG truck that had ferried them hundreds of miles across the desert. It was time to get as far away as possible before the fireworks began. But it was then that Reg Seekings noticed a target they had all somehow missed. Near by was a vehicle park crammed full of enemy trucks, a large number of which appeared to be fuel tankers. There were eighteen in total, each containing 4,000 gallons of petrol and 'just waiting for the order to head to the front line'.

With such a tempting target at hand, and with plenty of their Lewes incendiary bombs left, Stirling and his men got to work. Like wraiths in the night they darted from vehicle to vehicle, planting their charges and setting the timers. If there were any sentries in the area, they didn't show themselves, enabling the raiders to go about their deadly business unmolested. They could not believe their luck.

Charges set, the eight men were joined by Duncan and Barr, who had placed their bombs around the radio mast. Their work in the port done, Stirling gave the order to pull out. But there was still one tempting target. Noticing an anti-aircraft gun with its crew asleep beside it, Sergeant Pat Riley crept forward, being careful not to wake them. Taking out his one remaining Lewes bomb, he stuffed it down the gun's barrel. That done, he crept back to where his comrades were waiting.

As Johnny Cooper would reflect, even as they slipped away they were tensing themselves for 'the explosions to begin'. None of them had to wait for long. The first of the Lewes bombs detonated, the thunderous blast cutting through the air, ripping storage units and warehouses apart, reducing them to a mix of rubble and blazing timber. There then followed the biggest series of blasts of all, as one by one the petrol tankers went up, sending a series of massive mushroom clouds of smoke and flame billowing into the sky. The trucks had been rendered into twisted, mangled wrecks, the intense conflagration lighting up the entire sky as the fuel boiled and burned.

Their job done, it was time to bug out. Waiting for them, not too far away, was their ride home.

Sitting in the driver's seat of the Ford 4x4 V-8 was Guardsman Lewis 'Archie' Gibson, a twenty-two-year-old corporal serving in the LRDG. Gibson had been personally chosen by Stirling to be his driver. The honour had been conferred due to Gibson's truck having the words 'Wha Daur' emblazoned on its wing. It was a line taken from the Scottish folksong 'Little Jock Elliot', after the eponymous character fends off attacks from his foes, and asks the rhetorical question, 'Wha daur meddle wi' me?' (Who dares meddle with me?). With its Wha Daur monicker, Gibson's truck reminded the SAS commander of the regiment's motto, Who Dares Wins. Gibson went on to prove himself one of the best drivers that Stirling had ever encountered, becoming indispensable to their operations – so much so that he had been declared an honorary member of the SAS.

Upon reaching his vehicle, the raiders clambered into the rear, while Stirling jumped into the passenger seat. Wasting no time, Gibson put the truck into gear and pushed hard down on the accelerator. It was now up to him to get the raiders to their rendezvous with the remainder of the LRDG patrol, which was waiting in the desert to the south. From there the LRDG convoy would navigate the raiders through the desert and back to their base, over 600 kilometres away. Time was pressing. As much distance as possible needed to be covered before daylight, when the Italians and Germans would get on the hunt for the elusive raiding party.

As Gibson powered Wha Daur along the tarmac, Stirling, who, unlike the others still had a few Lewes bombs left, occasionally signalled him to halt. As Johnny Cooper, manning the quick-firing Vickers K machine gun positioned on the truck's rear, would remark: 'In the dead of night, miles behind enemy lines, our truck sped along, stopping every now and again when we saw a parked truck.' Those 'parked trucks' were given the same treatment as the fuel tankers. Shortly, they were likewise ablaze, thick palls of black smoke marking Wha Daur's progress along that desert highway.

But as the Ford thundered onwards, Gibson spied flashing lights on the road up ahead. No sooner had they seen them than 'shots whizzed through the air', narrowly missing the British raiders. The enemy were before them readying an ambush. From behind, Gibson heard the sound of the Vickers being made ready, as Cooper prepared to trade fire with fire. Seekings, to Cooper's side, lifted his Thompson sub-machine gun and pulled back the cocking handle, as the adrenalin began pumping.

Gibson figured he had two choices. He could either put the vehicle into reverse and try to find another way out of the danger, or he could continue dead ahead, and attempt to bludgeon a path through. Either way, he had to think and act fast. This was do or die.

Flicking on the headlamps in an effort to blind their attackers, he pressed his foot hard to the floor. The Ford lurched ahead, the sudden burst of acceleration forcing him back into his seat. Behind him, Cooper opened up with the Vickers K guns, letting fly with 'a devastating mixture of tracer and incendiary'. To his side, Seekings likewise blasted away with his Thompson, spraying deadly fire at their would-be ambushers. But the enemy here were no shrinking violets. Responding in kind, they let rip at the speeding vehicle with rifles and machine guns, bullets cutting through the air like swarms of angry wasps.

From Wha Daur, the raiders redoubled their efforts to return fire. Their lives were largely in the hands of their driver, who seemed blessed with nerves of steel as he endeavoured to break through. But it was then that the route directly ahead seemed to erupt in fire and devastation, as the enemy began dropping in mortar rounds, seeking to score a hit on the fast-moving truck.

'Get off the track!' yelled Stirling. 'Get off the track!'

Gibson was about to do as he ordered, when he 'noticed that the ground dipped away alarmingly at the side of the road'. Clearly, if he complied with the SAS commander's instructions, the truck would career down the drop and turn over, killing or wounding all on board. There was no alternative – he had to ignore Stirling's instruction, stick to the road and barrel on through.

As the men hung on for dear life, Gibson pushed the Ford to maximum speed, giving it everything he had, his total focus glued to the road. Throwing Wha Daur about, he swerved around the mortar craters that were appearing to his front. There was no time for panic, or even to think. Gibson was acting on pure impulse and instinct. After a few agonising seconds of running the gauntlet, they seemed to have broken free, the enemy positions now lying behind them.

From the truck's rear, Seekings continued to unleash with his Thompson, until their adversaries were out of effective range. They had done it. Better still, behind them, Bouerat was ablaze, the night sky glowing brightly as scores of fires burned furiously. A huge number of enemy trucks, and thousands upon thousands of gallons of fuel had been destroyed, and all destined for Rommel's Panzers. The port-side warehouses had been reduced to heaps of fiery rubble, and the radio mast lay in a heap of twisted metal and tangled cables.

As Gibson powered the raiders deeper into the desert, Stirling, sitting beside him, appreciated that this young driver had very likely saved all of their lives. Unbeknown to Gibson, the SAS commander had made the decision to recommend him for the Military Medal (MM) for his actions. Johnny Cooper would also be rewarded for his expert work with the Vickers K machine gun, earning a Distinguished Conduct Medal (DCM). As Stirling appreciated, he had chosen these men well. They were fearless warriors, as well as being the very essence of what he had hoped for when forming his elite fighting unit.

Gibson's route to joining Britain's Special Forces had been a long one. Shortly after finishing his initial training with the Scots Guards, he'd been posted to London for ceremonial duties. Being tall and good-looking, with a 'Douglas Fairbanks' moustache, he cut a dashing figure in his dress uniform and bearskin. No stranger to royalty, he did a stint guarding Buckingham Palace, meeting King George VI and the two young princesses, Elizabeth and Margaret, and taking part in the king's coronation in 1937.

It was around this time that he had his first brush with a tall, dashing Scots Guards officer, 'someone who would come to play a part in his life of which the young man could not possibly dream'. Gibson's first impression of David Stirling had not been entirely positive. While on manoeuvres in Hampshire, Gibson was tasked with collecting Stirling, so as to drive him to where the exercises were taking place. He was surprised to find the lieutenant in full dress uniform, when the situation required him to be in khaki service dress. Mistaking the good conduct stripe on Gibson's sleeve for a mark of rank, Stirling had declared, 'Thank you, Corporal.' Gibson had concluded that Stirling was 'something of a fool, which did nothing to change his opinion of authority being placed in the hands of unsuitable or undeserving people'.

It was only later that his opinion of Stirling would change, when their paths crossed again. Deployed to North Africa, Gibson had landed his dream job as a motorcycle dispatch rider. Given free rein to tear around Cairo, he became familiar with that city, making many friends along the way. Life for the young soldier simply couldn't get any better. But while there he heard news of Britain's declaration of war against Nazi Germany, realising that his easy and enjoyable life in Egypt was very likely over.

On 10 June 1940, Italy joined the conflict, its Fascist leader, Benito Mussolini, declaring war on Britain and France. Just days later, tens of thousands of Italian soldiers poured into Libya, with the objective of driving the British out of Egypt, and taking control of the Suez Canal, that vital link between the Mediterranean Sea and the Indian Ocean – Britain's wartime lifeline.

It was around this time that Ralph Bagnold started recruiting drivers for his new unit, the LRDG. He was looking for free-thinking men with a thirst for action, who had the skills to drive thousands of miles through one of the harshest environments on earth – the Sahara desert – while watching for signs of enemy movements. After a day's dispatch riding, Gibson discovered that the LRDG was recruiting. On return to his barracks, he found that three of his closest friends had been 'interviewed by an officer of a newly formed unit . . . the Long Range Desert Group. The sort of life they lived appealed to me enormously . . . I would have volunteered so forcibly they would have had to take me along.' Disappointed though he was to have missed his chance, he still had a role to play, one that shortly would take him into the heart of the action.

In just a few weeks the Italians 'had crossed over the border into Egypt and captured the town of Sidi Barrani', 500 kilometres to the west of Cairo. Hasty reinforcements were sent from Britain and, with the Italians advancing no further, 'by the beginning of December 1940, the British were able to go on the offensive'. Under the command of General Wavell, the Italians were pushed ever backwards, and by February 1941 the vital port of Benghazi was in British hands. But with their supply lines stretched, the British had to slow their pace.

'Startled by the sudden collapse of their Italian allies, the Germans had no alternative but to shore up the situation,' Gibson noted. A week after the British halt, German troops began landing at Tripoli, on the Libyan coast. On 24 March 1941 they struck, forcing the British into a fighting retreat. Benghazi was quickly retaken and by the end of May, Tobruk, which lay further east, fell to Rommel's Afrika Korps. It was here that the Germans had to call a halt. They'd hit the same problem that the British had just weeks earlier: they could not maintain their supply lines. For both sides, this would become the key issue as the war in North Africa raged.

Ralph Bagnold had been right. If those supply lines could be monitored and hit, then Axis forces would have major problems sustaining any meaningful advance. His LRDG should be the ones to make that happen.

For Gibson, still smarting from missing out on joining Bagnold's fledgling unit, his war was about to come to a violent, if temporary, end. Tasked with delivering ammunition to some frontline positions, he found himself alone in a truck filled to the brim with artillery shells. As it was a scorching hot day, he'd taken off his shirt and boots, using his bare feet to control the foot pedals.

With the truck thundering across the desert, he noticed a bright flash ahead of him, followed immediately by a puff of black smoke. At first, not realising just what it was, he pressed on. But a second later the shockwave of a massive explosion hit the truck, as a shell tore up the ground just ahead of him. Moments later, another hit, blasting a crater in the ground to his rear. Whoever was shooting at him had clearly found his range.

With no other option, and fearing the next shell would score a direct hit, Gibson slammed on the brakes and jumped free, sprinting away and hunting for some cover. It was a decision that saved his life. As the truck rolled on, its momentum carrying it forward, a third shell struck, tearing apart the cab in a massive blast. The concussive impact threw Gibson down into the sand, as the searing heatwave washed over him.

Slowly he got to his feet and stared in disbelief. The truck was blazing furiously, sending a thick pall of smoke high into the Saharan sky. Oddly, what annoyed Gibson most was that 'the flames were consuming a half bottle of whisky, a present from his friend back in Cairo'. Also trapped in that burning cab along with his shirt and boots was his 'baling out bag', a haversack which contained items he would need to survive – 'a water bottle, cigarettes, matches and other essentials of desert warfare'.

And then, 'over a sand dune, rolled a German armoured car'.

It came to a halt a few yards away. Three German soldiers jumped out. As they eyed the burning truck, the ammunition in the rear began to explode. Fearing for their lives, the enemy troops forced the half-naked Gibson into the rear of their vehicle and raced away at top speed. Inside, it was cramped and piping hot. Gibson was made to sit at an uncomfortable angle. The smell of petrol filled his nostrils, so strong he feared he might be overcome by the noxious fumes.

After a while, the Germans pulled to a halt and everyone got out. As Gibson's eyes adjusted to the blinding sunlight, he realised they'd paused to have a bite to eat and a cup of coffee. He looked around for any means of escape, but it was hopeless; they were in the middle of nowhere. Even if he did manage to dash away, he was barefoot and had no water. He wouldn't last five minutes out in the desert. Reluctantly, he realised he would have to stay with his captors if he was to survive.

Having eaten, they got back into the armoured car. But just as Gibson was bundled into the rear, his fortunes were about to change. As the German commander went to get in behind him, there was the sudden sound of machine-gun fire, rounds hammering into the vehicle's armour. Without a word, the Germans grabbed Gibson and 'unceremoniously shoved [him] out through the doorway and onto the ground below'.

Leaving their former captive sprawled on the sand, with the roar of its engine the enemy vehicle accelerated away, as long lines of fiery tracer chased after it. Gibson glanced up to see a number of British Army vehicles approaching. Getting to his feet he raised his hands. He was pleased to see that it was the 11th Hussars, a British armoured unit. His time in captivity had lasted a mere five hours.

Dressed only in shorts, at first the British soldiers refused to believe Gibson was who he claimed to be, repeatedly questioning him as to his identity. Of course, any evidence he had confirming he was a British soldier was long gone, destroyed in the fire that had consumed his truck. Becoming increasingly frustrated, Gibson 'let fly with some choice British Army language'. Shocked at this outburst, the Hussars 'quickly decided that no German spy would have such command of ripe vernacular, no matter how intensive his training'. Identity duly established, Gibson was 'sent back to his Guards unit in one of their ration trucks'.

Ironically, the loss of his truck and his spectacular, if brief, spell as a captive had come at an opportune moment. Upon returning to his unit, Gibson discovered that the LRDG were once again seeking recruits. As Gibson was now bereft of a vehicle, he was asked if he would like to be considered for the role? He 'was over the moon' and immediately stepped forward to join the unit that he longed to be a part of. The 'incident in the desert with the Germans' had proved to be 'a major turning point in my life,' he observed.

Arriving safely at the LRDG's Abbassia barracks, in the eastern suburbs of Cairo, Gibson was pleased to be reunited with his friends who had joined the unit a few months earlier. He couldn't have been happier. He 'knew instinctively that the LRDG was for him. It fitted my personality like a glove. For once, I was a round peg in a round hole,' Gibson would reflect. 'I had come home, as it were.'

Assigned to 'G' patrol, a 'body of men plucked from the Guards regiments', Gibson was given what was supposedly the 'runt' of the vehicles, with the patrol number G11. It was the slowest of all, apparently. An ugly-looking Ford 4x4 V-8, it had certainly seen better days. 'We tried everything possible to improve the performance, without result,' he would write. 'I was furious that she couldn't keep up with the remainder of the patrol when the going was fast.' As each of the vehicles had names painted on their wings, Gibson chose 'Wha Daur'. In time it would prove entirely fitting.

By November 1941, a mere four weeks after joining the LRDG, Gibson and G Patrol were on the move. With plans by Allied commanders for a new push against Axis forces, the LRDG were tasked to keep watch on enemy supply routes. Heading south along the banks of the River Nile, they drove for three hundred miles in the scorching heat, passing 'half-buried temples, overtaking slow-moving bullock carts and jostling peasants out of the way', as Gibson would describe it. After that, they swung west and headed for the town of Kharga, where they could refuel the vehicles for the onward journey.

Their stop in Kharga was brief. Soon they were on the move once more, heading deeper into the Libyan desert, crossing the Great Sand Sea – 'an area of towering dunes as large as Ireland' – and heading for the LRDG base at Kufra, a '20 mile long series of desert oases, which provided shelter, food and much needed water in inhospitable surroundings'. Kufra had been chosen wisely, for it was blessed with a seemingly unlimited supply of fresh water from an underground lake, which was lined with thousands of date palms, casting blissful shade. 'Together with the Egyptian oasis of Siwa, to its north-east, Kufra provided a base of operations for the LRDG throughout the rest of the North African campaign,' Gibson noted.

As the men of the LRDG had motored through the heat of the desert, 'clad in half-Arab, half-Army dress', Gibson knew he was exactly where he wanted to be. His lust for adventure had been assuaged. As he would reflect, 'I felt completely at home with the Desert Group.' They were a unique body of men, 'a collection of individuals', yet each welded together with the same single-minded determination and the 'unquenchable spirit of adventure' that made them 'nigh unstoppable'.

Throughout the month of November 1941, Gibson and G Patrol operated on 'the main road inland from the Mediterranean, along the Trigh-el-Abd, a track running south away from the sea, monitoring enemy transport'. Becoming experts in desert camouflage, they were able to work with a degree of impunity, radioing back to headquarters all that they saw. Some days were tedious, revealing no movement, but on others the roads were crammed with military hardware, the enemy totally unaware of the watchers' presence. From their desert hideouts, the LRDG was having an impact. Their work was invaluable, the intelligence they were sending back of immense value.

But as the enemy became aware that British forces were operating in the area, their warplanes were on the lookout for any signs of the LRDG's passing. To counter this, Gibson would note, they became 'extremely proficient at hiding their vehicles'. A passerby would never have noticed the small, apparently random humps in the desert. Indeed, the LRDG could boast that one of their observation posts lay only two hundred yards from the main road and in all the 'months it was in use, it was never discovered, not even from the air'.

Yet it was to prove a very different matter when the LRDG was on the move, as Gibson discovered to his detriment. On a journey to take up a position on the Via Balbia – the Libyan Coastal Highway – G Patrol was spotted by an Italian Savoia, a three-engine medium bomber. As the enemy warplane swooped to attack, the gunners on the LRDG trucks let rip, the salvoes from their machine guns forcing the plane to drop its bombs harmlessly in the sand some distance away. As the barrage of fire from G Patrol's gunners filled the sky, the Italian pilot saw sense and turned away.

But no one doubted that the pilot would have raised the alarm. A quarter of an hour later the sound of another aircraft rent the skies. Looking up, Gibson could see the unmistakable form of a Junkers Ju 87 B, otherwise known as the 'Stuka', heading their way. This was a more formidable aircraft, posing a far greater threat. With its two-man crew, the Stuka dive-bombers were the terror of the skies, causing untold damage to British and Allied forces. Equipped with sirens over the spats on their wheels, they produced a high-pitched wail as they came in to attack, putting the fear of God into anyone unfortunate enough to be caught below. Fitted to their wings were four 110lb bombs, with a much larger one tucked beneath the fuselage. The Stuka also boasted two MG17 machine guns on its wings, plus an MG15 at the rear. Unlike the Italian pilot, who had fled the scene as soon as those beneath had bared their teeth, the Stuka pilot seemed determined to cause as much damage to the British patrol as possible.

As the trucks of G Patrol scattered, the pilot focused on one vehicle in particular. Gibson was horrified to discover that it was Wha Daur. His heart pounding, he pressed the accelerator to the floor and threw the truck around, driving in whirls and circles, constantly changing direction as the Stuka's machine guns ripped into the sand all around. Fleeing at speed across the desert, Gibson noticed the aircraft swoop around to come in for another strafe, and he 'frantically tugged at the steering wheel, all the time expecting to feel a hail of bullets slicing across his back'.

The crazed way in which Gibson was driving meant that his gunner, positioned behind him, could barely return fire. Instead, he was forced to hang on for dear life. The Stuka unleashed its first bomb, missing Wha Daur by inches. Luckily, it had failed to explode. Had it done so, it would have blasted them all to smithereens. Still Gibson drove on, as the air was filled with the piercing wail of the aircraft's siren, which circled around for another attack.

By this time, Gibson's gunner had given up any hope of trying to shoot at the Stuka. 'Instead, he came down front and crouched on the running board, shouting "Left, left, left", while . . . my other passenger . . . crouched on the other running board, shouted "Right, right, right".' With his two comrades yelling out instructions, and the plane howling through the sky, still Gibson was unable to shake it off. Finally he opted to slow the truck down, telling his guides to jump for it. There was no point in them all being killed.

Now on his own, Gibson carried on with his deadly cat-and-mouse game, zig-zagging the kangarooing truck across the rough desert terrain. And then the Stuka pounced again, dropping a bomb that exploded just a few feet away, the powerful blast lifting the truck on its springs. Still Gibson managed to avoid being hit. 'Again and again he came at me,' Gibson recalled. 'On his final dive he fired two shots, he was out of ammunition. I have never been so frightened in my life . . . From that day until the end of the war, I had a very healthy respect for aircraft and a droning noise in the distance was enough to set my heart beating faster.'

With the Stuka disappearing into the distance, Gibson breathed a sigh of relief. It was the closest he had come to being killed, and was even worse than when the German gunners had blasted apart the cabin of the truck that he had been driving. Had it not been for his superior skills at the wheel, he didn't doubt that Wha Daur would have been blasted into oblivion. Upon checking the vehicle afterwards, the truck had suffered not a single shrapnel or bullet hole. The only damage seemed to be 'some bullets lodged in a bedding roll'.

Shortly, the extraordinary driving skills that Gibson had demonstrated were to be called upon by the SAS, who were desperate for a means to strike a blow against the enemy, and to prove that David Stirling's concept of deep desert raiding did indeed have merit.

On the night of 17 November 1941, Operation Squatter the SAS's inaugural mission, had been launched. It was an unmitigated failure. The plan had been to parachute a group of SAS deep behind enemy lines, to raid the airfields at Tmimi and Gazala on the Mediterranean coast. But disaster had struck. The would-be raiders were caught in one of the fiercest desert storms. Jumping into this *khamsin*, dozens were killed or badly injured. Unable to release themselves from their harnesses, they were dragged along the desert by the howling wind. Many were declared missing, never to be heard of again. Torrential rain turned wadis into raging torrents, soaking the explosives that the men carried, rendering them unusable. Of the sixty-odd who had jumped that night, just twenty-two made it back to safety. No enemy warplanes had been destroyed, as the raiders had failed to make it to the target airfields.

Worried that the misfortunes of Operation Squatter would

spell the end of the SAS, Stirling was desperate to have another go. A chance meeting with David Lloyd Owen, then the deputy commander of the LRDG, was to prove pivotal. Lloyd Owen suggested to Stirling that, rather than parachuting in, the LRDG, with their superlative driving skills, could ferry the SAS to target in their trucks. Of course, it would mean traversing thousands of miles of inhospitable desert, but they could pretty much guarantee to deliver the SAS safely. Once at their targets, the raiders would go in on foot to attack, before returning to the waiting vehicles, to ferry them back to their base.

Stirling readily agreed, and a famous partnership was born.

For Gibson, this turn of events proved pivotal. So far, his missions with the LRDG had largely been ones of covert intelligence gathering. Teaming up with the SAS was all about driving into the heart of enemy territory, hell-bent on seriously destructive endeavours. The adventurous life that he had sought since childhood was about to be lived to the full.

Linking up with the SAS brought Gibson a renewed acquaintance with David Stirling, of course, the man that Gibson had thought 'something of a fool' when first meeting him, back in Britain. This time, the SAS captain was to leave him with a very different impression. To his surprise, Stirling 'seemed to have changed character. No longer the slightly distant figure he once was, Stirling had an air of bustle and bounding enthusiasm for his new task.' The positive impression went both ways. When spotting Wha Daur scrawled across the battle-worn Ford, Stirling decided that it would be Gibson who would be his driver on forthcoming raids.

Theirs was to prove an enduring partnership, Gibson reflecting on Stirling's unique persona that 'he had the fortunate knack of being able to sleep in the passenger seat as we bumped across the desert on the way to the job and was fresh and ready to go when the fun started'.

In addition to Stirling, a handful of SAS stalwarts would have a major impact on the young LRDG corporal, men with whom he formed an inseparable bond. Like Gibson, the 'slight of frame' Johnny Cooper, 'a sensitive, well-educated lad', had lied about his age to sign up. At 'just nineteen years old, he still looked like something of a boy scout, but his fresh-faced, boyish looks belied a resolute inner toughness'. Cooper's strength of character had been clear to Stirling, who had recruited him personally, seeing in him the qualities he sought for his new unit. Described by Gibson as 'a delightful companion and a handy man to have in a tight spot', Cooper was to prove all that and more at Bouerat.

Alongside Cooper, Albert Reginald 'Reg' Seekings was another formidable SAS soldier with whom Gibson would form a strong friendship. With his 'stocky boxer's physique, sandy moustache and unruly brown hair', Seekings was 'irascible, combative, rebellious and a self-confessed brawler'. He would not be one to shy away from a fight, of that Gibson was certain. As he would later remark, 'Cooper and Seekings were wonderful characters and the three of us became firm friends.'

When Gibson had run Wha Daur through that fearsome ambush at Bouerat, part of what had given him the confidence to do so was knowing that he had such warriors as Cooper and Seekings manning the vehicles' guns, as they made good their escape.

For the remainder of the war in North Africa, Gibson would operate with Stirling, Cooper, Seekings and more, ferrying these men across the desert on missions of untold daring. His fearless driving skills and good nature endeared him to all, but first and foremost to David Stirling, the man who had founded the SAS and proved that this type of innovative, hit-and-run warfare could pay huge dividends.

The famous photographer Cecil Beaton, while visiting the SAS and LRDG in the early summer of 1942, wrote of them: 'A more frightening-looking band of chaps it would be hard to imagine. Dustier than you would have thought possible, with bloodshot eyes and strange head-dresses or hair standing on end, bearded, they have no connection with this period of history. They were like primeval warriors.'

They were, and Gibson was glad to be one of them.

By the spring of 1943, the desert war was drawing to a close. The Axis had begun to evacuate their forces from North Africa following defeat by the Allies. Caught between two armies, and retreating from both, Rommel had no option but to save what men and materiel he could. But in the process of chasing after the retreating enemy, David Stirling had been captured and carted off to captivity.

For Archie Gibson, that turn of events would lead to pastures new. Having suffered heavy casualties during the desert war, the Guards battalions looked to reinforce their strength with experienced soldiers, and sought to recall Gibson. But he was 'loath to return to the life of a guardsman in a regiment'. Instead, he sought advice from Jake Easonsmith, the second in command of the LRDG. Easonsmith had witnessed Gibson in action and he advised him to apply for a commission, and to return to the LRDG as an officer.

With Easonsmith's blessing, in the spring of 1943 Gibson went for officer training. Returning to the LRDG in late September that year, he would prove to the top brass that he was not only a fearless soldier, but also a formidable and capable officer, respected by all who served with him. A new mission awaited, one that would have an utterly profound impact upon Gibson for the rest of his life.

In the autumn of 1940, the Italian dictator Benito Mussolini had invaded Greece by way of Albania, moving his forces across the Adriatic from the Italian mainland. But 'Il Duce', as he was known, was to fail miserably, the Greeks forcing his troops into a full-scale retreat. To save the Italians from a humiliating defeat, on 6 April 1941 Hitler sent in troops to bail out his ally. In order to get to the battleground of Greece, the German Panzer divisions needed to pass through a number of countries. Hungary, Bulgaria and Romania were sympathetic to the Nazis, and Hitler had presumed that Yugoslavia, which bordered northern Greece, would likewise allow his legions unfettered passage through their territory.

It was a reasonable assumption, especially since the Yugoslav government had signed a Tripartite Pact that aligned the country with Germany and Japan. But everything was to change.

On 27 March 1941 a coup d'état, led by a group of Yugoslav air force officers, dislodged the government. The country's new leaders disavowed their pact with Nazi Germany. Incensed, Hitler launched a full-scale invasion, declaring that 'Yugoslavia as a nation should be wiped off the map of Europe'. Showing no mercy, and massacring innocent civilians in the process, the Germans forced a quick victory. By 17 April all Yugoslav forces had surrendered. Three days later, Greece capitulated to the German foe.

But then the forces of Nazi Germany turned eastwards, invading the Soviet Union. By way of response, the leader of the Yugoslav Communist Party, Josip Broz, more commonly known as 'Tito', called for a general uprising, for he allied his nation with the Soviets. Up and down the country partisan bands began attacking German units. But not all of the Yugoslav guerrilla fighters were loyal to Tito. There were some who still supported the Nazis: a ruthless band of fascists known as the Ustaše.

Despite such bitter enmities, by the end of the summer almost half of Yugoslavia was under Tito's control. Hitler's response was to order savage purges against the partisans and all those who harboured them, 'but as one resistance cell was mopped up, two more were born'. By the time the Italians had surrendered to British and American forces in September 1943, the Yugoslav partisan army was some 200,000-strong, and it was armed with much of the weaponry abandoned by the defeated Italians. With 'clandestine help from the British Mediterranean Command and the Americans, Tito's army was able to reclaim Croatia and Dalmatia', on the western coast.

It was against this backdrop that Allied Special Forces missions were mooted, spearheaded by the LRDG. As part of this initiative, Gibson was tasked to sort out a particularly vexing problem, one that was causing havoc to shipping in the Adriatic. Enemy aircraft from the Mostar area, which was under German control, were carrying out regular sorties against Allied vessels. It was a serious problem. If a small group of elite soldiers, who specialised in reconnaissance behind the lines, could be dropped into the area, then they could provide early warning of German aircraft movements.

Hence Operation Behemoth was born.

But there remained a lingering distrust between Tito and the British government. Until now, Allied aid had been limited. The British establishment was suspicious of Tito for his communist leanings. But, if Yugoslavia were to be liberated, then Tito and his partisans would be the ones to achieve it, as the British government fully appreciated. In essence, Britain had no option but to back Tito.

By early August 1944, Gibson and his team of six highly experienced men were preparing for their Yugoslavia mission. They were tasked to 'establish an Observation Post near Mostar aerodrome for the purpose of keeping a continuous watch and reporting immediately all aircraft movements during daylight hours by W/T special link'. 'W/T' signified wireless transmission, i.e. radio. Their reports would 'be received by an LRDG W/T post on Vis which will be in direct contact with Royal Navy and RAF. All messages will be passed on immediately to both,' thus ensuring a quick reaction to any intelligence gained.

With their first seaborne landing frustrated by the unwelcoming commissar, Gibson and his patrol had launched a second attempt. Finally on the move into the Dalmatian hills, by executing the long trek towards Mostar they hoped to make Operation Behemoth a reality.

They set off at night, crossing the coastal road. Gibson and his group – which included radio operator Ken Smith, Sergeant Jetley, Corporal 'Bombski' Cashin and Lance Corporal Johnny Metcalf – followed their local guides as they headed into the darkness of the interior. Despite the initial nervousness and aggression that Gibson and his men had encountered, the Yugoslavs now seemed happy enough. Partisans were carrying much of the British raiders' equipment, and seemed eager to assist their new comrades.

The going was tough with Gibson and his men heavily laden. As well as their personal weapons, there was also the added weight of 'ammunition, detonators, fuses and plastic explosives. Then there was the "compo" rations: corned beef, tinned fruit and sweets. And there was the battery charger,' a cumbersome bicycle-operated device, for recharging the patrol's all-important radio.

As they plodded through the pitch darkness, the terrain became steeper and steeper still. Ahead lay a mountain, rising to some 3,000 feet. They were making for a partisan camp that lay on the far side, the route taking them 'through scrubby woodland'. As they struggled upwards the ground got rockier, making for increasingly difficult going. For what felt like an age they laboured onwards, across gullies, around boulders, through bush and trees. At times they seemed to have doubled back. But, with Ustaše and German patrols on the prowl, this was all about foxing the enemy; they could not afford to leave the slightest traces of their passing that might be followed.

Indeed, their pre-mission briefings had left Gibson in little doubt that they were heading into a hornets' nest. There were a number of garrison towns scattered throughout the area, harbouring thousands of enemy troops. Intelligence reports had confirmed that 'elements of both 5 SS Corps troops and 369 Division will be doing garrison duty in this area', backed up with 'Ustaše troops in some strength'. The last thing they wanted was to fall into the hands of the SS or Ustaše.

After hours of 'climbing, falling and struggling to their feet again . . . stopping for alarm, pressing on when the going became better', finally the group came to a halt. They had reached a hut that clung to the side of a hill. Settling down to get some much needed food and rest, they could see how glad all were to be able to take a break.

Shortly after dropping all their kit, two figures emerged from the darkness. The first, who introduced himself as Major Ivan Gaco, was there on the orders of Tito himself, to ensure 'that the British were being properly looked after and were being taken to where they wanted to go'. But it was the second figure who caught Gibson's attention. Gaco introduced his comrade, Kapitan Smail Ćemalović. He was 'a Mostar Muslim, who knew the country like the back of his hand . . . tall, dark-haired . . . clad in battledress and with a moustache only a professional brigand could grow', as Gibson described him. As the British captain sized Ćemalović up, he knew he was looking at a fellow guerrilla commander of real aplomb, someone with whom he sensed he would have an innate understanding.

More figures came into view – male and female partisans, carrying an array of weaponry and looking every inch as fearsome as Kapitan Ćemalović. Gibson was surprised to see so many women among them, appearing no less tough than their male counterparts. He was to learn that these women, known as *drugaritsa*, not only fought alongside the men, but also acted as spies, and as couriers between the various partisan groups. As he was also to learn, discipline for the *drugaritsa* was draconian. If one should 'fall pregnant . . . she would be of no further use as a fighter, so she would be booted out' of the group. Even more shocking, 'the man who had made her pregnant would be sought out and shot for deliberately hindering the war effort'. Of course, this harsh treatment was meant to act as a deterrent, but inevitably love flourished among the hills, despite the threat of exile and execution that hung over all.

There was also an interpreter of sorts, a Yugoslav doctor who spoke French. Up until now a mixture of pointing and sign language had been the only way to communicate. As the doctor translated Gaco and Ćemalović's Serbo-Croatian into French, Gibson, having a basic grasp of that language, was able to conduct a conversation of sorts. Although not ideal, at least both sides were able to get their points across in a roundabout way.

Major Gaco seemed suspicious of his British charges and demanded to know 'why Britain hadn't aided him before'. This was a contretemps that Gibson was not prepared to get into. He was there for one sole purpose, to report on enemy aircraft movements, not to discuss the geopolitical situation with partisan leaders. Accepting this grudgingly, Gaco warned Gibson that movement in the Mostar area would be 'extremely difficult as it was entirely German and Ustaše controlled, with few partisan sympathisers among the villagers'.

Regardless, the group pressed on. The partisans had rustled up two mules, which were loaded with Gibson and his men's heaviest gear. Again, the going was 'very rough or very hilly', as they endeavoured not to leave the slightest trace that might reveal their presence. They walked in silence, the only noise being their laboured breathing and the mules' hooves as they clomped across the rocky ground. Gibson kept checking his surroundings. The only cover was the sparse scrub and small patches of woodland. The occasional hamlet broke the skyline, but many were abandoned, having been destroyed by the enemy. They passed 'small villages which had been almost completely burnt by fascists and were now empty except for one or two people', Gibson observed, grimly.

Atrocities carried out by the SS and Ustaše were evident all around. Gibson had been briefed about this at headquarters, and as he was to reflect of the Ustaše, 'we feared them much more than the Germans. They were masters at atrocity.'

At one point they reached a village whose inhabitants had befriended the partisan company with which Gibson and his men were travelling. But to their horror they discovered that nearly all the inhabitants were dead, and that the corpses of the women and children had been severely mutilated. The only survivor was an old woman who had managed to conceal herself. 'She had hidden in a chimney while the slaughter was going on,' Gibson recorded. By the time the killers had left, she had gone 'completely insane'.

By dawn on 28 August the party reached Bajto. It was immediately clear that this had once been a thriving village, but the 'deserted clutter of fallen buildings, shelled houses and blown-up roads' was evidence of a recent enemy purge. Even the sign to the village was riddled with bullet holes, as if the enemy sought to erase the place's very existence. This underlined Gaco's warning of how the area was crawling with enemy troops who were hell-bent on causing ruin and devastation.

Even so, Bajto was to be their temporary home, while Kapitan Ćemalović sought information about the area beyond. They would not move further without assurances that it was safe. And so, as Ćemalović's scouts set out to gather information, those that remained settled down for what might be a long wait, sheltering in the ruins and using their gas capes – thick, waterproof and gas-proof coats – as blankets against the cold.

Through the interpreter, Gibson tried to converse with Ćemalović. Disturbingly, he found the partisan commander aloof and unwilling to open up to him. As with many partisans he'd met so far, Ćemalović was suspicious of the British and just why they had decided to aid their cause now. He did reveal this much to Gibson: his orders were 'to keep the British out of trouble, render any assistance he could and, at the same time . . . make sure that they did not hinder the partisans . . . in any way'.

Wondering just how he would be able to 'get through to the man', Gibson sought to make him understand that they were there to support the partisans in any way they could. As matters transpired, their hosts' attitude towards Gibson and his men was about to change dramatically.

At 0700 hours, the sound of small arms fire woke many from an uncomfortably cold sleep. Immediately, Ćemalović roused his partisans, quickly setting up defensive positions against what looked to be a large body of enemy troops. Gibson grabbed his US-issue M1 carbine – a light, semi-automatic rifle favoured by British Special Forces by this stage of the war – as Sergeant Jetley and the rest of the men followed suit, calmly clipping in fresh magazines. But seeing what they were up to, Ćemalović put his hand up, gesturing for them to stay out of it. They were not to engage with the enemy. His partisans would take care of it. Gibson was disappointed. He knew that 'he and his men, with all their experience, could be of valuable help in the gun battle, but no amount of cajoling would get the Yugoslav commander to change his mind'.

Moments after Gibson gave up expressing his objections, 'incoming fire began to raise spurts of dust and stone chippings around the two of them'. As Gibson and Ćemalović ducked into cover, it quickly became clear that their attackers were the Ustaše, those Yugoslav fascists in league with the forces of Nazi Germany. More to the point, they looked to have the village surrounded with about eighty of their fighters. Ćemalović's partisans were heavily outnumbered, that much was clear.

Ćemalović was forced into a climbdown. Right now, he needed every fighter he could get, British included. For two hours the battle raged as the Ustaše closed in on the defenders, and Gibson, Jetley and the others blasted away with their carbines. Their accurate, controlled shooting forced the Ustaše to keep their distance, or die. Any who strayed too close paid the price in blood. At their sides, Ćemalović's partisans were likewise putting up a blistering fight. With bullets pinging and ricocheting off the walls, the ruins of Bajto still offered good cover, while the Ustaše, despite their numbers, were out in the open.

With the skills of the defenders starting to take deadly effect, a number of Ustaše fighters lay dead or severely wounded on the dusty ground. Replenishing their weapons with the ammunition they had dragged through the hills, the defenders fought on. But as the battle raged, the sheer weight of enemy numbers began to have an effect. As Gibson realised, there was a very real danger that they might be overrun. Something would have to give, for there were simply too many enemy.

Sensing the danger, Ćemalović moved out with a small force of his men, heading off to higher ground, from where he intended to carry out a flanking attack. As soon as the Yugoslav commander and his comrades were in position, Gibson and his men rose up and let rip with their carbines, forcing the Ustaše to keep their heads down, and providing a diversion. With the enemy's attention focused on them, Ćemalović and his men crept ever closer from the flank, primed to unleash hell.

All of a sudden Ćemalović's hidden force opened up. Now the enemy had bullets slamming into them from two directions – from Gibson and his men in the ruined buildings, plus machine-gun and rifle fire hitting them from a mystery force on their right flank. Almost immediately some of the Ustaše decided they'd had enough, breaking away and making a run for it back down the hillside. Soon enough the rest, realising they were in danger of being overrun, turned on their heels and fled. After many hours the assault had been beaten off.

As Gibson was to report later of the battle, 'the Kapetan, directing operations from a hill top ... managed, by noon, to partially surround the enemy. From then on the battle turned in our favour and the Ustaše were forced to withdraw, leaving several dead and wounded behind.'

Although the firefight had raged for close to five hours, the casualties on both sides were relatively light. One partisan and two civilians had been killed, with four wounded. Three Ustaše lay dead with a further seven wounded. Still, they'd proven that Ćemalović's partisans, supported by Gibson and his men, could achieve a victory against all odds.

With the battle won, Gibson and his men wiped the sweat from their brows and grabbed their water bottles, gulping down the contents. Shortly, Ćemalović rejoined them. As Gibson would write of the encounter, 'He looked at us for a moment, then permitted himself a half smile. "Good!" he declared simply, and nodded a couple of times.' Around him, his partisans likewise nodded and smiled. The British had proved themselves in battle. This was just the kind of endorsement they needed.

The dust settled, the wounded were taken care of and, in the evening, the dead were buried. Digging graves proved back-breaking work in the hard ground of the Dalmatian hills. But the battle had done much to cement the relationship between the British and the Yugoslavs. Ćemalović and his partisans now looked upon Gibson and his men with respect, all suspicion gone. In those few hours of action they had proved that they were formidable soldiers, more than capable at holding their own in a firefight.

News of the battle soon reached LRDG headquarters, relayed by Ken Smith, Gibson's signaller. In a top secret report, dated 31 August 1944 and entitled 'LRDG Daily Summary No. 72', it was noted: 'patrol engaged with Ustaše forces for four hours 29th August in Mostar area. They held their ground but lost 1 partisan killed and four partisans wounded. British casualties Nil.'

With many wounded, Gibson's medic, Lance Corporal Johnny Metcalf, joined the partisans' doctor in administering first aid, offering up any supplies they'd brought with them. Bit by bit, this small British team were becoming an integral part of Ćemalović's force.

For forty-eight hours the men waited at Bajto, seeking news that it was safe to continue on to Mostar. If the Ustaše had any intention of launching another assault on the village, they didn't show it. Time was spent eating and resting, Gibson and his team sharing their 'compo' rations with their new friends. These soon ran out, but food in the area seemed plentiful, the partisans sup-plying fruit, maize bread and a thick pea soup. There was also an abundance of wine, plus rakija, a strong fruit brandy.

On the afternoon of the second day at Bajto, a man was seen approaching the village. Immediately everyone was brought to high alert, taking up defensive positions. But, 'as the visitor was passed through the outer defensive ring by successive sentries, the partisans began to relax' and lower their weapons.

The newcomer was introduced as Frano Bundimier, who was well known to the partisans. As Gibson was to write of Bundimier, 'he was a very courageous man who was risking everything for the partisan cause.' The reason for this was quite simple: Frano Bundimier was a spy.

Tasked with infiltrating enemy units and gaining information as to troop movements and strengths, Bundimier presented himself as Ustaše to the Germans and as a German to the Ustaše. This brazenness had worked wonders, and he had managed to gain much useful intelligence, which he had sent via a network of couriers to the Allies in Vis. But this process of relaying information proved risky and time consuming. Now, with Gibson and his team embedded with Ćemalović's partisans, things were set to change, for the British had a radio and a direct link. Bundimier could get his intelligence to the right people in a flash.

But Bundimier also brought disturbing news. By now, the Germans and Ustaše were aware of the presence of Gibson's patrol and were about to step up the hunt. In fact, the Ustaše attack on the 29th had come about directly because of this. The assault on Bajto had been no chance thing. They had been specifically hunting for Gibson's patrol. Why they had not returned in greater numbers remained something of a mystery.

Bundimier's revelations gave Gibson a lot to think about. With enemy troops on the lookout for them, he reflected, 'any attempt to get into Mostar and carry out Operation Behemoth' seemed somewhat 'suicidal'. After discussing this with Ćemalović, and his own men, Gibson had Ken Smith radio their headquarters in Italy. 'Mostar was out,' he told them. 'What should he and his unit do next?'

The men settled down for a third night in Bajto, as they waited for HQ to get back to them. Would there be fresh orders, or would they decide to pull them all out, now that the Mostar mission was off the table? Sleep did not come easily.

At 0100 hours he was shaken awake. Immediately he grabbed his revolver. It was the doctor-cum-translator.

'The Ustaše!' he breathed urgently. 'They're coming. We have to get away from here quickly.'

'Can't we stand and fight?' queried Gibson.

'We're not strong enough. It is better that we go up into the hills. They will keep for another day.'

Gibson roused his men and got them organised. Minutes later they were ready to move. The enemy were already at the gates and, from what Bundimier had told him the previous day, it was Gibson and his band of warriors they were most intent on catching. They needed to slip away as quickly as they could.

They got going, heading south-east towards the foothills of the Biokovo and Sveti Mihovil mountains. Stealing through the pitch darkness, they had to feel their way around rocky outcrops and deep gullies. At times they found themselves caught in thorny thickets, their uniforms tearing, their exposed skin suffering deep scratches and lacerations. But if they were to survive, they had to put as much distance between themselves and their Ustaše hunters as they could. For hours they hurried on, careful not to make any noise. Finally, as the dawn began to cast an ethereal glow across the landscape, they slumped down exhaustedly into what would be their new camp.

Their passage through the hills had not gone unnoticed. As

the morning drew on, a group of people approached the small encampment. They were the inhabitants of the local village. They brought pots of food – stew and vegetables – plus maize bread, to be washed down with bottles of wine. Hungrily, the partisans and Gibson's men wolfed down the provisions, their first hot food in a number of days, as the villagers watched on.

For forty-eight hours they waited in this hillside camp for instructions from headquarters. At night, partisans would sally forth on the lookout for Ustaše or German targets to ambush. When Gibson approached Ćemalović to ask if they could tag along, his request was refused. The partisan leader shook his head with regret. 'My orders from Vis say that you should not be involved or put in danger,' he explained. This irritated Gibson and his men, who were itching to get into the fight once more. But the partisan leader had his orders.

On 3 September new instructions were received from head-quarters. 'In view of imminent operations ... and general disintegration German armies elsewhere, important you stay in area. Report German movements and concentrations. Inform me how long your rations will last.'

Gibson had Ken Smith signal back: 'Can stay indefinitely.'

The message from high command was invigorating. Instructed to stay in the area to provide intelligence on enemy troop move-ments, it looked as if operations against the Germans here were about to commence in earnest. Embedded with Ćemalović's par-tisans, maybe Gibson and his team could contribute in a really meaningful way.

As food was running low and the weather was growing notice-ably colder, Ćemalović decided to move camp. They would return to Bajto, the very place where the Ustaše had attacked them. The ruins would give them a degree of protection from the elements, and it was unlikely that the enemy would think that they might return to such a place so quickly. That evening, they made the long trek back down the mountainside and once again took up camp in the deserted village.

Shortly, they were joined by Frano Bundimier, desperate to pass on his latest intelligence. He also had with him a civilian radio set that he'd managed to pilfer. Reluctantly, the diminutive Ken Smith, Gibson's signaller, handed over his battery charger to the Yugoslav spy, so he could try to fire up his radio.

If Gibson had any misgivings about returning to Bajto, they were quickly assuaged. The following day they were joined by a second band of partisans, a large force with an abundance of weaponry, including 'fifteen Bren guns, a PIAT and numerous automatic weapons', a PIAT being a British-made anti-tank weapon.

Leading this band was Cudra Assiz, 'the commander of the Dalmatinska Brigade'. From this point on, Assiz and his men would be the ones to look after Gibson and his patrol, for they had 'more knowledge of the areas in which the British would be operating'.

Assiz looked every inch the formidable partisan leader. He was 'stocky, dark, mustachioed', and wore 'a smartly tailored tunic, battledress trousers and a leather Sam Browne belt'. Right away Gibson sensed that this was someone with whom he could work. After their introductions, Assiz turned to a group of partisans who were standing near by. Raising his hand, he beckoned one of them forward.

'Drugaritsa Zara Menko,' he announced with a smile, 'good for you.'

For a moment Gibson thought he must be dreaming. Stepping towards him was a young, petite woman, 'stunningly beautiful, in a Slav kind of way', as he would describe her. At first he did not know the reason for the introduction. That was until she started speaking.

'I learned English at Belgrade University,' she explained, 'but please forgive me if I get any words wrong when I translate. I could not complete my course because of the war.'

Gibson was taken aback. 'Your English is good,' he declared, once he'd recovered his wits. 'I think that we'll get along just fine.'

Secretly, Gibson was relieved. The awkwardness of using the Yugoslav doctor with his rudimentary French was over. From here on, things would surely run more smoothly. To add to his seeming good fortune, Zara Menko was both stunning to look at and pleasant company. With Assiz's band of impressive-looking fighters to hand, Gibson had a feeling that their mission was going to go from strength to strength.

The camp at Bajto became a hub of intense activity. More partisans gathered, passing on intelligence for Ken Smith to relay to Vis and Italy. At night, small bands set out to patrol the surrounding area, on the hunt for enemy units. Johnny Metcalf had attached himself to the doctor, and he would occasionally head out to nearby villages to administer first aid to the sick and injured. They also set up a regular clinic where they could treat both partisans and civilians.

But such activity did not go unnoticed by the Ustaše. No longer willing to assault the heavily defended village, they kept their distance, using snipers and small patrols to launch short-lived, probing attacks. These minor skirmishes were usually over quickly, the partisans, plus Gibson and his men, forcing them back with their superior fire power. On one occasion, with the partisans running low on food, 'a handful of local women struggled towards them, carrying a huge cauldron of steaming soup'. As they got closer to the camp, a sniper opened fire, causing them to drop the container and dive for cover. Moments later, the cauldron was peppered full of holes, the soup pouring out onto the dusty track.

It was galling, but in truth the Ustaše could do little more than loose off potshots from the sidelines. Repeatedly, they failed to stop the partisan spies from returning to the camp bearing choice intelligence, which was quickly relayed back to Allied headquarters at Vis and Rodi.

Over time, Gibson's men grew closer to their new comrades. One evening the partisans decided to hold an impromptu dance in a nearby village. After drinking more than his fair share of wine, Corporal 'Bombski' Cashin had to be carried back to the camp, whereupon he was dumped in an untidy heap. When one of the partisans asked what was the matter with him, Sergeant Jetley replied, 'Drunk on duty. The skipper had him shot.' Believing this to be true, the partisans informed their commander. It was only the following morning when Cashin emerged, bleary-eyed and hungover, that they realised it was all a joke, one they found highly amusing.

Cashin was an invaluable member of their team. Described by Gibson as 'a compact man with the twinkling eyes of a malevolent, but ultimately well-intentioned' gremlin, and with a 'sense of humour as dry as the Oklahoma Dustbowl', Cashin was an expert in all things explosive, hence his nickname 'Bombski'. He took great delight in spreading his gospel of causing 'maximum damage for the minimum of effort', becoming a popular figure with the partisans as he taught them all he knew about his explosive craft.

Shortly, Gibson was to receive a surprising request from Commander Assiz. One of his men hailed from a local village and his wife had just given birth. 'Would Archie care to act as godparent to the new baby boy?' Assiz asked. Not only that, would he also be so kind as to oversee the baptismal ceremony, for there was no priest available. Gibson readily accepted. This gesture from Assiz reflected how completely he and his men were becoming accepted, by both partisans and locals alike.

With Zara at his side to act as interpreter, he made his way to the village. Water was brought from a nearby stream and somehow he managed to muddle through the service, baptising the infant Malik Andrović, much to the delight of his parents and all in attendance.

But at the same time Gibson fully appreciated that they were not here in Yugoslavia to party and to carry out baptisms. With Zara translating, Gibson approached Assiz and told him that there was a lot more that he and his men could do, than simply relaying intelligence from his agents and spies. He could organise a supply drop of weapons, and anything else the commander needed. All he had to do was give him the word.

Assiz thought for a moment before replying in Croatian. Zara turned to Gibson. 'The commander wants to know if you can bring cannon from the sky?'

Gibson was bemused. 'Cannon?'

After she had translated back to Assiz, the partisan commander 'made a gesture with his hands, as though dropping a hot potato. Then he ducked his head sideways, closed his eyes and clapped his hands over his ears. "Boom!" he roared. Then, just as swiftly, he opened his eyes and his arms described a high arc.'

Realisation dawned on Gibson. Assiz meant a mortar, not a cannon. He nodded his head. Yes, it could be arranged. No sooner had Zara translated, than Assiz jumped to his feet and took Gibson's hand, pumping it up and down enthusiastically.

Gibson had Ken Smith radio through an order to headquarters. And so, on the afternoon of 16 September 1944, the British, along with their Yugoslav comrades, set out the short distance to what they had designated as the drop zone, 'a flattish area where there were few trees but a fair amount of scrub'. After setting up a large letter 'V' on the ground, spelled out with sticks and branches, they settled down to wait.

Around 2100 hours, as darkness was falling, the sound of an aircraft could be heard approaching from the east. Quickly, torches were lit as the partisans gazed to the sky. And then they saw it, a single RAF C-47 Dakota transport plane was heading towards them, right on cue. It circled, the pilot acknowledging they had been seen and, moments later, the side door was flung open and the aircrew started to eject a series of drop-canisters.

The air was filled with the silk canopies, as the supplies drifted towards the ground. With so many canisters being released, the aircraft had to swing around for a second run. One or two 'chutes failed to open, the canisters breaking on impact to spill their contents onto the hillside. Even so, the 'sortie was a complete success', Gibson declared. With a tilt of its wings, the Dakota turned and headed for home, job done.

For the remainder of the night and well into the next day, the partisans dragged the canisters and crates back into Bajto. Eager hands removed the much needed supplies. Among their contents were new battledress for Gibson and his men, to replace their worn and lice-infested uniforms. They were also pleased to receive more suitable footwear, for their American-made boots were full of holes, the rubber soles wearing through. With the weather growing much colder and decidedly wetter, warm clothes were a priority.

Crucially, the supplies included a 3-inch mortar, as Assiz had requested. 'In the afternoon we sorted everything out,' Gibson noted in his diary, 'while the Commandant and his mortar experts played with the 3 inch ... The clothes were all distributed to the partisans and the food taken and hidden in the rocks.'

There was no doubting the prize: it was the mortar, along with a generous supply of bombs. Immediately, Assiz wanted to put these to good use, and he had the perfect target in mind. Two hours' march to the south-east lay the town of Kokorići, host to a large body of German troops. It was an important location for the enemy, for it provided a base from which to guard traffic heading north and south along one of the main arterial routes. It was along this road that reinforcements for the enemy's armies to the south had to come. In short, it was an ideal target.

This was too good a mission for Gibson to be left behind. He insisted that he and his men come. They had proved their worth many times already and were well-versed in the use of the mortar. Hearing his arguments, the partisan commander relented, but he insisted they could come along as observers only. The fighting was to be left to the Yugoslavs. Agreeing to the compromise, at dusk the band of marauders set forth.

In the still of the night they crossed the main road, heading for a large hill to the west of Kokorići. From there, they would have a clear view into the town. Slowly they made their way up the slope, lugging the heavy weapon between them, the trees providing good cover. Soon, the attackers had found the perfect spot from where to unleash their attack. Quickly, the mortar team set up the weapon, while others checked and cleared their rifles and machine guns.

Gibson watched on as Assiz gave the order to commence firing. Seconds later, a round was dropped into the tube. 'With a metallic "tonk", the first bomb hit the firing plate and shot out of sight in a high, arching trajectory,' Gibson observed. Moments later came the unmistakable crump, as the bomb struck right in the heart of the German garrison, the ringing explosion reaching their ears clearly on the hillside. Gibson was impressed. The very first round had landed exactly where Assiz had wanted it to.

With the range perfect, the mortar team began to pump round after round into the tube, each of the bombs landing within the enemy garrison, tearing the buildings to rubble and causing carnage among the sleeping troops. Soon enough the corpses of enemy soldiers lay strewn around the area, while more perished inside buildings as the flames took hold.

Seeing the destruction being wrought on the enemy, and wanting to press their advantage, Assiz gave the order to attack. A long line of partisans broke from the cover of the trees and ran down the hillside, firing their machine guns from the hip as they went. After a couple of minutes they were inside the garrison itself, wreaking havoc and offering no quarter. From the hillside Gibson and his men watched as the Germans, caught completely unawares, were routed. Those who could retreated, while a mere handful returned fire. In just a few minutes scores of enemy soldiers lay dead, the rest having fled, getting as far away from the partisans as they could.

With the enemy in full retreat, Assiz and his men gathered together as much equipment as they could. Weapons, ammunition, sacks of flour, cigarettes and, much to Gibson's surprise, a pair of typewriters – for 'forging German passes or letters of authorisation' – were brought back. Their booty gathered, Assiz gave the order to pull out. They had to get back to the safety of the hills, before enemy reinforcements were brought up.

As dawn began to break on what was the 18 September 1944, the band of guerrilla fighters snaked across the hillside, leaving the smoking ruins of Kokorići behind. They returned to their camp at Bajto, encumbered by an enormous amount of booty. But, Gibson observed, the added weight didn't seem to bother them, for each carried 'something for which they could find a better use than the hated Germans'.

Unsurprisingly perhaps, the partisan assault on Kokorići could not go unanswered. Two days later word reached Bajto that a significant body of German soldiers were assembling to the north of Kokorići. Gibson was informed that the Germans had with them large numbers of horse-drawn artillery. What the intelligence lacked was the exact numbers of troops, plus the calibre of their weapons. Whether they were there to prevent further partisan attacks, or were readying themselves for something else, no one could be certain. With so many questions unanswered, there was only one thing for it, Gibson decided. He would have to go and take a look for himself.

In the early hours of 19 September, together with Zara and a small party of partisans, he set off. Following narrow goat tracks and sticking to the trees, by dawn they had reached a position on a hillside that overlooked Ravča town, where the enemy forces had gathered. Finding a concealed vantage point, Gibson lay down and took out his binoculars. What he saw shocked him.

He had not expected anything like such a large body of German troops. Then he frowned. Mixed in with the artillery were at least a dozen tanks, plus a large number of ground troops. He was confused. Tanks could do nothing in the hills against the partisans. Why were they here? It didn't make the slightest bit of sense.

As Gibson relayed what he was seeing to Zara, she translated for a partisan who jotted it all down in a notebook.

'I can't tell how many men they have down there, but it's a hell of a lot,' he declared. 'I've spotted officers too. Nearly as many chiefs as Indians.'

This expression seemed to confuse Zara, and she stopped her translation mid-flow. 'Chiefs? Indians? What does this mean, please?'

Gibson laughed. As he began to explain that he meant there were as many officers as men, a thought occurred to him. This was clearly a far more potent force than a regular field unit. It was likely that their attack on Kokorići was not the sole reason why they were here. It looked to Gibson like a Headquarters Company. But what were they doing in Ravča and where had they come from?

Once he was sure that Zara had taken down all the information, he sent a runner back to Bajto, with instructions for Ken Smith to radio all they'd learned back to headquarters. With his colleagues in Italy being privy to the bigger picture of all that was happening in Yugoslavia, maybe they could make sense of it.

For the rest of the day, he sat on the hillside with Zara and the others, watching as the Germans dug in around Ravča. It seemed clear that they were there to stay. Fearing that to remain on the hillside would increase the danger of being detected, he gave the order to pull out and head back to base.

The information that Gibson had sent caused a stir of excitement. Allied intelligence experts recognised the forces settling into Ravča. It was the Headquarters Company of the German 118th Division. The reason for their appearance was telling in the extreme. It had to signify that the war in Greece was going so badly that the Germans were pulling out. Their retreat would take them through Yugoslavia. They had to be seeking to 'extricate as many men and as much equipment as they could before the final collapse,' Allied headquarters concluded. That 118th Division headquarters unit were there to prepare the way for the withdrawl of all who were to follow.

Accordingly, Gibson was given fresh orders. He was to move to the hills near Ravča, and set up an observation post, from where he could relay intelligence on enemy troop movements, passing on targets for air strikes, for this was the perfect way to frustrate the German retreat. Gibson's chosen vantage point lay some 26 kilometres to the south-east. It would entail a long trek over tough terrain. Hard-going in the extreme. To make matters worse, it had started to rain. And not just any old rain. The heavens had opened.

At dusk on 21 September Gibson set off in torrential rain, accompanied by Zara, a small group of partisans, plus 'Tashy' Smith and another of his trusted men, Ron Mitchell. Gibson knew that to operate effectively, he would need the assistance of the partisans local to the area he was heading for. It was his intention to try and make contact with them, for which Zara's presence would be indispensable.

The going proved punishing. The heavy rain made it treacherous underfoot and they were soon soaked to the skin. A cold westerly gusted off the sea, adding to their discomfort. They moved only at night, trying to rest during the day. But the atrocious weather made it difficult to sleep and impossible to stay warm. They huddled together, sharing what body heat they could, shivering against the cold, as the incessant rain lashed down.

Progress was at a snail's pace, as the steep, waterlogged terrain became impassable. Finally, Gibson was forced to accept that their only option was to turn back and hope they could reach Bajto. Four days after setting out they made it, only to find that those they had left behind had had it equally bad. Gibson had left Sergeant Jetley in charge of his men. A couple of nights previously they had decided to move to Turić, a small village, to find better shelter. En route they had been spotted by the enemy, who had proceeded to target them with artillery fire. Fearing they would all be killed, and having no means by which to fight back, they too had retreated to Bajto.

Despite the awful conditions, Gibson's spirits lifted. He was heartened to hear that the intelligence garnered by his team was starting to really bite. 'Every single target which had been identified . . . had been hit, damaged or destroyed by rocket-firing Typhoons', the Typhoon being a potent ground-attack aircraft. On 20 September, the day after Gibson's initial reconnaissance had revealed the leaguer of the German 118th Division HQ, those forces had been hit in a series of airstrikes, the RAF destroying numerous vehicles. Sustained air attacks had followed, with devastating effect.

As Gibson and his men awaited a break in the weather, Frano Bundimier, the partisan spy, entered the camp. He had news that would cast Gibson's radio reports into sharp perspective. Greece was poised to fall, with the Allies advancing from the south. At the same time the Soviets were approaching from the east, heading for Belgrade, the Yugoslav capital. The enemy were in danger of being caught in a pincer movement. According to Bundimier's sources, they were pulling out as many of their troops as they could, fighting a rearguard action as they went.

'If we are further south, watching,' Gibson mused, 'we may catch them trying to slip by . . . If they attempt a sudden move across country, we can signal the change of direction and the Typhoons will soon have them.'

The urgency of reaching such a vantage point was powerfully made. They selected the village of Bijača, which seemed ideally suited as a lookout point. The following day, 26 September 1944, Gibson and his small force moved out once more. This time, the whole of his patrol went with him, along with Zara, plus Kapitan Ćemalović and a party of partisans, to act as escorts and guides. As he gazed around Bajto, Gibson understood that this would probably be the last time he would see the place. It was unlikely he would be returning. He turned to the friends he had made while there, Commander Assiz and the French speaking doctor among them – two figures for whom he had the utmost respect. This was goodbye.

Facing Assiz, Gibson drew himself to attention and saluted. 'Smrt fašizmu!' he declared. Death to fascism.

Assiz returned the salute. 'Sloboda narodu.' Freedom to the people.

As a parting gift, some of the partisan women had fashioned small red stars, which they sewed onto the British soldiers' berets. They were one and the same now, Yugoslav partisans and

British raiders. From initial mistrust and suspicion had grown an unbreakable bond. Friendships and comradeship had been forged in these war-torn hills, forming a fellowship that would endure.

In the late afternoon twenty-odd men and women set out heading for Bijača. This time the going would be harder, for they were weighed down by all of their equipment, including weapons and ammunition, grenades, rations and the radio with its cumbersome battery charger. At Gibson's side walked Zara. From their very first meeting he'd felt a special closeness with this young partisan woman. She carried her fair share of equipment, despite her diminutive size. Strapped around her waist was a thick leather belt, attached to which were a number of hand grenades and ammunition pouches. She also brandished 'a fiendishly long knife which she did not hesitate to use'.

Despite spending so much time together, Gibson realised he knew very little about her, and how she had come to be a partisan. He was also intrigued by one of her friends, a giant of a man who was never far from her side, looking out for her, and watching over her much as would a bodyguard or a protective big brother. Curiously, this man, Mario, wore a long coat with the sleeves cut off at the elbow, giving him an almost comic appearance. Gibson described him as 'a hulking giant of 6' 6",
ungainly but immensely powerful'. As they trekked through the hills Gibson realised that although it had been difficult saying goodbye to Assiz, when it came time to part from Zara, the sadness would be magnified tenfold.

In single file, the group marched through the night, skirting around villages they thought might be held by the Ustaše. Whenever any suspicious noises were heard they'd stop still, waiting for the moment to pass, before moving on again. 'At one point, they had no option but to cross the main road. If not, then they would be walking straight into a cluster of enemy-held positions.' Their chances, if spotted by an enemy unit, were not good. They would be given no quarter.

But, of course, Gibson had been in similar situations before. The raid on Bouerat was nearly two years ago, the time spent in the North African desert seeming all too distant. But his experiences with those fearless warriors had made him the man he was. From a somewhat naive and reckless teenager, he'd grown into a special operations warrior of long-experience, one who was both admired and respected by his men and the partisans whom he'd befriended. He had come a long way, he reflected, and he was all the better for it.

By dawn they had reached the small village of Radonjići, some eight kilometres from where they had set out. Unlike most settlements, it looked to be untouched by the war, the buildings showing little sign of conflict. The villagers took them in, providing hot meals, while at the same time keeping watch for any Ustaše, who were known to be operating in the vicinity. Once the party had eaten its fill, the owner of a local tobacco warehouse allowed them to use his building to rest and get some sleep.

At dusk, the group set out again, walking a further nine kilometres to the small town of Draževitići. There, they were met by the partisan commandant for this area, Tolić Drinko. He was a short, stocky individual, dressed in 'a British soldier's standard battledress, topped off by an animal fur hat with huge dangling flaps which rose and fell about his ears in the wind', as Gibson described him. 'Dark haired, dark mustached and dark skinned, his squat and stocky body bulged with muscle. He had

the over-developed biceps and thighs of a weightlifter.' His gait
was so that he had to walk with his legs well apart, 'like a flesh
and blood robot'.

Drinko had news for Gibson and none of it was good. As Zara
translated, he warned the British officer that to carry on to Bijača
would be foolhardy in the extreme. Desperate to keep the road
open, the Germans were clamping down on partisan activity on
every side. 'Everyone is moving out,' Drinko declared. 'It is no
longer safe.'

It made sense, reflected Gibson. If the Germans were pulling
out of Greece, they would need to ensure their escape route was
clear of partisans. But that did little to detract from his mission.
'Any intelligence I can pick up about their troop movements will
have immense value to the Allies,' he argued to Drinko. With
the RAF controlling the skies, they just needed to know where
to strike. Those target coordinates could be furnished by Gibson
and his team.

By way of answer, Drinko suggested they join him at his
headquarters in Trklje, which lay a further 15 kilometres to the
south-east. As this was heading in the right direction, Gibson
agreed. Looking at his map, he could see that Trklje stood in a
wooded, hilly area, and was serviced by a single track, meaning
any motorised vehicles had only one way in and one way out,
making it 'easier to guard'. It appeared to be the perfect place
from where he could continue with his mission.

Aware of the extent to which matters had taken a dangerous
turn, he figured the area was likely to be thick with Germans
and Ustaše. They would have to tread carefully and remain on
high alert. Even so, it was decided to risk moving during daylight
hours, to make traversing the hilly, rain-lashed terrain a little

easier, and to speed their progress. Shortly after breakfast, the group, led by Drinko, gathered their things, as a heavy deluge of rain continued to fall.

They stuck to the track that snaked across the valley floor, aware that enemy outposts were in the heights above. With the Germans occupying the high ground – a range of hills known as Mali Prolog and Veliki – they sought an area less exposed to the enemy observers. Using the cover of the trees, they pressed on. To their right, and higher up the hill lay the small partisan-held village of Pasičina.

Suddenly, the screech of an artillery shell filled their ears. As Gibson and his men dived for cover, an explosion ripped apart the ground further up the slope. The air was filled with screaming ordnance, the village above seeming to be the target. Had the Germans seen them, and concluded it was to Pasičina that they were headed? Gibson couldn't be sure. One thing was for certain – they couldn't risk moving from their present position, lest they be seen, and the shellfire brought to bear directly upon them.

As Gibson and the rest looked on, the small village was seen to be taking a terrible pounding, the shells tearing buildings to pieces, rubble and debris being blasted out and rolling down the hillside. Flames took hold as the houses began to burn, sending thick palls of smoke high into the September sky. As Gibson lay in the rain-soaked undergrowth, with Zara at his side, he knew there was nothing they could do other than wait for the bombardment to finish.

Noticing the giant figure of Mario observing them from a discreet distance, Gibson spoke to Zara. He was intrigued to know the story behind the odd-seeming coat that the man was wearing.

Why did it have no sleeves, he asked, and why did the huge partisan pay so much attention to her, watching over her like some kind of guardian? He was also keen to learn how she had come to be fighting with the partisans in the first place.

Lying on that rain-soaked hillside, as the German barrage pulverized Pasičina, Zara relayed her story to the young Scottish captain.

She had been a student in Belgrade up until the German invasion, she explained. Her boyfriend, an ardent anti-Nazi, had become involved in the Yugoslav Resistance. One day, the Gestapo had raided his apartment and arrested him. Fearing they would come back for her, Zara had fled to her uncle's village in the countryside. On arrival, she found the place deserted. 'The Germans must have attacked it during the advance on Belgrade and a lot of the houses were in ruins . . . my uncle's house was empty,' she remarked. As she wandered through the ruins of what had once been a thriving village, a shot rang out, causing her to scream. 'I could not move. I was frozen,' she recalled. Thinking she was about to die, she suddenly heard a voice near by. It was a man calling out to her from behind a low wall. As she looked over, she saw a raised hand.

'I ran towards it. When I reached the wall, I tried to climb over but I slipped . . . Then this big, strong arm reached out and dragged me over . . . And there was Mario.' At first the huge man scared her, but soon she realised he had no ill intentions. He was armed and he began shooting back at the sniper who had tried to kill her. Fearing they might bring up reinforcements, Mario headed into the hills. With no other option, Zara went with him.

After a while, Mario noticed that Zara's shoes, which were unfit for this type of terrain, were broken and her feet were bleeding. Making her sit down, he took off her shoes and threw them into some nearby bushes. Removing his greatcoat, he 'pulled a great knife out of his pocket . . . and cut off the sleeves at the elbow.'

Intrigued, Gibson asked why he would do such a thing.

She smiled as she recalled the moment. 'Then he lifted my feet again, one by one, and bound them in the cut-off sleeves, to make new shoes for me.' This single act of kindness ensured she no longer feared the huge man, instead seeing him for what he was – a gentle giant and her saviour. From that point on, she had committed herself to the partisan cause.

Gibson found himself immensely moved by her and Mario's story.

After an hour, the shelling came to an end. There was no way they could make their intended destination by nightfall. To make matters worse, further along the route, on a hill named Mali Prolog, lay a German observation post. They could not take the chance of being spotted, especially as the enemy could bring in artillery strikes seemingly at will. It was most likely the guns of the 118th Division that had been brought to bear on Pasičina, with devastating effect.

Once it was deemed safe to move, Drinko led the band deeper into the hills, towards Radaljica, 'a tiny village sequestered in the pine trees'. There they would spend the night. But Gibson and his men were to get little sleep. 'There were sounds of shelling all night, often fairly close but seemingly with no fixed target,' he would report. At 0200 hours they were shaken fully awake. Due to the increased enemy activity, Drinko had decided to complete the journey in the hours of darkness, such were the number of Germans moving across the valley. And so, three hours later, they finally entered the small hamlet of Trklje to be greeted by the rump of Drinko's forces.

Still Gibson felt he couldn't drop his guard. As his men settled into their new place of abode, he felt the need to get a feel for their surroundings. He also wanted to figure out any escape routes, should the Germans mount an operation to corner them. After all, the enemy had been aware of the British patrol's presence from the day of their arrival in Yugoslavia. Should they know Gibson's team were here, then they would hunt them remorselessly, especially since the stakes were so high.

With Drinko acting as his guide, Gibson made his way to the summit of the hill on which Trklje lay. From there, they could see over the treetops and clearings to the valley beyond. Putting his binoculars to his eyes, Gibson immediately saw something that made his heart beat faster.

There was movement. Scanning the area, he spied a large body of enemy soldiers creeping through the trees. Horrifyingly, they were moving in towards Trklje. It seemed impossible to put up any kind of effective fight against such a concentration of German troops.

Reacting on instinct, Drinko and Gibson sprinted back down the hill. Even as they entered the camp they were yelling out their warnings. They had to move, and fast, for German troops were almost upon them! They had to get away! They had to escape! Hastily, the partisans and Gibson's men made ready to move out.

No sooner had they began to evacuate, than the first shells started raining down all around. Artillery support for the advancing infantry. They were being fired upon not only by the forces creeping towards their base, but by the big guns sited across the valley. The bombardment became intense, as the enemy fire concentrated on the small hamlet they had once thought to be safe. As the shells slammed in, the partisans and Gibson's band fled for the hills, weaving a path through the blasts. Behind them, the hamlet of Trklje was pounded into ruin. Within minutes each of the buildings was reduced to nothing more than burning timbers and pulverised heaps of masonry.

For the remainder of the day, as German patrols searched high and wide, British soldiers and Yugoslav partisans lay hidden on the highest slopes. With nightfall the shelling petered out and the enemy began to withdraw. They seemed to baulk at continuing the hunt come darkness. A group of partisans headed back to Trklje, to see if anything might be salvaged. Gibson warned his men to remain where they were. His sense was of an enemy closing the trap. No sooner had the thought crossed his mind 'when shots rang out, scattering the Yugoslavs'. Although the artillery bombardment had ceased, a number of snipers had remained in Trklje. They had opened up on Drinko's men, and with lethal effect, for several were cut down. Gibson's medic, Johnny Metcalf, did the best he could with the casualties, patching up the worst. But a number lay dead, for the German sniper fire had proven precise and deadly.

Drinko decided to pull out and head north into the hills. But first they would need to drop off the wounded with the friendly villagers at nearby Štrbići. Gibson agreed this was the only viable option, for there was no way they could stand and fight a pitched battle with such an enemy. They would be annihilated. At the same time, he knew that by withdrawing and heading north, the hopes of him executing his mission would be dashed.

He felt deeply frustrated. 'All that night-marching, all the discomfort, all the injuries sustained, now seemed to have been in vain.' But ultimately, he had no choice. Their mission had become one of survival – to stay one step ahead of the enemy and avoid capture.

Strapping the worst of their injured onto makeshift stretchers, and helping the walking wounded as best they could, they got on the move. With a badly injured partisan slung over his shoulder, Gibson trudged ahead, the blood from the man's wounds seeping through his shirt. The route to Štrbići proved incredibly punishing. Now, not only were they weighed down by their weapons and kit, but they were burdened by wounded comrades.

The nightmarish trek continued deep into the dark hours. After what seemed like an age, they finally reached their destination. Having dropped off the wounded with the villagers, they set out once more, for there was no time to tarry. Drinko, leading from the front, steered the party of fugitives along narrow tracks that wound through the woods, and over innumerable hills. It proved exhausting, for they had had little sleep or proper sustenance for a number of days. But if they were to escape the enemy, then they needed to keep moving, and fast. They could barely risk a moment's rest.

By the time they arrived at their intended destination, Baranovac village, they had covered a further ten kilometres. Here they finally got to enjoy their first hot meal in days and were able to snatch a few hours' precious sleep.

Sunday 1 October 1944 proved a chilly and damp morning. Barely had Gibson and his men had time to clean their weapons and repack their kit, when from out of nowhere the German artillery opened up on them once more. As British soldiers and Yugoslav partisans dived for cover, word reached them that German troops were once again surrounding their position. The net was closing and they needed to move now, if they were to stand a chance of slipping away.

The hunt was relentless. No sooner had they settled in one place than the enemy were upon them. It was exhausting, both mentally and physically. Breaking cover, they made for the woods. Moments later, German troops were sighted at the edge of the village, opening fire with their weapons. As Gibson and his men raced hell for leather for the trees, where 'a breathless courier caught up with them . . . heavy enemy concentrations were moving in', he warned. As Gibson sprinted for the woodlands, he 'gave silent thanks' for Drinko's alertness and quick thinking. His sharp mind and tactical awareness had saved the lives of every one of them.

But they were far from safe yet. All around, shells began to tear into the earth, scything down trees and blasting rocks into the air, deadly shrapnel spraying in all directions. Dropping their rucksacks, Gibson and his men made a dash for the shelter of a nearby pile of boulders. Reaching it unscathed, they hunkered down, attempting to make themselves as small as possible as the bombardment intensified.

Suddenly, one of Gibson's men broke cover and ran to where their packs had been dumped.

'Get back, you idiot!' Gibson yelled.

But he doubted whether the man had heard him. The packs contained all their vital equipment, including the patrol's radio. He'd dashed back aiming to retrieve it. Before the runner reached the rucksacks, 'a shell landed right on our cluster of packs and the whole lot disappeared in a mushroom cloud of dust and flame,' as Gibson would recall. Luckily, Gibson's man had dived for cover before the shell hit.

The moment the bombardment ceased, they dashed out to retrieve what kit they could. Following the fearsome barrage, they knew that enemy troops would be moving in, hot on their heels. For miles they slogged uphill. At one point they looked down upon the ruined village of Pasičina, nearby which they had sheltered just two days earlier, as it was reduced to rubble by the German artillery fire. They had pretty much gone full circle, at every juncture being pursued by a relentless and determined foe.

Finally they reached another village, Trnovo, where Drinko hoped they might find sanctuary. It was remote, set deep in the hills and, as yet, untouched by war. As the exhausted partisans and British soldiers plodded in, they were greeted by the locals. 'There were no Ustaše or Germans there,' they declared, confidently. 'Never had been.' As Gibson noted, 'This village had not been shelled . . . and the locals were confident that it was not under observation from anywhere.' For the moment, at least, it seemed as if they had evaded the enemy. As they settled down to rest their aching limbs, it looked like Trnovo was a place where maybe they could muster their strength, as they prepared for whatever fate might throw at them next.

A short while after reaching Trnovo, Gibson was approached by Ken Smith, his radio operator. The man looked uncharacteristically downcast.

'Skipper, the radio's packed in,' Smith announced. It had been damaged during the bombardment.

'Any chance you can repair it?' Gibson queried.

Smith shook his head. Not a chance. 'I've stripped it down and done what I can, but I really need some parts that I don't carry with me.'

This was all Gibson needed. With the radio kaput, the raison d'être of their mission was over. In short, there was little point in any of them being there. During the last few weeks, the partisans had managed to procure a couple of German radio sets, but they were unreliable and next to useless. As Gibson appreciated, somehow they would have to get their own set fixed. There was only one way to do that – they would have to head back to Vis to have it repaired, or get a new one parachuted in.

He approached Drinko and explained their predicament. Together, they hatched a plan. Gibson and Smith would head north for Brikva, a small town serving as partisan headquarters. It lay close to the Adriatic coast, from where they should be able to catch a boat across to their headquarters at Vis. There, they could get the radio repaired. Zara would go with them, along with her protector, Mario, complete with his coat with the 'ludicrously short arms'. They would act as guides, for they knew the route well. The four would travel light and fast. If they set off now, they could be back within a week.

Drinko assured Gibson that the rest of his team would be safe. The partisan commander also saw an opportunity. If Gibson was going to Vis, then he could take some of the worst injured and evacuate them into the care of the Allies. Gibson demurred. That would only slow them down, and they'd have to move fast if they were to get there and back safely. But Drinko was adamant. If they were to go, then the worst of the wounded would go with them. Finally, a compromise was reached. Drinko agreed to send the walking wounded only. Gibson accepted, for retaining good relations with the partisan commander was vital to all that he had planned.

But then Drinko dropped a second bombshell. A group of Italian prisoners had been gathered together, those who had been part of the Italian military before their country's surrender. All they wanted was to get back to Italy. These too would tag along with Gibson and his group. When Gibson made to protest, Drinko made it clear it was a deal-breaker. 'Either they go, or you don't.' To sweeten the pill, he suggested that he'd send a stronger partisan escort.

The die was cast. Gibson's initial band of four had swollen into a far larger, and decidedly ragtag, column. He told those of his men that he was leaving behind to try to raise headquarters on one of the captured German radio sets, to let them know what Gibson and party were up to. Having ordered the Italian prisoners to carry all of the heaviest kit, the group set out. It was the afternoon of 2 October, and they were starting a 22-kilometre trek north-west towards the coastal town of Brikva.

Despite being encumbered with the wounded, Gibson and his group managed to make relatively good progress, especially as the Italian prisoners were serving as porters. With Zara and Mario taking the lead, they threaded their way through the rough terrain, moving away from the area where the enemy were conducting their intensive seek and destroy missions. They were soon some distance from the place they'd left Drinko, plus the remainder of Gibson's patrol, at Trnovo.

Little did they know that there, all hell was about to break loose.

At 0800 hours on the morning of 3 October, the day after Gibson and his group had set out, those of his men who had remained behind were preparing their breakfast when a partisan came dashing into sight.

'Get out quickly!' he yelled. 'The Germans are here. They've almost surrounded us.'

Gibson's men leapt to their feet, abandoning their cooking. Hiding what kit they could among the rocks, and covering everything with groundsheets and branches, they grabbed their weapons and as much ammunition as they could carry and sprinted for the woods, even as machine-gun fire ripped up the ground behind them. The enemy were almost upon them. Sprinting for their very lives, bullets tore through the air, smacking into trees, ripping bark from trunks and sending splinters flying in all directions.

All around there were figures dashing to escape, as the enemy tried to close the net. On and on the partisans and British soldiers ran, 'pushing through the rough grasses and thorny bushes' and plunging 'deeper into the sheltering forest'. Moments later, the artillery opened up, ripping into the once peaceful village. Shortly, the guns began hitting the woods where they had taken shelter. Abandoning the attempt to reach higher ground, the fugitives burrowed behind rocks, for there was nothing they could do now other than seek cover from the barrage.

Below, German spotters radioed back to their artillery officers the coordinates of where they believed their prey had gone to ground. The shelling proved so fierce that the hunted were forced to remain hidden for most of the day, nailed under the murderous precision of the German guns.

With nightfall, at last there came the opportunity to slip away. Led by Drinko, they made a break for Brikva, the same destination to which Gibson and his party had set out. It lay deep within partisan-held territory, and it was unlikely the Germans would venture so far. Half an hour later, having left the ruins of Trnovo behind them, the shelling began once more, hitting the very hiding place which they had just vacated. For the moment at least, it seemed that the enemy had lost them.

Knowing they had to keep moving if they were to evade the Germans' relentless pursuit, they pushed onwards. By one o'clock in the morning they'd covered eight kilometres, their progress quicker now, for they were carrying only their weapons and ammo. Finally they stumbled into yet another village. This one, Tilovina, was long deserted. Seeking shelter in the empty houses, they bedded down, desperate for some precious rest.

Meanwhile, Gibson and his group had reached their destination, being unaware of what had befallen their comrades. At one stage they had come across an enemy patrol, with whom they had briefly traded fire, but they had 'managed to hide in a wooded area', after which they had pressed on 'without further excitement'. Having reached Brikva, they needed to offload their Italian prisoners, before finding a way to cross the Adriatic to Vis.

The coast was teeming with activity. There were people everywhere, and for the first time in a long while all of them were friendly. As they approached the dock area, Gibson was informed by a Yugoslav guard that the majority of the people were Italian prisoners of war, all of whom were desperate to get back to Italy.

Eventually a ferry arrived and the prisoners surged towards it, eager to get aboard. There was little the partisan guards could do to stop them. Before long, the boat was full to capacity. Gibson had no intention of boarding that ship. It looked over burdened and decidedly dangerous. He had not come all this way, repeatedly escaping death at the hands of the Ustaše and the Germans, only to go down with a sinking ship. He opted to hand over his prisoners to the local partisans and to seek out more suitable transport.

Finding a small hamlet, which had a 'panaromic view of the Adriatic and the neighbouring coastline', Gibson and his group were given food and shelter by the locals. At last, after weeks in the Dalmatian hills, they felt they could finally relax a little. They had escaped the German net by the skin of their teeth, and now, for the first time in an age, Gibson and his comrades felt relatively secure.

His thoughts turned to the trip across the water. Just himself and Ken Smith would be going. There was no need for Zara or Mario to accompany them. At hearing the news, the young partisan woman appeared downcast. Gibson asked what was troubling her.

'Tomorrow you will be leaving and I have to stay here,' Zara explained, simply. 'We may never see each other again.'

Gibson tried to remain cheerful. 'Don't worry. I'll be back before you know it. I'm only going to get this radio of ours repaired . . . You'll not have time to miss me.'

Yet Zara was not to be so easily consoled. 'Suppose something happens? Suppose the boat is attacked? Or it sinks in a storm. What then?'

Drawn to her inexorably, Gibson stroked Zara's 'deep brown hair tenderly' and pulled her close. 'He could feel the warmth of her slender body enveloping him and he suddenly felt very protective. He wanted, above all, to shelter this vulnerable-looking girl from any harm.' How he could best do so was anyone's guess, but one thing was for certain – he could do little when separated from her by a large tract of the Adriatic Sea. He would have to get on with the journey, get the radio fixed double quick, and get back to his mission . . . and to this woman with whom he was falling in love.

A while later two vessels pulled into the harbour. One was a supply ship, the other a partisan gunboat providing escort. Gibson seized upon the opportunity. With the rain pouring down and darkness cloaking them, he and Zara walked the short distance to the harbour-side. Guided by torches, they made their way to the water's edge. Once Ken Smith and the wounded partisans had climbed aboard the cargo ship, Gibson turned to Zara.

He was shocked to find her crying, as he later recalled:

The rain had flattened her hair to her head, making her look even more of a waif. She shivered a little in the cold dampness of the evening air, her arms clutching her body tightly. Instantly a pang ran through me, a pang so painful that it felt as though someone had punched me . . . I experienced a sudden and lurching sensation of emptiness as I realised that the two of us were going to be parted for the first time in a month: a month when we had shared our lives, sleeping together under the same blanket, eating together, at each other's side when sheltering from enemy guns, shoulder to shoulder when firing our carbines or throwing grenades at the Germans. It would feel very strange without her.

Unable to hold back any longer, he wrapped her in his arms and held her tight. Over Zara's shoulder, he could see Mario, her protector watching on 'like a benevolent grandfather would his grandchildren'.

With shouts from the ship that he needed to board, Gibson tried to prise himself away, but Zara clung on desperately, unwilling to let him go.

'I have to go,' Gibson explained, kissing the top of her damp head. Looking into her tear-filled eyes, he whispered, 'Come on. Cheer up. Remember I'll be back in two shakes of a lamb's tail.'

The expression made her giggle and, as Gibson pulled away, his hands ran 'softly down the length of her arms until all he was holding were her small hands, warm despite the iciness of the night air'.

This parting was especially hard. Without tarrying another moment, for fear he would tell the captain he was simply not going, Gibson turned and leapt aboard ship. As the vessel pulled away from the quayside, he gazed down upon this woman who had captured his heart, and with whom he had shared a lifetime's worth of experience in just a few short weeks. With the boat drawing further away, Zara turned to Mario 'and buried her face in his greatcoat with its short arms'. Moments later, they were lost to sight, enveloped in the darkness of that rain-lashed Yugoslav night.

Gibson felt someone beside him.

'Are you all right, Skipper?' It was Ken Smith.

'Yes, of course,' Gibson replied, trying to brazen it out. 'Just a bit sad at saying goodbye, you know.'

He tried hard to hide the lump that had suddenly appeared in his throat, but Smith knew the truth of course. With the Yugoslav shoreline fading into the night, Gibson took hold of himself and turned to check on the wounded.

Back in the Yugoslav hills, Sergeant Jetley and the rest of Gibson's patrol were doggedly making their way towards Brikva, conscious that the enemy were still on their trail. Although they were doing their utmost to hide their tracks, a partisan courier managed to locate them. Along with bringing them some much-needed food, he also had a rare piece of good news. The Germans, it seemed, had managed to shell their own troops, at the very place where Gibson and his men had come under fire just two days before. In the process they'd suffered thirty-five casualties.

With a renewed spring in their step, Jetley and the rest of the party pushed on to Brikva, only to discover that they had missed Gibson by twenty-four hours. There, Jetley was able to locate a working radio. 'The partisans had a No.22 wireless set . . . and I tried several times to contact our HQ without success,' he would report. 'I did, however, receive a broadcast message from head-quarters telling us to return immediately.'

The reason for their recall was not yet clear. Either way, forty-eight hours after Gibson had left Yugoslavia, the remainder of his men boarded a ship to take them across the Adriatic. Despite all their efforts, the Germans and Ustaše had failed in their attempts to capture Gibson and his men. With the help of some exceptionally brave and resolute partisans, they had managed to remain one step ahead of the hunters, all of them making it out safely.

The withdrawal of Gibson's men signified that Operation Behemoth was over. They learned as much upon reaching head-quarters. Gibson and his fellows were due some well-earned leave, but Gibson could not settle. He felt compelled to return to Yugoslavia as quickly as possible. Of course, it was more for personal reasons than for any military objective, for there 'was someone he desperately wanted to see'. Over the coming days he badgered his superiors; as far as he was concerned, there was unfinished business in Yugoslavia. But no matter how much he might argue, there was simply no way they would allow him to go. In truth, all British forces were being pulled out and it was highly unlikely that any would be returning. It seemed that Zara's fear that she and Gibson would never see each other again was well-founded.

The reason behind this sudden change in priorities was political. In recent weeks Tito had aligned himself with Soviet Russia, and, as the Germans were now pulling out, his bands of communist partisans were in 'a position to take over local government as soon as the war ended; to fill the vacuum before anyone else had a chance'. In short, the British were no longer welcome, despite the brave and courageous assistance they had provided. As far as Tito was concerned, they, and their American allies, were becoming his political adversaries. As Gibson began to appreciate, Tito wanted it to be 'his troops who would mop up the final German resistance', so he would be 'borne to power on a wave of public rejoicing and gratitude'.

Sadly, this spelled the end for Gibson and Zara's love affair. No matter how much he might argue for the need to go back, his every request was refused. Gibson felt deeply frustrated, not to mention heartsick. He and his men had fulfilled a key military function in Yugoslavia and there was still more they could do; 'the information which we had picked up, deep inside enemy held territory, had enabled Allied firepower to be brought to bear where it could most hurt the Germans.' They had done a job and done it well, while all the time being hunted by the enemy. He hungered to return to such work, but every request was rebuffed.

Distraught as he was that he might never see Zara again, there was still a war to be fought. His patrol was given another task.

They were to proceed to the island of Ist, lying off the Dalmatian coast, to monitor German naval movements. For Gibson, it was on Ist that his war would come to an abrupt end. Having witnessed the sinking of a British motor launch by a German E-boat, he rowed out in a small boat to retrieve the bodies of the dead, some of whom he had been with just the night before. While bringing one to shore, he fell awkwardly between rocks, damaging his back in the process. His pain was so intense, he had to be evacuated to an RAF hospital in Italy to recover.

While in hospital, Gibson received two pieces of news that would break his heart.

One day, he had a visitor – a familiar face whom he was overjoyed to see. It was Gilbert Jetley, his patrol sergeant. But Jetley brought terrible news. Ken Smith, their radio operator and Gibson's close friend, had been killed on 10 January 1945 on the island of Ist, in an act of unparalleled heroism.

Knowing there were British troops on the island, one night after Gibson's evacuation a party of German saboteurs had come ashore and planted a number of bombs in and around the houses being used by Gibson's men. Waking up early the following morning, Smith had discovered one such device lying on the kitchen table of the place in which he was billeted. It was serving as their radio room. With so many people still asleep upstairs, and the bomb's fuse burning down to detonation, Smith calmly picked it up and carried it outside. He had not gone far before the bomb exploded, blowing him to pieces. The death of such a well-liked and courageous comrade hit them all hard.

Further terrible news was to follow. Hearing that a Yugoslav partisan had been admitted to the hospital, Gibson sought him out. After introducing himself, he asked if the young man knew of the partisan group with whom Gibson and his men had served. The man replied that he did. Excitedly, Gibson asked him if he knew of the female interpreter, Zara Menko. The reply was to shake him to the core.

'Oh, yes, I know Zara,' the partisan confirmed. Then, almost as an afterthought he added, 'She was killed at the battle of Pag, earlier this month.'

Gibson could not believe his ears. The news cut him to the core. Was the partisan possibly mistaken? Surely, he had to be. A figure with the life force and zest of Zara simply could not have been killed. She and Gibson had so much left to do in this life, for he had vowed to track her down come war's end. He refused to believe she could be gone. 'And yet in my heart of hearts, I knew that I had just been told the truth,' Gibson would confess.

Falling into a deep depression and in constant agony from his injured back, Gibson was evacuated to Scotland, to recuperate at home, a place he had not seen for close on eight years. By the time he was fit for duty again, the war was over. Sent to Hilden, near Düsseldorf, in Germany, as the Motor Transport Officer of the 53rd Reconnaissance Regiment, he would see out his military service there, finally returning home in 1947 following demobilisation.

For his actions at Bouerat with the SAS, Gibson, then a corporal, was awarded the Military Medal. His citation, written by David Stirling and endorsed by General Auchinleck, reads:

On the night of 25th Jan 1942, Guardsman GIBSON was the driver of a truck containing LRDG and parachutist personnel returning from a raid on the coast road between

Sirte and Misurata. When proceeding south . . . the truck was ambushed, machine guns opening up from both sides of the road, and mortar and grenade bombs falling close to the truck. Guardsman GIBSON drove his truck with great determination through the fire, and it was largely due to his coolness that no casualties were sustained . . . On all other occasions the work of Guardsman GIBSON has been of an exceptionally high standard.

A decorated officer and a garlanded army veteran, Gibson decided to spend his demob money on a beautiful Rolls-Royce, which was in immaculate condition. He drove it home to his native Scotland, where he began working as a bus driver. Sadly, he was forced to sell the Rolls after only a few months, for he couldn't afford to run it on a busman's pay. Bored of driving buses, and having married his sister's friend, Joan, in 1946, he started in business, firstly selling agricultural equipment and then building up a highly successful company supplying the DIY superstore trade. It would go on to employ a hundred people across the UK.

In his spare time Gibson taught himself to be a magician, entertainer, folksinger, and music promoter across Scotland. Among other famous visitors to the family home in the Scottish market town of Crieff, were Billy Connolly and The Corries, many of whom became close friends. To add to his busy schedule, he opened a business marketing motorbikes, becoming the first BMW motorbike dealership in Scotland. His innate wanderlust eventually getting the better of him, he left his businesses in the hands of his son, Paul, plus business partner, Duncan Wallace, before moving to Ireland. There he renovated an old farmhouse in County Cork, before moving to warmer climes in the Algarve, where he cultivated a 'hippy' lifestyle, making and selling jewellery on the street and honing his magician's skills. In that spirit he travelled the world, mostly hitchhiking, with a folding bicycle, and with a guitar strapped to his back.

Finally, he returned to Scotland and his 'long suffering and very patient wife'. In retirement he typically got bored again, so rekindled his love of motorcycling, buying a Harley-Davidson Electra Glide for his seventieth birthday. He rode motorbikes until his final days. Archie Gibson died on 4 April 2005, at the age of eighty-five, survived by a son, Paul, and granddaughter, Emma.

Ken Smith, Gibson's friend and radio operator, would receive a posthumous George Cross for his actions on Ist. His citation reads:

On the night of 10th January 1945 . . . Signalman Smith was a member of the Long Range Desert Group, which was attacked by saboteurs, who laid time-bombs in the vital houses of the island . . . Signalman Smith entered the wireless room and found one such bomb on the table. Realising that there were a number of partisans in the room and young children elsewhere in the house, Signalman Smith immediately picked up the bomb, which was ticking. He intended to move it to a place of safety behind a nearby wall, but he had only gone a few yards outside the house when the bomb exploded and he was blown to pieces. There is no doubt that Signalman Smith's action saved the lives of many of his comrades, partisans and civilians, and that he showed superb courage and complete disregard for personal safety in lifting a time-bomb which was already ticking when he knew it might explode at any moment.

Smith was twenty-four years old.

Whether Zara Menko had been killed shortly after Gibson left Yugoslavia remains unclear, but there is little reason to doubt that what the partisan had told him was true. This brave young woman, forced into the fight following the Nazi invasion of her country, was so typical of many who fought for their country's freedom and liberation. What happened to the rest of the brave partisans whom Gibson encountered in Yugoslavia remains unknown.

Lewis 'Archie' Gibson's adventures with the LRDG and the SAS in North Africa and Yugoslavia shaped him for life. After the war he wrote a memoir, which included tales of his months spent soldiering with the LRDG and SAS in the North Africa desert, and leading his team in their dramatic operations against German and Ustaše in the Yugoslav hills. In all of his writing, his youthful enthusiasm, supreme martial skills and his zest for life shines through. Gibson endeared himself to all with whom he served, including his SAS comrades in North Africa, and its founder, David Stirling, who valued him as a driver so very highly. He saw in Gibson the true attributes and the never-say-die attitude that he sought in his men.

Gibson was a young man in the prime of his life when war broke out. He was an intelligent and deep-thinking individual, with a penchant for poetry, penning many lines of verse while in the desert with the LRDG and SAS especially. One such poem, entitled simply 'G Patrol', relates an event that took place in December 1941, expressing just how quickly and without warning death can strike in times of war:

What deep surprises lie in store,
For those who blunder on.
How swift can be the crushing blow.
How soon one's comrades gone.

'Twas dawn on the sixteenth December,
The patrol had been travelling all night.
They slept on the brink of a wadi;
In the early morning light.
They saw figures down on the opposite bank,
Where our troops should have been.
The Captain went forward to parley,
But alas! he had not seen
That the figures down there were German
A colossal mistake had been made
They captured both him and a sergeant
Then a cunning plan was laid
The patrol all unsuspecting
Were waiting for the P.U.
Which came racing up behind them
Manned by a German crew.
Too late to fire the Vickers gun
Too late to turn and fly.
For fifteen Bredas opened up,
And the shots came whizzing by.
Four trucks managed to start away,
As Gibson shouted 'run'!
But only two got out of the trap,
That was laid by the wily Hun.
The Bofor truck was riddled,

And the other trucks were still.
The patrol hadn't a dog's chance,
As the enemy made their kill,
Long will the memory linger,
Their comrades will never forget;
That fatal day at U. Sedra,
And those who were caught in the net.

Yes, deep surprises lie in store
And swift the crushing blow
That's here and gone and all is lost.
Ask me now; I know!!!

The spirit of men like Archie Gibson endured, as the last Great Escapee featured in this volume powerfully demonstrates. Deployed on the aptly named Operation Pistol, his mission and the remarkable getaway that followed was to be executed at the very gates of Nazi Germany itself.

Chapter Five

OPERATION PISTOL –
THE IMPOSSIBLE GETAWAY

September 1944, RAF Keevil, UK

The autumn sun hung low on the horizon, casting the last of its rays over RAF Keevil, an airfield lying to the east of the town of Trowbridge in southern England. Gathered on one of its three concrete runways, groups of soldiers checked their jump-kit one last time, before boarding the Short Stirling bombers of 299 Squadron. It was 15 September 1944 and fifty-one men of A Squadron, 2 SAS, were about to embark on a flight deep into enemy occupied France.

For a number of these soldiers, and especially for twenty-six-year-old Squadron Quartermaster Sergeant (SQMS) John 'Jack' Alcock, there was a degree of déjà vu to the whole thing. Just over a week earlier, some of these warplanes had made a similar journey, aiming to drop reinforcements to their SAS comrades engaged in Operation Loyton, a mission to disrupt and harass German forces battling the US Third Army in the heart of the Vosges mountains of north-eastern France.

But things hadn't gone quite as planned. Following a successful drop by the lead warplane, 'immediately afterwards . . . ground fog obscured the lights they were using on the DZ as a rallying point'. With mist rolling in to envelop the area, the pilot of the second aircraft had been unable to see the markers below. Unwilling to drop his charges blind, he'd made the decision to abort the mission, leaving Alcock and the rest of those riding aboard his aircraft burning up with frustration.

As a foil to their disappointment, a satellite mission to Operation Loyton was hatched by Allied commanders, code-named Operation Pistol. This time, the SAS raiders would be dropped to the north of the Loyton area, with 'the intention of harassing the enemy's road and rail communications running eastwards from the front, between Metz and Nancy and on the approaches to the Rhine Plain'. Once on the ground, Alcock and the rest of the force were to cause as much havoc and mayhem as possible, before making their way back to Allied lines by whatever means they could.

At 2200 hours on 15 September the flight of Stirlings took to the skies. The men riding in Alcock's aircraft were split into two sticks, with the callsigns 'C1' and 'C2'. C1 was to be led by SAS Captain M. W. Scott, with Alcock picking up command of C2. They were detailed to operate near the towns of Zabern and Saarburg respectively, and once safely on the ground they would be the closest Allied troops to Nazi Germany itself.

The throaty growl of the Stirling's four Bristol Hercules engines proved deafening, but for Alcock it was of little matter. While waiting to board the aircraft, he'd felt 'more like a spectator . . . resigned to whatever the mission would throw up', even if it resulted in a second aborted drop. That feeling of otherworldly calm was pretty much the norm for him these days. A seasoned warrior, he'd seen action many times, and by now was used to the vagaries of war.

It was around midnight when the Stirling reduced speed and descended to some 800 feet. They were approaching the DZ. The order was given to make ready. The RAF dispatcher threw open the bomb bay doors by which the jumpers would exit. With the sudden increase in noise, coupled with the cold air hitting them like a blast from a giant refrigerator, the thirteen-men tried to stretch and loosen cramped limbs. Minutes later, the red signal lamp blinked on, casting a dim glow throughout the fuselage. In response, each man steeled himself for the jump, dragging his cumbersome leg-bag along the floor, and shuffling forward to bunch-up as close as possible to the drop-hole.

Suddenly, the light switched to green-for-go. Without further word or hesitation, the first figure stepped forward and dropped into the void, the others piling after. 'There had been no hesitation by any man,' Alcock noted. 'It had been a good clean exit.'

As Alcock floated earthwards, he studied the area that stretched out below. By the dim light of a waning moon he could make out a couple of small villages, and what appeared to be a river cutting through the landing field. The whole area looked distinctly flat and open, with only the occasional clump of trees or distant hamlet to break up the uniform landscape. Far from ideal territory to be conducting raiding operations. Added to which, the weather was far from favourable – it was lashing with rain and the gusting wind threatened to blow them off course.

No sooner had he landed than Alcock hit the release button at his chest, shook off his para-harness and gathered in his olive-green parachute. Replacing his jump-helmet with a woollen commando-style hat, for the warmth, he set out to locate the others. First thing he came across was a drop-canister. Stooping down he opened it, to discover one of their precious radios. Retrieving it, he wrapped it in his 'chute, to protect it from the elements and from any knocks, making a mental note to collect it later. His key concern now was finding the rest of the men. They had to identify a suitable hiding place pronto, for they'd dropped into terrain that was known to be crawling with the enemy.

Even as he searched for the others, something struck Alcock as being amiss. The Stirling was supposed to have made a second run, dropping the majority of the canisters containing most of their kit: food, explosives, ammunition. That was to supplement the limited supplies and weaponry that each man carried on his person. Disconcertingly, he'd neither heard nor seen any sign of it. And the more he searched, the more the drop zone looked nothing like where they were supposed to be.

Even as he was wrestling with such concerns, a soldier appeared from out of the darkness. Alcock recognised him instantly – it was Corporal Hill. Shortly, more figures emerged, including Private Fawthorpe who bore some disturbing news. He'd located their commander, Captain Scott, but he was lying in a ditch at the edge of the field and was in some distress. Scott had landed awkwardly, and it looked as if he'd broken his ankle. It was causing him severe pain.

Alcock made his way to Scott. Although someone had strapped-up his injured leg, the SAS captain still found it diffi-cult to stand or to walk. Despite his obvious pain, Scott was clear minded enough to issue orders, and to muster the men. Having drawn together the remains of the scattered stick, he dispatched individuals to knock on the doors of any households near by, to try and find out where they were, for right then it was anyone's guess.

A while later those men reported back to Scott and Alcock. While many of the locals had proved too fearful to open their doors to a mystery knock in the night, one or two had been persuaded. It turned out that they had landed close to the village of Audviller, some fifteen miles north of their intended DZ. Injured as he was, and dropped in the wrong place, Scott decided to split his force into smaller groups. In twos and threes they would attempt to sneak through to their area of operations and execute their mission, before making for Allied lines.

Alcock found himself teamed up with a Corporal Hannah. Shouldering their US-made M1 carbines, the two men set out into the dark, rain-lashed night. Shortly, they stumbled upon a couple of stragglers – Corporal Holden and Private Lyczak. Lyczak, a Pole, had joined the SAS a year earlier, after being liberated from a concentration camp in southern Italy, in what had been one of the most daring and audacious SAS missions of the entire war. Ordering the two men to tag along, Alcock led his patrol onwards through the pouring rain.

He pressed ahead, weighing up their options. The terrain thereabouts provided little natural cover. Unlike the Operation Loyton patrols, those on Op Pistol had no jeeps, and there were no plans to parachute any into their area. As the name suggested, Pistol had always been envisaged as a short, sharp initiative – travelling light and on foot, they were to hit the nearest railway lines and communications, before heading west towards the American frontline, which was believed to lie between the cities of Nancy and Metz.

They'd been warned not to trust the locals, so there would

be no fraternising with the French Resistance or the Maquis. 'The group's orders had been to avoid contact with civilians,' Alcock observed. For years this area, Alsace, had been fiercely contested between France and Germany. Following the Franco-Prussian War, in 1871 Alsace and Lorraine had become part of Germany. But with Germany's defeat in the First World War, those areas had been ceded to France under the Treaty of Versailles. Unsurprisingly, many of the locals still considered themselves to be German. Indeed, the German language was in use in much of the area, hence the orders to avoid civilian contact wherever possible.

With dawn approaching, Alcock decided they needed to find a place to hole up. The area was known to be thick with enemy troops, stiffening their defences against the much-feared American advance. Finding a small copse, the four men busied themselves fashioning a shelter from their gas capes – waterproof smocks that supposedly also offered protection from a poison gas attack. Beneath that meagre shelter they unrolled their sleeping bags, settling down to try to get some rest.

But the downpour continued unabated, and their gas-cape shelter proved woefully inadequate. To Alcock, these were the worst possible conditions in which to keep body and soul together, especially when they had been dropped in the wrong place, their forces had been split up, and most of their cold- and wet-weather gear was stowed in the missing drop-containers. Still, Alcock reminded himself, it was not in his nor his men's character to shy away from the toughest of challenges.

Jack Alcock was born in the Yorkshire town of Goole, on 4 March 1918. His father, 'a typical working-class Yorkshireman with strong family values', was a 'riveter at Goole shipyards'. In the 1930s he'd suffered periods of unemployment, and Jack had been forced to leave school aged fourteen, becoming 'a butcher's boy to help with the family finances'. But that was never going to be enough for the adventurous young lad. In 1936, at the age of eighteen, he'd enlisted into the army, joining the Coldstream Guards.

He was sent to France with the British Expeditionary Force (BEF) shortly after the outbreak of war. It was during the bitter retreat to Dunkirk that Alcock learned the harsh and horrifying realities of soldiering, and especially those of defeat. With the BEF being forced to evacuate from the beaches, Alcock found himself fighting a desperate rearguard action, as British forces plucked survival from the jaws of defeat. Volunteering to head back to shore to help some of the final evacuees, Alcock was one of the last to be plucked to safety. He'd returned to his parent unit, the Coldstream Guards, battered and exhausted, having lost much of his kit. His reward for his sterling efforts was to be put on a charge for losing items of British Army equipment.

In early November 1942, Alcock was back in action, being sent ashore in Algeria as part of the Operation Torch amphibious landings in North Africa. A few months later he was in bloody combat again, taking part in the 'Battle of Longstop Hill' in Tunisia, a ferocious struggle to seize a ridge of high-ground – commonly known as 'Longstop Hill' – that saw some two hundred men of his parent regiment lost in action.

A keep-fit fanatic, Alcock was made one of the Physical Training (PT) instructors at the Allies' Philippeville base in Algeria, running PT drills for various units. With Philippeville adopted by the newly formed 2 SAS regiment as a training camp, recruits were sent there for SAS selection. The first part of the process entailed the 'Jebel Run', and Alcock invariably led the charge. Along with his pal from the Coldstream Guards, Fred 'Dusty' Rhodes – who would also go on to join the SAS – Alcock would lead the recruits up a punishingly steep hill, the 'Jebel', and back again. Those who failed to complete the Jebel Run in an hour would be promptly RTU'd – Returned to Unit.

With Alcock's interest in the SAS duly aroused, he sensed that the adventure and independence it promised were right up his street. In fact, Alcock's attributes were just those sought by Bill Stirling, 2 SAS's commander and the brother of SAS founder David Stirling. Here was a man who had fought bravely in two theatres of war, and whose fitness was at the very highest level. As 2 SAS were forever seeking volunteers, Alcock put his name forward and shortly after was sent for parachute training.

His SAS induction complete, Alcock joined Bill Stirling on a recruitment drive, travelling far and wide in an effort to select more soldiers for the elite unit. In September 1943 he'd found himself in Taranto, southern Italy, where the SAS were carrying out scouting missions and combat sorties at the vanguard of the Allied Operation Husky landings.

In a break from such work, the men of 2 SAS were given specialist training by Colonel Hector Grant-Taylor, an expert in 'close-quarters combat', something that was to benefit Alcock greatly in all that was to come. Alcock and his pals had gathered in a room, awaiting Taylor's arrival. An unremarkable-looking man had pitched up, having more the demeanour of an ageing school master than an expert in close-quarters battle. Taylor had decided his pupils weren't paying sufficient attention. He'd proceeded to lift his Tommy gun and shoot out all the lightbulbs in the room. He sure had their attention then.

After seeing action across Italy, 2 SAS had returned to Britain to prepare for operations across Nazi-occupied France. That in turn had led Alcock and his men to parachute into the Alsace region, to a rain-drenched patch of woodland that was crawling with the enemy.

With daybreak there was yet more rain. Rest had not come easy. Despite their makeshift gas-cape awning, their sleeping bags were soaked and had done little to keep them warm. From their place of hiding, Alcock and his three men could see that they were close to what looked like an enemy pillbox. Hoping it was simply an abandoned part of the Maginot Line defences – the series of French fortifications built in the 1930s to deter a German invasion – Alcock and his men spent the day on high alert. Here and there they spied German work parties busy constructing more defences. Alcock used the time to plan. They would make their way gradually south-west, he reasoned, heading towards the American frontline, but sticking to the heavily forested Koecking plateau, and seeking out targets of opportunity along the way. 'The Alsace railways, their mission targets, would dictate the route.'

Although the Koecking plateau would be patrolled by enemy troops, it was less exposed than the flatlands on which they'd been dropped, so offered better cover. At times it should provide a panoramic view of what would be the main battlefield in the coming weeks, and should furnish a vantage point from where to observe the best route to cross the lines. At least, that was what Alcock hoped.

With nightfall it was time to get moving. Dumping their sleeping bags, which had become 'useless after being soaked by the rain', the four men set out, making for a railway line and an anti-tank ditch. They came to a swollen stream. Unable to find a bridge to cross it, they were forced to turn south, a direction that barred them from climbing to the Koecking plateau. As dawn approached, Alcock began to get seriously worried. They were still in open countryside, and would need to find shelter fast. Reaching what he figured was the Kappelkinger-to-Insming road, which linked those two local towns, he spied what looked to be a half-decent hiding place in a large orchard.

Concealing themselves under the branches of a massive pear tree that provided a modicum of shelter from the incessant rain, they settled down to watch. They'd found cover only just in time, for shortly they spotted activity. 'From there we could see the main road which was being used by a lot of SS and SA cyclists,' the SA being Hitler's *Sturmabteilung*, or Brownshirts, paramilitary Nazi thugs.

Two hours later, disaster seemed upon them. A pair of young children approached, clearly looking for fruit. As their eyes searched the pear tree's branches, the four hidden soldiers were spotted. Immediately the kids yelled out a warning and ran away. Fearing they would return with a search party, Alcock and his men evacuated the pear tree and sprinted across the road, making for a thick copse standing in the middle of 'cultivated land'. It was far from ideal as a place of concealment, but what other choices were there?

Lying low, Alcock feared the area was just too densely populated and too devoid of cover to slip through unnoticed. Sure enough, a lone figure wandered across to their place of hiding. It turned out that he was a local farmer and he promised to fetch them food. Deciding they had little option but to trust him, they let him depart. Shortly, he returned as promised, bearing provisions.

He'd also brought a friend, who, somewhat alarmingly, spoke German. The warning not to trust the locals, due to their questionable loyalties, was foremost in the SAS men's minds. Yet the two farmers not only gave them a decent meal, but also proved to be a fine source of information. As Alcock questioned them, they made every effort to show that their loyalties lay firmly with the Allies. Locals were being forced to construct defensive positions for the Germans 'under threat of a machine gun', they told him. Understandably, this did not sit well with them. Helping the SAS was their way of hitting back.

The farmers alerted Alcock and his men to an ideal target, for close by lay a busy railway line. With nightfall, the raiders listened to goods trains lumbering to and fro, as they sheltered from the pouring rain. This, Alcock reminded himself, was the reason they were here in the first place, enduring such sodden, freezing conditions. That railway would make a perfect target, and Alcock focused his senses on trying to work out the busiest times, and the best moment to launch their attack.

During daytime the railway fell silent. Nothing seemed to be on the move. With the Allied air forces ruling the skies, the enemy looked to be moving their locomotives only during the dark hours, when there was far less chance of being spotted. Alcock decided a night attack was called for, so they could hit the railway when it was at its busiest. As darkness fell, the four men gathered their kit and set out. The rain had not let up, and they had long since abandoned any notion of trying to keep dry.

A kilometre east of the town of Insming, they flitted towards the rail tracks, checking for any signs of the enemy. Ironically, the terrible weather turned out to be a blessing. What sentry would want to be out in conditions such as these? With their senses on high alert, they crept towards the iron tracks, which glistened wetly in the ambient light. There, they prepared to lay their charges. Using the tried and tested fog-signal system, which was designed to trigger the explosives well in front of a speeding train, so guaranteeing a derailment, they worked away in silence. Alcock checked and rechecked their handiwork to ensure that all had been configured just right.

With the only noise being the dripping of rain on leaves, they pulled back from the railway line, finding a place of concealment among some trees. Now, the wait.

Two hours later, they detected a distant rumbling: it had to be a train. As the locomotive drew closer, they could see that it consisted of three sections, 'an engine, tender and one truck'. Watching on, the four hoped for the best. The fog-signal system had been invented by SOE, and it was used widely by Allied saboteurs. But the enemy had grown wise to it, and had started to fit their locomotives with equipment designed to flip any such device off the line before the locomotive could trigger it. Should the approaching train have been so modified their efforts would go unrewarded. Alternatively, should the charge be noticed by an observant driver, he might bring his engine to a halt, and shortly the area would be awash with enemy troops.

As the seconds ticked down, there was a sudden blinding flash followed by an almighty boom. It was as if a bolt of lightning had hit the line, for as the explosives detonated they ripped the steel tracks from their wooden sleepers and blasted them into a heap of twisted metal. With a terrible grinding noise, and a thunderous roar that echoed around the terrain, the locomotive hit the torn-up section of track, powered onwards, ploughed into the embankment and flipped onto its side, coming to a rest in a mangled heap. As Alcock was to report, 'The engine and tender fell to the left and the truck fell across the right-hand track.'

As the noise abated and the billowing dust and smoke began to thin, the cries of the injured became audible. Shortly, there came the pounding of running feet, as the survivors struggled through the dark trees in a blind panic. Some passed perilously close to where the four saboteurs were hiding, and as Alcock was to learn later, two German officers had been killed in the blast.

It wouldn't be long before the derailment was reported and the area swarmed with enemy troops. Now they had success-fully wrecked a train and put the line out of action, it was time to move, and move fast. The four saboteurs slipped away, being careful to stick to the shadows and the trees, all the time on the lookout, and listening for any signs of pursuit. Pushing south-west, they passed the small town of Albestroff, noting the fresh trenches that had been excavated in the woods – more defences against the expected American advance. But, strangely, there seemed to be no signs of any kind of pursuit. Oddly, not a soul appeared to be on the hunt for them.

To Alcock, it didn't make the slightest bit of sense.

What he and the rest of his men couldn't know was that by a stroke of good fortune they'd been given a clean shot at making a getaway. But what was lucky for them proved quite the opposite for a local man, one Michel Pottier. The Frenchman 'had been falsely accused . . . of sabotaging the train', and had been arrested by the Gestapo. As Pottier was interrogated for forty-eight hours, that gave Alcock and his men ample time to put a good distance between them and the scene of their attack.

By the time the Gestapo had realised their error, the SAS were long gone.

As they moved on, Alcock sensed that things were becoming dire. The rain had not let up one bit and the cold chilled them to the bone, plus their meagre rations were running low. If they didn't find proper shelter and a decent meal, and get to dry their clothes and to sleep, then the chances of them making it safely across the lines were minimal at best. By now it was approaching the fourth week of September, and the autumn chill was setting in. Not only were they hungry, wet and freezing cold, but they had no way to call for any resupply or reinforcements.

Alcock remembered the radio he had so carefully wrapped in its cocoon of parachute silk, several days earlier. Figuring the wounded SAS captain was far more in need of it, Alcock had left it for Captain Scott and his comrades. But that meant Alcock had no way of calling in any air drops. The only option he had was to fall upon the charity of the locals, despite the warnings they had been given to trust no one.

From his map Alcock identified an isolated farm, which he figured had to be worth a go. On the way to the farmstead, they came across a section of railway that was polished with use. Alcock figured it was the same line as they had blown earlier, back near Insming. With that line already out of action, it would serve little purpose to plant their remaining explosives here, and it risked bringing the wrath of the German military down upon them. Pressing on, by dusk they'd reached a road. On the far side lay L'Allewald woods, an expanse of forest that offered good cover.

They were about to cross the road when they heard movement. Shortly, a large convoy of horse-drawn artillery appeared, 'moving south from Neufvillage', a small settlement that was about a kilometre away. Enemy troops streamed past. It would take just one alert German soldier to cast his eye in their direction, and the four fugitives would surely be spotted. Alcock and his men 'released the safety catches on their carbines and made ready'. Though hopelessly outnumbered, they would make a fight of it.

As they hunkered down and kept watch, their German counterparts looked as tired and miserable as they were. They too were dripping wet, rivulets of rainwater running onto their grey-green uniforms from their steel helmets. Steam rose from the haunches of the horses as they plodded forwards, and the enemy troops looked in no mood for a fight.

Once the last of them had passed, Alcock made a note of their position on his map, aiming to pass it on to Allied commanders, should they ever get the opportunity to do so. That done, they darted across the road and headed for the 'Ferme Besville', the farmstead that Alcock had identified as offering uncertain, if longed-for, sanctuary.

A while later they reached the edge of the woods and settled down to watch. As Alcock noted, the 'farm's location was ideal . . . not located near a main road so there would be little chance of being surprised suddenly by the arrival of an enemy vehicle'. Seeing nothing untoward, at dusk they approached the building and knocked on the door. It was opened by a 'short man with a weathered face and broad hands'. It turned out they were in luck. The farmer declared himself willing to help. He gave his name as Pierre Canteneur, telling the four men that they could stay in his barn for the night. His wife would dry their clothes and make them a hot meal.

Like many of the locals, Canteneur resented the German occupiers with a passion. Since early 1943, young men from the region had been 'forcefully drafted into the German army', and many had been sent to the dreaded Eastern Front, which was little short of a death sentence. The Alsace region had been gripped by 'a Nazi regime of suppression', leading to 'growing resentment within the local . . . population'. Hence any Allied soldiers in the area, including the SAS, could hope to be well looked after by the local populace.

As the four fugitives settled down to their first hot meal and proper shelter in a week, Canteneur briefed Alcock on all that he knew. He had spotted a group of Allied parachutists a couple of days earlier, passing through the area to the north of his farm. They could well have been SAS, and very possibly another of the Operation Pistol patrols. While there was no way of knowing, who else could they possibly be? Canteneur was also able to alert them to another farm on their route, at which they would be guaranteed help and assistance. It lay adjacent to the rail junction at Bénestroff and Rodalbe villages, a few kilometres away from their present location.

Early the next morning, 22 September 1944, with their clothing 'still a little damp', but their bellies blissfully full, the patrol headed into L'Allewald woods once more, this time making for Ferriendel farm, where Monsieur Canteneur had assured them they would be welcomed by his friend, Jean Koenig.

They were almost there when they noticed movement along the tree line. A large body of men were going into and out of what looked like some kind of workshop. After observing it for a while and making a note of its coordinates, Alcock led Hannah, Holden and Lyczak across the nearby railway line and away into cover. It was broad daylight and the danger of being spotted was very real.

It was midday by the time they arrived at Ferriendel farm. Knocking on the rear door, it was opened by a 'stockily well-built man of about five foot six'. At first, he gazed upon them suspiciously. But once it was established that they were bona fide British soldiers, and Alcock had confirmed that the man facing them was indeed Jean Koenig, they were invited in. There they joined the farmer's wife, Marguerite, and their four-year-old son.

Koenig had very good reason to be cautious. The Gestapo were making regular calls to the farms in the area, searching for Allied parachutists. Knowing now that it had been Allied saboteurs who had carried out the attack on the train, the hunt was very much on. Koenig was also harbouring Lucien Tilly, a young Frenchman on the run from the Gestapo, who was trying to avoid forced conscription into the German army. Koenig was risking a great deal by doing so, and even more now by sheltering Alcock and his men.

Shortly, there was a fierce banging on the door. Peering through the window, Koenig was aghast to see it was the Gestapo. Quickly, he ushered the four SAS men out of the kitchen and into the downstairs toilet. Hidden from sight in what was a small and cramped room, all Alcock and the others could do was wait and put their faith in the Frenchman. Fumbling with their carbines, they made them ready, muzzles menacing the door.

In the kitchen, Koenig was having a heated quarrel with his unwelcome visitors. They were demanding the use of his horses for military purposes, but the Frenchman was having none of it. Putting on a haughty demeanour, he argued that there was no way they were taking his animals. Answering their questions in 'fluent German in a confident manner', his assertiveness seemed to work. In light of the French farmer's front and his stubbornness, the Gestapo began to relent. Koenig's bravado seemed to have worked, for eventually they left the property empty handed.

Once they were gone, Koenig asked Alcock what he would have done if the Gestapo had opened the door to their hiding place.

'I would have shot them,' was Alcock's measured reply.

'What about us then?' Koenig had demanded. Alcock explained he would have taken Koenig and his family with them and through to the Allied lines.

With the Gestapo gone, Keonig introduced the four men to Tilly, the young Frenchman hiding out on the farm. He proved keen to join the SAS on their journey towards the American lines. Alcock weighed up the pros and cons of letting him do so. The youngster spoke both French and German fluently, which could come in useful. By taking him with them, it would also relieve Koenig of a huge burden. The brave Frenchman was risking all he held dear by helping these fugitives, French and British alike. It was the least they could do by taking Tilly along.

Koenig was able to pass on invaluable intelligence to Alcock and his men. He possessed a vast knowledge of enemy troop positions. The workshop that Alcock had spied in the woods was being used to repair German machine guns, he advised. He was also able to provide the names of other farmers who would be able to help them, pointing out their properties on Alcock's map. Upon learning that Alcock had left a radio at the drop zone near Audviller, he volunteered to cycle over to see if he might retrieve it.

As Alcock and his men rested up and dried out their clothes, Koenig set out on the long bicycle ride. He returned several hours later but was empty handed. The radio was nowhere to be found. Undeterred, the following morning, 23 September, the four SAS men, plus their new companion, Lucien Tilly, set forth, bidding farewell to Koenig and his family. The brave farmer had arranged a rendezvous with a friend of his, Gaston Forfret, at Bérange farm, some nine kilometres to the south-west – nine kilometres closer to the Allied frontline.

With the weather worsening still, the fugitives were assailed by storms. Some way along their journey, the sound of an artillery barrage cut through the rain-lashed skies. As explosions rent the air, they spied two dozen German tanks withdrawing into the cover of some nearby trees. It was clear that they were in among the heart of the German positions right now, with all the inherent dangers.

It was now that Corporal Holden began to complain that he was feeling unwell. As Alcock quickly realised, the curse of Philippeville had struck again. It was malaria, that debilitating disease that had plagued many a man who had been put through SAS training in Algeria. With Holden gripped by fever and delirium, there was no way they could press on. He needed shelter and proper care, if he was to stand any chance of pulling through. There was nothing for it, Alcock reasoned: they would have to head back to Ferriendel farm and rely on the goodwill of Jean Koenig.

It took hours to retrace their steps. They had to stop repeatedly not only due to Holden's weakened state, but also to avoid the enemy, as German troops appeared at every turn. Typically, Koenig welcomed them back as old friends. While Holden recuperated in the warmth of the farmhouse, Alcock and the others rested in a shelter in the woods, drying out as best they could.

Several days passed before Holden felt well enough to continue. The five escapees bade their goodbyes to Koenig and his family once more, and set out. This time they stuck to the edge of the thick woodland that grew all along the flank of the Koecking plateau. They'd pushed ahead five kilometres or so, when they heard voices close by. Two figures appeared from the trees. Fortunately, they were not enemy soldiers but unarmed Polish woodsmen, who were being used as slave labour by the Germans. With Lyczak being Polish, he was able to chat fluently with them. The Poles informed the SAS fugitives that there was a cottage near by where they could dry themselves out and get a cup of hot coffee. With the rain continuing to lash down, the offer seemed too good to resist.

With the Polish woodsmen acting as their guides, it was midday by the time Alcock and his men arrived at a group of buildings making up Koecking farm. Approaching the rear of the farmhouse via a steep slope, they slipped indoors and began stripping off their sodden uniforms. Inside, they were met by two Polish girls, who looked no more than sixteen years old. Employed to carry out chores for those who lived at the farm, they were soon handing out steaming mugs to the appreciative British soldiers.

Eventually, the woodsmen rose to leave, explaining that they needed to get back to work before their absence was noticed. Thinking nothing of it, Alcock and the rest thanked them for their hospitality. But not an hour later, Alcock heard the distinctive revving of a heavy vehicle making its way towards the farmstead. Dashing to the window, he spied a truck pulling up at the end of the driveway, loaded with a party of German troops.

Ordering the others to grab their clothes and reassemble their weapons – they'd broken their carbines down to dry and to clean them – he ushered all into the rear hallway. Hurriedly dressing, they readied themselves for whatever was to come. With his mind racing, Alcock could only imagine that the Polish woodsmen had betrayed them, fetching the enemy. The timing was just too suspicious to think otherwise.

As the enemy troops leapt down from their truck, the first two raced around to the cottage's rear and began to hammer on the door. Firmly bolted shut, they'd have to shoot it open, which should buy Alcock and his men a little time. Sensing what was coming, Alcock grabbed the two young Polish girls and man-handled them towards the front door. If he could shove them out, then he might save them from any firefight that was bound to ensue, for the interior of the cottage was about to become a killing zone.

As the girls were thrust through the main entrance, they drew the instant attention of the German troops mustering themselves at the truck. Even the two soldiers at the cottage's rear were seen to dash around to the front, keen to discover what was going on. Alcock and his men finished slotting together their M1 carbines, as they prepared for what seemed inevitable – a close-up firefight with a far superior enemy force.

Moments later they heard the front door shoved open, as the first of the enemy troops piled inside. They moved into the kitchen, and Alcock could hear them yelling at the Polish girls. He had little doubt what they were demanding to know. Then, with a sense of dread, he remembered something: he'd left a magazine of ammo and a glove on the kitchen table. It was bound to be seen. As the yelling escalated, Alcock could tell that the girls were replying from outside, which meant that this was the moment to strike.

The SAS favoured the M1 carbine in part due to its ease of use in close-range battle. With its short barrel, folding stock and comparatively light weight, it was far easier to wield than any traditional rifle, including the kind that the enemy troops carried. Highly effective in confined spaces, Alcock and his men had the added advantage of the instruction that Colonel Hector Grant-Taylor had given them, teaching the art of how to kill at close quarters. The time to put that superlative training into action was now.

Giving the enemy little time to react, Alcock booted open the door leading from the rear hallway into the kitchen and opened fire. He was joined by Hannah, Holden and Lyczak, blazing away with their weapons. The bullets tore into the enemy, throwing them to the floor in a bloody tangle. It had taken just a few seconds, but now there were six German soldiers lying lifeless on the kitchen floor.

Their work done, Alcock ordered the others to make for the rear exit. As his comrades made a dash for the back door, Alcock moved towards the window. Alarmingly, another truckload of troops had just arrived, coming to a halt at the front of the cottage. Already, soldiers were pouring off the back, no doubt having heard all the gunfire.

Then he detected a noise to one side. It seemed to be coming from the stairs leading to the cottage's first floor. A figure appeared. It was a German soldier that they had somehow missed. He must have gone to search upstairs when the rest of his comrades had entered the kitchen. Oddly, he was bareheaded, his bright red hair seeming to stand out dramatically, and Alcock noted that his rifle was slung uselessly over his shoulder.

For a brief second they locked eyes, the German evidently in total shock.

Breaking the man's stare, Alcock turned and made a run for it, following the others out of the back door. For some reason he had decided to let the red-headed soldier live.

From behind him, Alcock could hear the noise of pounding feet, as the newly arrived troops gave chase. He had to get into the sanctuary of the woods, for only there might he lose them. The route of escape lay over a low wall at the rear of the house and down the steep slope that they had walked up, less than two hours earlier.

As Alcock vaulted over the wall, he caught his foot on a capstone, dislodging it, and putting himself off balance. Righting himself, he sprinted for all he was worth. Ahead of him his comrades likewise ran for their lives. Moments later the sound of gunfire filled his ears, as the enemy, now at the wall, and with their rifles resting on it for better aim, opened fire. Alcock and his men began to zig-zag, to prevent the shooters getting an easy fix on them. As they sprinted for the distant tree line, a hail of hot lead cut through the air, thwacking into the nearest trees, or kicking up sods of earth around their feet.

Doubting whether any of them would make it, somehow Alcock found himself among the trees miraculously unharmed, whereupon he dived into cover. Glancing behind, he saw the enemy giving chase. With no time to slot in fresh magazines of ammo into their M1 assault rifles, the four SAS – along with the young Frenchman, Tilly – were up and running again, weaving through the trees. They followed what appeared to be a well-worn path that snaked through the thick forest. Rounding a corner, which put them out of sight of their pursuers, Alcock called a halt.

They had to eliminate the threat, or they stood little chance. Slotting in fresh magazines of ammo, they dropped into ambush positions, two on either side of the path. Moments later, the first enemy troops appeared. There were four of them, and they clearly hadn't been expecting to be ambushed by those that they hunted. Alcock gave the order to open fire, and just as their comrades in the kitchen had been caught off guard, so were these German soldiers. In an instant three of them had been cut down, their bloodied forms slumping into the undergrowth. The fourth, seeing the fate of his fellows, turned tail and ran.

But no one was kidding themselves that the danger was over. Alcock and his men had just killed or badly wounded nine of the enemy. The hunt would be resumed in earnest. On they ran, heading deeper into the woods. If they could only get to the farm that Jean Koenig had told them about, maybe they could lie low and figure out what to do next.

After several minutes hard running, they reached the edge of the forest. Ahead lay a road that stretched from the town of Rodalbe to Dieuze. Beyond it lay open terrain. With no sign of any pursuit, Alcock decided to grab a short breather. Their adrenalin levels were off the scale and they needed to calm and compose themselves. As the five men paused to catch their breath, there was a sound that made Alcock's blood run cold. It was the distant echo of two single gunshots.

He didn't doubt what had just happened. The Polish girls who had helped them had paid the ultimate price. Convinced that the Polish woodsmen had informed on them, Alcock reckoned that he and his men should have moved out, as soon as the Poles had departed. But he had never once imagined that they would go straight to the enemy. Until now, everyone had proven so trustworthy. The Poles were serving as slave labour, so surely the Germans would be their hated enemy? Why they had acted as they did was anyone's guess. And now, because of their betrayal, two innocent Polish girls had been murdered.

While it was all so unnecessary, Alcock couldn't dwell on any of that now. He needed to focus. They still had to get to the safety of Allied lines.

Rest done, they pushed on. Under cover of a low mist, they slipped across the road and forded a canal. Hitting another patch of woodland, they kept to this for two kilometres, hugging the tree line. Alcock was navigating them towards Bérange farm, where Jean Koenig had organised a rendezvous with its owner, Gaston Forfret, a man that he'd promised was of unshakeable integrity.

After a while they came across another road. From the far end came the sound of a vehicle, which seemed to be struggling up a hidden incline. Hiding in the long grass at the roadside, the fugitives watched and waited. Slowly it came into view, the engine whining and the gears crunching as the driver fought against the slope. It was a *kübelwagen* – an open-top German military field vehicle, not too dissimilar from the SAS's jeeps. Taking a grenade from his pocket, Alcock gripped it firmly. Glancing to his side, he saw the others were also preparing for action, their carbines at the ready.

As the *kübelwagen* neared their place of hiding, it stopped. An officer stood up in the rear and took out some binoculars. As he put them to his eyes and scanned the area to his front, each of the five lay as low as they could. After a while he sat back down again and ordered his driver to continue. With a collective sigh of relief, Alcock and his men watched until the car was well out of sight.

Pressing on, the terrain seemed thick with enemy on all sides. 'We saw a German truck back into the woods, fill up with artillery ammunition, and go off again ... We could hear repairs being carried out ... it sounded like a tank repair shop.' But there were too many troops for them to risk any sabotage there and then. To do so would inevitably lead to their capture and, as they all understood, that would result in almost certain execution.

As all on Operation Pistol understood by now, Hitler had issued his infamous Commando Order. This illegal instruction, signed off by Adolf Hitler himself, had been handed down to German officers, decreeing that any Special Forces combatants caught on operations were to be passed to the Gestapo for questioning, and then eliminated. Even if they were captured in uniform on legitimate military operations, they were not to be spared. Armed with this knowledge, Alcock and his men knew that capture spelled the very worst.

Rather than attacking the enemy positions all around them, Alcock and his men made careful note about dispositions and strengths, marking the coordinates on their map, for passing on to Allied high command should they ever make it through the lines.

Moving on, the fugitives climbed up to the Koecking plateau, the hilly, wooded terrain making it easier to move without being seen. Following forest tracks they probed forward, each listening intently for any signs of the enemy. Stopping whenever they heard voices, and scooting around the enemy positions so revealed, they kept pressing west towards Allied lines. But their nerves were on a knife edge, and they would stop stock still at even the slightest sound.

Now and again the throaty roar of Panzer engines revealed enemy armour, enabling them to give it a wide berth. Yet it made for slow and nerve-racking progress. From far to the west they caught the booming of artillery guns, as the Americans shelled German positions in readiness for mounting their next offensive. The din from those weapons combined with the incessant rain helped mask what little sound they were making.

Eventually they reached a clearing. Six hundred yards away lay what Alcock reckoned had to be Bérange farm, the home of Gaston Forfret. To the right, gathered at the edge of the trees, they could make out a row of German tanks. They were in an utterly precarious position, right in the midst of a mass of German armour. As yet, their luck had held out, but to get to the farm they would need to break cover. To do so would put them in full view of the enemy. For the moment they would have to wait and put their trust in fate.

After a while there was movement on the open field. Stealing a glance in that direction, Alcock saw a farmer approaching. He seemed to be searching for something. This had to be Forfret, he reasoned. After a while, the Frenchman must have noticed them, for he approached slowly. Careful not to appear too obvious, he stopped with his back to Alcock and his men. With Lucien Tilly translating, he spoke over his shoulder in whispers, telling them to wait for early morning, and then to make their way via a nearby ditch to the rear of his farmstead. A German sergeant was billeted in his house each night, he explained, hence the exacting instructions. With that, Forfret wandered off.

That night the rain sheeted down, making sleep impossible.

The occasional report of a rifle being discharged only added to the collective anxiety. At dawn on 26 September, the five men crept closer to the farm to mount a watch. Sure enough, they saw the back door swing open and a lone German soldier exit, making his way towards the nearby woods. Once he was gone, the five men crawled through the ditch and were soon out of sight inside the brave Frenchman's home. Totally exhausted, the SAS and their companion, Tilly, stripped off their soaking clothes and settled down to some desperately needed rest, Alcock sleeping in the bed that had been recently vacated by the German sergeant.

Rested, fed and with dry clothes, Alcock and his men listened to Forfret, as he briefed them on the route ahead. Six kilometres south-west lay Salival farm, which was owned by a member of the Resistance. It was very close to the frontline, and looked to be the perfect jumping off point for the final leg of their escape. Shortly, the fugitives resumed their journey, moving with extreme caution, for the entire area was crawling with enemy troops.

In a sense it was no surprise when they were spotted, just a kilometre short of their destination. Approaching through the long grass were ten soldiers in their distinctive German uniforms, carrying some large cooking pots. Even though Alcock and the others were crouched in the grass, it was clear that they'd been seen. 'We immediately stood up and Corporal Holden shouted "Halt!"' Alcock would report. That was enough to stop the Germans in their tracks, especially since they faced four battle-hardened SAS, each menacing them with an M1 carbine at close range.

Dropping the food containers the enemy raised their hands. 'Don't shoot, don't shoot – Americans six kilometres!' one of them, their commander, cried, pointing out the direction of Allied lines.

As Alcock and his men soon discovered, these weren't German soldiers at all. They were Serbs who had been press-ganged into German military service as cooks. In fact, they were carrying food to Salival farm, for German troops billeted there, and that of course was exactly where Alcock and his men were heading. Alcock was placed in a tough dilemma. He couldn't take prisoners. Likewise, he couldn't shoot unarmed men in cold blood. With no other option, he waved them away. Grateful at not being gunned down, the Serbs turned tail and were soon out of sight.

Carrying on to Salival farm was now out of the question. At the same time, they urgently needed to get away from the immediate area, for the Serbs were sure to raise the alarm. Studying his map, Alcock picked out another place, around two-and-a-half kilometres south through the woods, at which they could possibly seek shelter. It was marked as 'Voitrebolle farm'.

As they edged through the forest, they came across what looked like a telephone cable snaking through the undergrowth. Curiosity getting the better of him, Alcock told the others to remain hidden, while he set out alone to find out where it led. After a few minutes he discovered a large body of German troops in what appeared to be an artillery command position. After observing it for a while, Alcock retraced his steps to the others. Taking a set of wire cutters from his pack, he snipped the cable and they moved off. Each time they came across any telephone wires he repeated the process. 'We cut several signal lines before proceeding to the east side of the wood,' he would report. It was a simple act of sabotage, but he knew it would cause the enemy considerable upset.

Once darkness had fallen, they moved in towards Voitrebolle farm. Again, they were in luck, for the farmer welcomed them in. He was also able to provide choice information about enemy positions, for his farm lay at the bottom of a ridge, 'which was heavily defended by the Germans'.

Knowing that Voitrebolle was to be the jumping off point for their final foray towards Allied lines, Alcock had to be sure of the route. He couldn't allow them to fall at the final hurdle. Accordingly, he decided to carry out a recce of the area that lay ahead.

It was almost two weeks after parachuting into Alsace, when Alcock borrowed a set of civilian clothes from their host, grabbed a hoe, and he and Tilly went forth. Posing as farm workers, they climbed to the top of the nearby ridge. Towards the west, and what was freedom, a canal cut across the landscape. To get to the American lines they would have to cross it. But where? To their right lay the village of Haraucourt-sur-Seille. A bridge stretched over the waterway, but it looked to be closely guarded. They would have to find another way. As Alcock considered their options, his eyes came to rest upon the village of Marsal, less than two kilometres to the south. It was at that moment suffering an artillery bombardment from the American heavy guns, the smoke from the resulting fires billowing into the air.

On their return to Voitrebolle farm, their host advised them of another, more secluded bridge, which might be a better place to attempt to cross the canal. Marking it on his map, Alcock figured he now had a workable plan, one predicated on the best intelligence he could muster.

For two days they remained at the farm, mustering their strength for what they hoped would be the final push, and making sure the 'equipment on their persons made little noise'. Briefing the four on the coming night's plan of action, Alcock traced the route he intended to take, highlighting the bridge where they would cross the canal. They were to avoid all villages and use the cover of the heavy rain to mask their movements. Fully briefed, the escapees settled down for a final few hours of rest. It was not just their bodies that were fatigued. Alcock had to be sure that each of them had the psychological strength to endure this one last trial.

It was 0230 on the morning of 1 October 1944 when they finally set out, following a stone track and sticking to the cover of the hedge lines. Once they had reached the canal, they traced its bank, searching for the elusive crossing point. Finding the bridge miraculously unguarded, one by one they crept across. On the far side one of the men spied a telephone line leading back to the German positions. Taking out his wire cutters, Alcock snipped it, in his final act of sabotage on Operation Pistol.

Using the darkness and night mist as cover, the five fugitives pressed on. They were now at the most dangerous point of their journey. Ahead lay the German frontline, and beyond that, no-man's-land, while on the far side lay the American positions. There was a very real risk of being shot by either side. Whenever they heard voices, Alcock would slowly lead his men towards them, to locate the source of the sound, before boxing around and continuing forward. This way he hoped to weave a route between the German frontline positions. But it made for heart-stopping progress. At any point the mist might clear and they would be revealed for what they were – British soldiers trying to escape to Allied lines.

On every side they could hear German troops excavating their slit trenches and foxholes, voices loud and clear in the darkness. They could only be a matter of a few yards away, yet still they hadn't been seen. Once again, perversely, the bad weather proved to be their friend, for it obliged the enemy troops to hunch their shoulders and keep low, and to show little interest in what was going on outside of their immediate area.

Then Alcock saw two groups of German soldiers up ahead. They were digging in, their silhouettes clear in the light of an almost full moon. Slowly, the five men stole forward, barely daring to breathe as they slipped between the two positions. A few minutes later, they were clear.

With the sun threatening to reveal itself, Alcock figured they needed to find somewhere to hide. He didn't doubt that they were almost there. But with sunrise, any American soldiers who spied five men creeping towards them would be bound to think they were the enemy and open fire.

'With daylight approaching we made for a bush at the bottom of a hill, but found freshly dug positions,' Alcock would report. Surely these had to be American fortifications? They were on the wrong side of the hill to be German defences. Then he saw something of far more concern. At the top of the hill was what looked to be an observation post (OP). Inside was a soldier with a light machine gun. Disconcertingly, it was pointed directly at Alcock and his men.

Expecting a hail of bullets to rain down on them, the escapees were astonished when the gunner refrained from shooting. Had he somehow missed seeing them? Or was he unsure as to who exactly was hiding in the bush directly below his position?

Alcock was convinced they had reached Allied lines, and that the figure on the hill above had to be American. But if that machine-gunner decided to let loose a burst, then there was no way he could miss, and 'friendly fire' was just as lethal as that of the enemy. There was nothing for it, Alcock decided. They would have to execute one last attack, seizing and subduing that American machine-gun post.

Quickly, Alcock gave his orders. Corporal Hannah and the Frenchman, Tilly, were to outflank the position, while he, along with Corporal Holden and Lyczak, would make a move in full view of the gunner. As Hannah and Tilly crawled into position, Alcock clambered to his feet with the intention of yelling out something suitable in German, for he'd picked up a few words during the war. That should draw the gunner's attention, as Hannah and Lyczak made their move to subdue him.

But as Alcock revealed himself, he inadvertently yelled out in English, as the drama of the moment got the better of him. It was of no matter. Suitably distracted, and doubtless utterly confused by the whole thing, the American gunner failed to spot Corporal Hannah creeping up from behind. With an M1 carbine levelled at him, the American quickly put up his hands in surrender. Moments later Alcock and the rest were called forward. As all this was taking place, a second US soldier remained fast asleep to one side of the OP, only becoming aware he was a prisoner of the SAS when he was roughly shaken awake.

Putting down their weapons, Alcock explained exactly who they were, before asking to speak to their commanding officer. He had vital intelligence about German positions to hand over as soon as possible. Shortly, Alcock found himself standing before Colonel Bruce Clark, the commander of Combat Command A of the US 4th Armoured Division, into whose lines they had escaped. Colonel Clark gratefully accepted the intelligence Alcock had garnered. Their advance was scheduled to start soon, and Alcock's target coordinates would lend the Americans a major advantage.

Target coordinates handed over, Alcock took a moment to reflect. Somehow, against all odds, he had done it. He had led his men to safety through the lines, evading the enemy at every turn. It had been little short of miraculous that they had managed to navigate their way through. Since they had dropped near Audviller on the night of 15 September, their mission had been plagued by bad weather, lack of supplies, and terrain that was crawling with the enemy. Even so, they had successfully blown a train, causing an important German supply line to be severed, and had emerged carrying priceless intelligence on key enemy positions.

And while they had accounted for at least eleven enemy killed or wounded, not a single man on Alcock's patrol had suffered so much as a scratch.

Of the four SAS patrols dropped into theatre on Operation Pistol, only three made it onto the ground. The 'D Patrol' never got to deploy. As the official mission report stated, on the night of 15 September: 'D party returned because fog prevented recognition of the DZ. Five more attempts . . . were made to drop D, but all were unsuccessful.'

Operation Pistol had, in the main, been a success. Not only did Alcock's patrol score its victories, but the intelligence they had gathered proved invaluable. Other groups had likewise scored signal successes. One had blown a concrete pylon and derailed a train. Another had laid charges in a train tunnel and put the line out of action for days. Another had managed to lay charges on two railway lines, while ambushing various roads and knocking out enemy vehicles.

Two days after Alcock's escape through the lines, a second Pistol patrol made a successful crossing, arriving at the American frontline positions at 0800 on 3 October. But not all on the mission would make it out safely. Of the thirty-eight soldiers who parachuted into Alsace on 15 September, only half had made it back across the lines by mid-October 1944.

For Captain Scott, the SAS commander who had broken his ankle upon landing, things did not get a great deal better. Scott would be 'wounded in the thigh during an encounter with a German patrol, by whom he may have been taken prisoner . . . According to local rumour . . . the Germans in Dieuze alleged at the same date that they had captured British parachutists.' With so many Germans on the hunt for the SAS, it was little short of a miracle that Alcock and his small patrol had successfully evaded capture.

Operation Loyton, the sister mission to Operation Pistol, would become infamous. Thirty-two SAS soldiers were taken prisoner, and duly murdered under Hitler's Commando Order. Many of them were personal friends of Alcock. Fred 'Dusty' Rhodes, Alcock's friend from the Coldstream Guards, would form part of the SAS team investigating the fate of the Operation Loyton missing. Together with Major Eric (Bill) Barkworth, the commander of the SAS War Crimes Investigation Team, Rhodes would discover the bodies of ten SAS men buried in the woods around Moussey village, in the Vosges. Among them was Sergeant Robert Lodge, a.k.a. Rudi Friedlander, the German Jew who had executed the daring escape attempt along with Roy Bridgeman-Evans, when captured in Sicily. Later, he had gone on to conduct his own intrepid escape, rejoining the SAS. Here in the Vosges, Lodge had been captured when fighting a rearguard action to allow his brother soldiers to escape. He was murdered shortly after.

For his daring exploits on Operation Pistol, Alcock would be Mentioned in Despatches. In April 1945 he was awarded the Croix de Guerre with Silver Star, a high valour French decoration proposed by Brigadier Rory McLeod, then commander of the SAS, and endorsed by General Koenig, the former commander of the French Forces of the Interior (Free French). For the remainder of the war Alcock served with the SAS in Germany and Norway, and continued his military service thereafter, becoming the Regimental Sergeant Major (RSM) of the 3rd Battalion, the Parachute Regiment (3 PARA). Alcock left the army in 1966 and worked for the East Riding Education Service until his retirement at the age of sixty-five.

In 1982, he made a visit to the Operation Pistol area with his son, Graham, where he met up with some of those who had assisted him and his men during that time. Reunited with Jean Koenig, of Ferriendel farm, he learned that the brave French farmer had been awarded the King's Medal for Courage in the Cause of Freedom by the British, for his wartime daring. Without Koenig's spirited help, the outcome for Alcock and the others may well have been very different. John 'Jack' Alcock died aged seventy-eight on 1 January 1997, at Holme-upon-Spalding-Moor, Yorkshire.

Other than Koenig, there were many who had helped Alcock and his group on their journey to Allied lines. But it was perhaps the two young Polish girls who had lost their lives at the Koecking farm to whom they owed the greatest debt of gratitude.

Without their actions, which had caused the German soldiers at the rear of the cottage to leave their posts, Alcock and his comrades might well have failed to get away. Those two young Polish women had paid the ultimate price.

The courage, tenacity and strength of will displayed by Alcock and his comrades typified the *esprit de corps* of the SAS during the Second World War. There was no other unit quite like it. The legacy left behind by men such as the Great Escapees depicted in these pages underpins the standard by which today's elite forces soldiers are measured, and will continued to be measured in future.

For the freedoms we enjoy today, we owe such individuals an immense debt of gratitude.

Acknowledgements

First and foremost, thank you to my esteemed readers. You go out and buy my books in the hope that each will deliver a rewarding, illuminating read, bringing a story to life in vivid detail. Without you, there could be no author such as myself. You enable individuals like me to make a living from writing. You deserve the very first mention.

A huge thank you to all family members of those depicted in these pages, without whose assistance and support I could not have written this book. Especially forthcoming and helpful were the Verney family, principally Sebastian Verney, who shared with me a rich correspondence and many special moments concerning his father's wartime activities, and who kindly read and commented upon an early draft of this book. Thank you also to Nicholas Verney, for setting me on the right path.

Thanks to Ged Basson, who provided research into the Mouhot family tree, and to Paul McKay who cast an appraising eye over the early draft of this book. Thanks also to Sandra Stocker of The Worshipful Company of Tobacco Pipe Makers and Tobacco Blenders, who furnished research relating to Bridgeman-Evans life post war.

Equally vital was the kind assistance provided by the family of Captain Lewis 'Archie' Gibson, and especially Paul Gibson, who shared with me his father's excellent unpublished manuscripts of the war years, plus the family's incredible wartime archive, and who provided superlative feedback upon reading an early draft of this book.

Graham Alcock, the son of John Jack Alcock, was likewise hugely helpful in corresponding with me over his father's wartime service, and in providing me with an early draft of his book *Operation Pistol: Raindrops in Alsace*, which inspired me to write his father's story of escape.

Michael Gibbs proved immensely helpful in corresponding with me over the Gibbs family wartime service, and Catherine von Schenk, the daughter of Captain Martin Gibbs, was equally gracious in helping me tell her father's escape story.

Huge thanks to Allan Hunn for our discussions in person and remotely regarding Sergeant Jacques Mouhot's incredible escape, and for your guidance, comments, leads and suggestions regarding the same. These proved invaluable.

Thank you to David Farran, son of SAS commander Roy Farran, for your kind permission to quote from your father's excellent writings, and for our correspondence over the years regarding his outstanding wartime service. I am most grateful.

Thanks to Eric Lecomte for corresponding with me over various aspects of the SAS service in France, as covered in this book. Special thanks to Thomas Liaudet and all at the AFPSAS, for your kind help concerning my research into the French aspects of the story told in these pages. Thanks also to Anthony Watrin for your correspondence and insight into French SAS operations.

A very special thank you to the late, great Pierre-Jean Cabut, for the help and guidance you were able to provide to me from you home in France. Sadly, 'P-J', as he was known to all, has sadly passed away. You were a champion of the cause of the French SAS, doing so much to commemorate their operations.

Thanks to Dave Robertson, whose excellent podcast *For You The War Is Over* (Series 5, Episode 8) helped steer me onto the right path regarding Sergeant Jacques Mouhot's epic escape.

Thank you to Will Ward, of CART Dorset, for providing the various insights and vital leads that you did during my research. These again proved invaluable.

I have benefited greatly in the research for this book from the resources that the British, French and other governments, and related institutions, have invested into preserving for posterity the archives from the Second World War era. The preservation and cataloguing of a mountain of papers – official reports, personal correspondence, telegrams, etc. – plus photographic, film and sound archives is vital to authors such as myself. Devoting resources to the preservation of this historical record, and to making it accessible to the public, is something for which these governments and other institutions should be praised.

I extend a special thank you to the Imperial War Museum (IWM), whose archives are a treasure trove, including oral histories and collections of private papers, all of which proved immensely helpful in my research. The IWM archivists deserve special mention, for reaching out to the families of those whose archives they hold, to secure the kind permission that I sought to quote from their private papers.

Equally, all at The National Archives, Kew, deserve fulsome praise for preserving and presenting to the public a wonderful trove of wartime documents, which are vital to authors such as myself. We could not write the books that we do without the wonderful service that you furnish.

Thanks to Julie Davies, ace researcher and translator, for your fine translations that I relied upon to tell some of these tales, and your astute and pertinent observations, assessment and guidance regarding same.

   Finally, I extend a massive thanks to fellow historian and author John McKay for his contribution to this book. His encouragement, insight and inspiration once again proved invaluable.

Enormous thanks to all at my publishers for their committed, enthusiastic and visionary support of this project from the get-go. In the UK, Richard Milner, my long-standing editor, provided seminal guidance and feedback. The wider Quercus team also deserve the highest praise, especially Elizabeth Masters, Dave Murphy and Jon Butler. Huge thanks to my agent, Andrew Gordon at DHA, for his guidance, support and fine judgement. Special thanks again must be extended to Sophie Ransom, of Ransom PR, for all her fine efforts to help me tell this story.

I extend my heartfelt thanks to my eldest daughter, Teän, for her sterling efforts and immense skills as applied to the Great Escapes series – you were there at the very start, and enabled me to bring what was then only a concept and a dream to a published reality. For that I am immensely grateful. Again, I crave your indulgence and understanding for a father who spent too many years away in the world's most obscure places and war zones when you were young. I owe much to your love and forbearance.

Finally, my deep thanks and gratitude to my wife, Eva, and to David, Damien Jr and Sianna, who once again had to put up with 'Pappa' spending far too long locked in his study trying to do justice to this story. That I have – if I have – I owe to you all: to your love and support and kindness, and for putting up with me through it all.

This is a special story for the Lewis family, if for no other reason than my wife has played a very hands-on role in the research, archiving and transcribing the revisions of this book, not to mention overseeing the administration side of things. You stayed the course over the long months that it has taken to come to fruition, for which I am hugely grateful.

Acknowledgements on Sources

I am indebted to the following authors (and/or estates), who have covered some of the aspects of the story I have dealt with in *SAS Great Escapes Four* in their own writing. I extend my gratitude to all those who kindly granted me permission to quote from their material. For those readers whose interest has been piqued by this book, these authors and their titles in particular would reward further reading:

Gerhart Friedlander & Keith Turner, whose gripping account of the wartime service of Rudi Friedlander (Robert Lodge) is entitled *Rudi's Story*. Regrettably it is long out of print.

John Verney, whose excellent accounts of his wartime service and of his escapes are the books *Going to the Wars: A journey in various directions*, and *A Dinner of Herbs*. Both are sadly long out of print (see Bibliography below for full details).

Lewis 'Archie' Gibson, whose wartime memoirs, *Humdulallah, A Personal Memoir*, and the other which is untitled, are enthralling narratives of Gibson's wartime service. Both remain unpublished.

Graham Alcock, whose memoir about his father's wartime service, *Operation Pistol: Raindrops in Alsace*, is a detailed chronicle of his life and gripping wartime adventures (see Bibliography below for full details).

*

I am grateful to the publishers, authors and estates for granting me permission to quote from the following works (full details in Bibliography):

John Verney, *Going to the Wars: A journey in various directions*, Collins, 1966, and *A Dinner of Herbs*, Collins, 1966 – all rights reserved.

Lewis Gibson, *Humdulallah, A Personal Memoir*, 1961, and *Untitled*, undated, both unpublished – all rights reserved.

Graham Alcock, *SAS Operation Pistol: Raindrops in Alsace*, 2024, Pen & Sword – all rights reserved.

References to Sources

Material quoted from the UK archive files listed below, is by kind courtesy of the UK National Archives. This book contains public-sector information licensed under the Open Government Licence v3.0.

Material quoted from the French archive files, and other sources listed herein, is by kind courtesy of the Service historique de la Défense (Ministère des Armées, France).

The National Archives

WO 218/175 – Operation Chestnut report (inc. personal accounts from those involved)

AIR 23/5549 – Operation Chestnut second outline plan

HS 9/9490/2 – Roy Bridgeman-Evans

WO 208/3316/1557 – Bridgeman-Evans escape report/Long escape report

WO 208/5450/13 – Webb report

WO 208/3315/8 – Lt. Norman Johnson escape report

WO 208/5439 – de Beer escape report

WO 373/94/199 – Bridgeman-Evans/Long MC recommendation

WO 208/3314/1394 – Jacques Mouhot MI9 escape report

WO 208/3702/40 – Jack Sibard escape report

WO 218/174 – Operation Hawthorn

TS 26/778 – La Maddalena: assault on Major J Verney and Captain
EHB Imbert-Terry

WO 416/137/100 – Martin A Gibbs Liberation Questionnaire

WO 373/94/597 – Verney/Imbert-Terry MC Citation

WO 204/6810 – LRDG Operations in the Balkans Admin
Instructions & Reports

WO 204/8512 – LRDG Operations against the Italian, Yugoslav
& Greek Coasts

WO 204/8459 – LRDG – Daily Summaries of Ops on the Albanian
& Dalmatian Coasts

WO 373/19/446 – Lewis Gibson MM citation

WO 373/69/682 – Ken Smith George Cross citation

WO 218/205 – Operation Pistol

WO 361/727 – Operation Pistol

WO 218/209 – Post-Operational Investigations Loyton & Pistol

Service Historique de la Défense

GR 16P 433726 – Mouhot wartime papers, Service

Imperial War Museum

Document 19040 – Private Papers of Lieutenant J P Cochrane

Unpublished Sources & Miscellaneous

http://www.worcestershireregiment.com/wr.php?main=inc/o_brooke_johnson

Les Amis de la Fondation de la Résistance – www.memoresist.org/resistant/georges-guillemin/

https://www.conscript-heroes.com/escapelines/EscapeLines.htm

London Gazette, Military Notice 1944

London Gazette, 24 January 1946

Probate Calendar 1858–1995, ref. Roy Harvey Bridgeman-Evans

https://www.tobaccolivery.org/our-company-who-we-are.html

commandoveterans.org

UK and Ireland, Incoming Passenger Lists, 1878–1960

Georges Roger Pierre Bergé Obituary, *The Independent*, 21 September 1997

https://www.podbean.com/login?url=https%3A%2F%2Ffor youthewarisover.podbean.com%2Fe%2Fseries-5-episode-8-sgt-jaem-mouhot%2F&error=Channel%20lockeduploads/2020/04/Oscar-LIEVAIN.pdf

https://www.geni.com/people/Oscar-Lievain

https://www.france-libre.net/jacques-mouhot/

Monte San Martino Trust archives – https://archives.msmtrust.org.uk/

Verney Private Papers, courtesy of Sebastian Verney

https://uboat.net/allies/commanders/438.html

Oxford Dictionary of National Biography, 2004

Sir John Verney Obituary, *The Independent*, 4 February 1993

Sir John Verney Obituary, *The Times*, 5 February 1993

Gavin Mortimer article 'Only the Best', Key Military website, 2018

Captain Martin A Gibbs MI9 escape questionnaire (MI9 108605)

Lewis Gibson, first unpublished memoir

Lewis Gibson, unpublished memoir

Lewis Gibson, Yugoslav diary, August–October 1944

Lewis Gibson, unpublished handwritten report

Lewis Gibson, unpublished poetry

https://www.tobarandualchais.co.uk/track/26916?l=en

Captain Archie Gibson Obituary, *The Times*, 17 May 2005

https://www.tracesofwar.com/persons/68957/Alcock-John-Jack.htm

https://www.specialforcesroh.com/index.php?threads/alcock-john.28904/

Selected Bibliography

Graham Alcock, *SAS Operation Pistol: Raindrops in Alsace*, Barnsley: Pen & Sword, 2024

Anon., *The SAS War Diary*, London: Extraordinary Editions, 2011

Johnny Cooper, *One of the Originals: The Story of a Founder Member of the SAS*, London: Pan, 1991

Virginia Cowles, *The Phantom Major*, Barnsley: Pen & Sword, 2010

Henry L. deZeng IV, *Luftwaffe Airfields 1935–45: Italy, Sicily and Sardinia*, 2014

Roy Farran, *Winged Dagger*, London: Weidenfeld Military, 1986

Raymond Forgeat, *Ils ont choisi de vivre la France Libre*, Paris: Atlante, 1999

Gerhart Friedlander & Keith Turner, *Rudi's Story*, London: Jedburgh Publishing, 2006

Malcolm James (Pleydell), *Born of The Desert*, Barnsley: Frontline Books, 2015

Keith Janes, *They Came from Burgundy*, Market Harborough: Troubador Books, 2017

Nicholas Jellicoe, *George Jellicoe*, Barnsley: Pen & Sword, 2021

W. B. Kennedy Shaw, *Long Range Desert Group*, Barnsley: Frontline Books, 2015

Brian Lett, *An Extraordinary Italian Imprisonment*, Barnsley: Pen & Sword, 2014

Damien Lewis, *SAS Brothers in Arms*, London: Quercus, 2022

——, *SAS Forged in Hell*, London: Quercus, 2023

——, *SAS Great Escapes Two*, London: Quercus, 2023

B. H. Liddell Hart, *The Rommel Papers*, New York: Harcourt Brace & Company, 1953

Gavin Mortimer, *2 SAS Bill Stirling and the Forgotten Special Forces Unit of WWII*, Oxford: Osprey, 2023

Tom Petch, *Speed Aggression Surprise*, London: WH Allen, 2022

John Verney, *A Dinner of Herbs*, Philadelphia: Paul Dry Books, 2019

——, *Going to the Wars*, Philadelphia: Paul Dry Books, 2019

Ex-Lance-Corporal X, QGM, *The SAS & LRDG Roll of Honour 1941–47*, SAS-LRDG-ROH 2016

Index

CHARITIES ENDORSED BY THE AUTHOR

Who Dares Cares supports our Armed Forces, Emergency Services and Veterans, including their families, who are suffering from Post-Traumatic Stress Disorder (PTSD). They provide weekend retreat facilities for individuals and families, Walk, Talk and Brew Groups where teams of volunteers across the United Kingdom meet with groups of people who maybe just want to clear their head and feel supported through participating in some gentle exercise; attending a PTSD awareness session to gain a better understanding of what the signs and symptoms of PTSD are; learning how to manage symptoms and ways that families can better support in a way that is helpful to the individual. The charity recognises the importance of exercise as part of recovery and they work to encourage this and make it accessible for those who are struggling with PTSD and anxiety related issues.

The charity was founded in Hamilton, Scotland in 2016 by two former serving soldiers, Calum MacLeod (King's Own Scottish Borderers) and Colin Maclachlan (Royal Scots and Special Air Service). After Calum and Colin met, sharing their own stories, and becoming friends, bound by their own experiences, they both realised they could help so many other people, who were left 'alone' to deal with their experiences, thoughts and traumas. They decided to build a platform that would provide help and support to individuals and their families, all in the way of Who Dares Cares.

There are a number of volunteers that support the charity, all with varying skills, from military backgrounds to nurses, who offer help and support to all of their followers in many different ways. The volunteers are just that, volunteers. They are dedicated to the charity and give up their own time and effort to support other people in so many different ways. Without them, Who Dares Cares wouldn't be able to provide the dedicated support that they can.

Anyone with a service record and a history of PTSD should apply for support, even if you're not sure you meet the criteria; each application is assessed on an individual basis. For more details, please email the Who Dares Cares Support Team Mailbox on wdc@who-dares-cares.com and if you wish to learn more about this amazing charity and how you can support its vital work, please visit www.who-dares-cares.com.

It is not about suffering from PTSD, it is about learning to live with PTSD!

AFPSAS

WHO DARES WINS

The AFPSAS (Association des familles des parachutistes S.A.S. de la France Libre), includes the Free French SAS from 3rd and 4th SAS (Special Air Service) regiments and their families.

The 'French SAS Squadron' traces its origins to 1940 when the 1ère compagnie de l'Air (1ère CIA) was formed by Capitaine Georges Bergé. Initially operating in North Africa, its men joined David Stirling upon the creation of the Special Air Service (SAS). They would return to the UK in 1943 and form the 3rd and the 4th SAS squadron. They would operate across Nazi-occupied territories and in particular in France. Along with the men of 1st and 2nd SAS, they would be the first forces to land on French soil on D-Day, parachuting during the night of 5/6 June 1944. The Regiment would continue to operate throughout the war, undertaking daring missions in occupied territories, harassing enemy troops by organising sabotage and ambushes as well as training the local resistance. The French SAS squadrons would complete their final missions helping to liberate Holland.

The AFPSAS promotes the social well-being of the veterans from those units, as well as supporting their families. It also aims at commemorating the history and *esprit de corps* of the SAS regiment and passing that on to younger generations. It works with the media, researchers, historians and writers focused on the history of the SAS regiment during the Second World War. It also supports specialised re-enacting teams and relevant museums.

The association operates out of France with a local liaison in UK and also works in partnership with the Belgian and Dutch associations. It supports commemorative events across those countries. In November 2022, it co-sponsored the unveiling of a commemorative plaque dedicated to the 3rd and 4th SAS regiments, in London. In recent years, the AFPSAS has set-up the first freely accessible, online memorial listing of the men of the 3rd and 4th SAS regiments. It can be viewed here: https://memorial.afpsas.fr

The AFPSAS is affiliated to the Souvenir Français au Royaume-Uni a.k.a. the French War Graves Commission in the UK, a registered Charity in England and Wales, charity number 1185088.

It can be contacted at the following address: getintouch@ afpsas.fr

Alabaré

Alabaré believes no veteran should call the street home. Since 1991, Alabaré has been helping people who are homeless or vulnerable by providing safe accommodation and a pathway of support to help clients move on to bright futures, homes and minds.

Today Alabaré are a national charity with homes and services across the south of England and Wales supporting 3000 people a year. Their support includes dedicated help for street homeless, young people, those leaving the care system, young parents and their babies, Armed Forces veterans and those struggling with their mental wellbeing. Alongside Alabaré's supported accommodation, the charity offers training and activities to help clients to live the fulfilling life they choose.

Alabaré opened their first dedicated Homes for Veterans in Plymouth in 2009, and have since gone on to open houses across the South and South West of England and Wales. Veterans benefit from the camaraderie and understanding of shared experiences that comes from living with others who have served in the British Armed Forces.

Alongside their supported housing, Alabaré's Boots on the Ground programme uses outdoor activities to build confidence, self-esteem and team endeavour, and the charity's Veterans' Self Build Scheme offers veterans training in the construction industry while building a home that they can live in.

Alabaré have given me a lifeline, I felt like I was stranded at sea and Alabaré were the buoyancy aid. Alabaré have provided me with knowing that there are people there who care and are willing to go the extra mile. I am loving life again and feel every day is a positive day and on point. I no longer go to sleep praying I don't wake. I am again hopeful for the future and look forward to what is to come.

Alabaré veteran client.

For more information or to donate go to www.alabare.co.uk